Telling Bible Sto

Telling BIBLE Stories

Tales to Tell Aloud

BOB HARTMAN

MONARCH
BOOKS

Text copyright © 2006, 2010, 2011, 2021 Bob Hartman

This edition copyright © 2021 Lion Hudson IP Limited

The right of Bob Hartman to be identified as the author of this work has been asserted by him in accordance with the Copyright, Designs and Patents Act 1988.

Published by
Lion Hudson Limited
Wilkinson House, Jordan Hill Business Park
Banbury Road, Oxford OX2 8DR, England
www.lionhudson.com

ISBN 978 0 8572 1986 2
eISBN 978 0 8572 1987 9

Materials first published in *Telling the Bible* © 2006, *Telling the Gospel* © 2010, and *Anyone Can Tell a Bible Story* © 2011.

First published in this edition 2021

Acknowledgments

Scripture quotations are taken from the *Holy Bible, New International Version*, copyright © 1973, 1978, 1984 International Bible Society. Used by permission of Hodder & Stoughton, a member of the Hodder Headline Group. All rights reserved. "NIV" is a trademark of International Bible Society. UK trademark number 1448790.

Images © i stock/LueratSatichob, i stock/babushka_p90, i stock/appleuzr

A catalogue record for this book is available from the British Library

Printed and bound in the UK, February 21, LH29

Contents

The New Testament

Introduction

If you do something long enough, you're likely to do a lot of it.

And that has been the case with the Bible retellings/reimagining/reflections that I have written over the past thirty years or so.

By the same token, if you have done something long enough, you will also find that some of that work holds up really well, and some not so much!

So when Lion Hudson approached me to do a compilation of the three storytelling books of mine that they had published – *Telling the Bible, Telling the Gospel*, and *Anyone Can Tell a Bible Story* – I saw it as a golden opportunity to sift through that material and pick out what I thought were the best pieces.

Those of you who have used those books might disagree with my choices, of course. And all I can do is say "sorry" if a piece you liked or used a lot didn't make the cut. Having said that, you probably still have the original, so it won't make much difference!

As for me, I was happy to cut pieces that were rooted in a specific time or place or situation and no longer had much relevance. And it made sense to leave out material that just didn't work for me anymore, assuming that if I didn't much like it then you probably wouldn't either.

On the other hand, this compilation gave me the chance to include all of the stories from *Angels, Angels All Around*, a book I have loved since it first came out and which is unlikely to come back in print again. I was particularly pleased to find a new home for the "Angel of Death and Life" story that so many people have used and enjoyed.

I suppose that is the other reason for this compilation. Folks who have used the material in this book will likely have copies of the three books from which it's sourced. But I'd like to think that this book will appeal to an audience that has no experience with the originals and that is coming to these stories for the first time. I'd like to think that I have chosen pieces that can stand the test of time and be a source of inspiration to a new generation of readers.

And so I hope it's not being too forward to see this as a kind of "Best of..." collection, not forgetting for a moment that there are hundreds of other stories in all those other books (the ones written mostly for children) that I still treasure, as well.

Like I said, you do something long enough, you do lots of it.

Here's hoping that you enjoy that the "lots" that is left in this book!

Bob Hartman
January 2021

Part One

The Art of Storytelling

1

A Storyteller's Story

I can't remember exactly when it began.

Was it that time under the blankets, late into the night, with the dimming torch and the second-hand copy of *The Call of the Wild*?

Was it the junior boys' Sunday school class and my grandma's grizzly account of Ehud's left-handed execution of evil King Eglon?

Or was it those prizes I received on the last day of school, the year I turned eight – the plastic dinosaur that I lost before the summer ended and the book about the magic umbrella that my mother still reads to her grandchildren?

I can't remember exactly when it started. It just seems that I have always loved stories. And I suppose that is why I became a storyteller. It's the essential requirement, surely!

You see, I can't really claim to be an expert in the field of storytelling – not in the sense that I've read all the texts and manuals, attended all the seminars, and know all there is to know about the subject.

All I can really say is that I love stories, I tell stories, and when I do, people lean forward and listen and seem to love those stories too. So what I can share are the tips and techniques and, particularly, the attitudes and approaches I have picked up along the way. I can tell you what has worked and what has failed, where I find stories, and how I tear them apart and put them back together again as I prepare to tell them. And if you're willing to accept, from the start, that all storytellers are different, and that their storytelling is as much a reflection of their personality as it is of the stories themselves, then I think we can go somewhere together. So if you find something that's helpful along the way – brilliant! And if something else just won't work for you – then that's all right too. Because that's how I learned to tell stories. By watching and listening, trying and failing, and starting all over again!

Kids' play

When I was twelve, my younger brother, Tim, came home one afternoon, desperate to do something in the school talent show. He found a Muppet pattern in a women's magazine (you can tell how long ago that was – *Sesame Street* was brand new, then!), and stitched together a few puppets on my grandmother's old sewing machine. All he needed was a script. So I wrote one for him. I can't honestly remember what it was about, but it began an eight-year run of puppet shows in churches and camps and community festivals in the Pittsburgh area.

My other brother Daryl and a few other friends joined in as well. And my mum ferried us around in her beaten-up old Studebaker. We were just kids, but that experience taught us a lot about storytelling.

We discovered, first of all, how important it is to have interesting characters. Tim is a natural comedian, and very quick-witted, so it didn't take us long to start building the stories around the puppets that he controlled. We countered his cheeky irreverence with a collection of "straight man" type characters – typical stand-up fare – which helped us learn the place of conflict in storytelling too. Bit by bit, we discovered the ways that characters can work together to create both humour and tension, and build the story to a satisfying conclusion.

We also learned how important it is to build a relationship with an audience. Puppeteers can only tell how their audiences are reacting through what they hear. We discovered, very quickly, how helpful it is to see those reactions as well. So we started putting someone "out front", at the side of the stage, to be our eyes. He would sometimes act as a narrator, sometimes as a straight man, sometimes even as one of the characters. But, best of all, he would watch the crowd, gauge their reactions, and move things on or slow things down, depending on what he saw.

We learned a lot about story pacing and story length as well. Our early stories were short and punchy, largely because we were pretty insecure and wanted to get in there and get out as quickly as possible! But as our confidence grew, so did the stories. And that was a mistake. It was the era of rock opera, and I suppose I fancied myself in that light – writing huge puppet extravaganzas. But they just didn't work. They meandered on and on, losing their point and their tension, and worst of all, the audience! To this day, I would still rather do several short stories than one long one – because it gives me the chance to adapt and adjust (or simply bail out!) instead of being stuck in the middle of some epic.

Yes, we made mistakes – loads of them! Inadequate practice. Incomprehensible messages (more than one parent or teacher or pastor wanted to know what "that story was about"). And inappropriate humour (although I still wet myself over most things scatalogical!). But the most important thing was that we learned from those mistakes and we improved, year by year.

There's one thing I can't emphasize enough – the only way you learn to tell stories and improve your storytelling abilities is to do it. Because I'm an author, people often ask me, "How do I get a book published?" My usual response is, "What have you written?" And you would be amazed at how many of them haven't written anything at all! Sometimes it's fear, sometimes it's uncertainty, and sometimes it's a lack of confidence. And I understand all those feelings, because I've been there, myself. But unless you actually put those things behind you and have a go, you'll never write a book. And the same thing is true of storytelling. You have to try, accepting from the start that you'll make mistakes, face difficult audiences, forget where you're going, and not always get it right. But you have to start somewhere. You have to take that leap. Maybe it's because we were just kids and didn't know any better – but we had a go. And because we had a go, we learned a lot about telling stories.

University challenge

I learned a lot about stories at university, too. I was studying theology, preparing for a career in ministry, and was surprised to discover that this helped me to understand even more about the way that stories work and the power they have to affect us.

The Bible is essentially a collection of stories. It contains other genres, I know, but the bulk of the Bible relates events in the history of Israel and then in the life of Jesus – stories, that are meant to help us understand both who God is and who we are. Preaching, therefore, has a lot to do with storytelling. Yes, I tried some of the other approaches – three points and a conclusion, unpacking the apostle Paul's tightly knit theological arguments, wrestling with the imagery in the psalms. But what I discovered, even in the churches where I preached as a student, was that people responded best to stories. They leaned forward, they listened, they laughed, they cried – they got the point! So I just kept on telling stories. And not just as illustrations so much as for the Bible stories themselves.

One of my biggest inspirations in this regard was a book I stumbled across in the seminary library while I was doing some research for my first homiletics class. The book was called *Telling the Truth*, but what really caught my attention was the subtitle – *The Gospel as Tragedy, Comedy and Fairy Tale*. It was written by Frederick Buechner, who is both an award-winning novelist and a theologian. Buechner's premise is pretty simple. Preaching is all about telling stories. It starts with recognizing the tragic stories that are a part of each of our lives – by acknowledging them and taking them seriously. It moves on to the comedy of the gospel – the holy foolishness of a God who speaks his light and laughter into that tragedy. And it finishes with what Buechner calls the truest fairy tale of them all. He contrasts the story of the Wizard of Oz with the gospel story. In the former, there is no magic in the end – nothing beyond our own power to redeem ourselves, just a man pulling levers behind a curtain and a lot of self-belief. But in the gospel, Buechner argues, we find true magic – a power at work in us that accomplishes what we could never have done for ourselves.

Buechner's book excited me in a way that no other book on preaching had ever done before (or has done since). It convinced me that I could be a preacher and a storyteller, taking the thing I loved and weaving it into my calling. And that's what I took to my first church.

As it happens, my first church was in the UK (how I got there from a seminary in the hills of East Tennessee is a story in itself – or maybe the makings of a country and western song). And, to be fair, telling Bible stories there was a bit of a challenge, at first, because the people in that church were older, on the whole, had mostly been raised in Sunday school and had already heard a lot of those stories. I'm not complaining. I think it's marvellous when Christians know a lot about the Bible. It's how things should be. But, on the other hand, there's nothing worse than that "Oh, here's THAT story, again" look. As any parent knows, you can tell the same story to a small child time and time again. But it's different with older children and adults. A familiar story is a lot like a joke when you've already heard the punchline: you know how it's going to end, so you don't pay as much attention along the way. It's the old "been there, done that" thing.

So I had to work a little harder to find a way around that problem. If I were retelling a familiar Bible story, I tried my best to find a unique way "in" to the story. Sometimes I told it from a different perspective (from the "bad guy's" point of view, perhaps!). Sometimes I introduced a character who could be an objective observer of all that went on. Sometimes I started the story at an unfamiliar place. Anything to keep the listeners guessing, so that when they finally realized which story it was, they were interested enough to see how that particular slant would bring them round to the ending. There's nothing original about this of course – the spate of reworked and re-imagined fairy tales that have appeared over the last several years, both in print and on film, attests to the fact that this works with other kinds of stories as well. And that's the important thing – it re-establishes the kind of tension and expectancy that pulls an audience through a story.

The other thing that preaching in my first church taught me was the way that an audience relates to the characters in a story. Many people who aren't familiar with the Bible assume that it's a pious, holier-than-thou kind of book. The fact of the matter is that the Bible is brutally honest about the people whose lives it chronicles. We see them – even the "heroes" – warts and all. And that means that people can identify with the characters in a Bible story, both at their best times and at their worst. Because the stories are human and honest, they encourage people to be honest about themselves.

One Sunday, I told the story of the prodigal son, and when the service had finished, one of our older ladies said that she wanted to talk with me about the message, some time during the coming week. A few days later I went to visit her, and following the obligatory tea and cakes and snooker match (that's right, for some reason, in the mid-eighties, all my elderly parishioners were glued to the TV in the afternoon, watching snooker. Steve Davis was, of course, their hero – "What a nice young man" – and the villainy usually came in the form of the late Alex Higgins), she proceeded to tell me (as if she were addressing the diabolical Alex himself) how much she had disliked my sermon. I couldn't for the life of me see the problem, and I couldn't get a word in edgeways. Then came the punchline.

"When I was a young woman," she explained, "all my brothers and sisters moved away and left me at home to care for my parents. I was like the son who stayed with his father, but when you told the story, you did what everyone does – you turned him into the villain!"

That made everything clear. Stories invite us to relate to particular characters, but a storyteller can't control the choice that someone makes in that respect. So we talked about the story again and how the mercy shown by the father extended to the older son as well – and could also extend to her.

Ministry to museum

My children were both born in England, and when that ministry came to an end, we moved back to Pittsburgh, primarily so that my wife and I could raise the kids near their extended family. My brother Tim was working in children's theatre, at the time, but was interested in developing his career in a new direction. He had done some storytelling at one of the big Pittsburgh libraries and thought that, by telling stories together, he and I could recreate the same dynamic that had worked so well with the puppets, years before. So I took a "break" from ministry and joined him.

We took one of the stories he had been telling – "Joe Magarac", Pittsburgh's tall tale about a heroic steel worker – and adapted it to our own style. What we came up with was a kind of "tag team" approach to storytelling, taking it in turn to tell the narrative. Sometimes we would cross over into drama, with each of us taking different "parts". And sometimes it would look more like a stand-up comedy routine as we borrowed the "straight man", "funny man" stuff from our puppet days.

I suppose the purist would argue that it wasn't straightforward storytelling. And it wasn't. It was a fusion of a lot of different styles and approaches. But the bottom line was that it worked! Kids loved it. Teachers did too. And I continued to learn more about telling stories.

First of all, I learned about the importance of structure, control, and rules in a storytelling context. This was essential for our work in school assemblies. In the US, these usually last for forty-five to fifty minutes, and are either made up of the whole school together, or the school broken into two big groups (corresponding roughly to Infants and Juniors in the UK). So the average session was 200 to 300 children, although I can recall times when that number jumped to 500 or 600! In addition, we were usually working in rooms that were not the best, acoustically – barn-sized gymnasiums where the sound echoed everywhere or ancient auditoriums with squeaky folding seats. In that kind of a situation, we found that we needed some way to keep the children as quiet as possible, or to re-establish that quiet following some participation activity that we had instigated!

In his children's theatre work, Tim had come across a device that many teachers use – and we found that it worked for us, as well. He started each programme by telling the children that they were going to have a great time. They would see things that they liked, and maybe even things that they didn't like. But most of all, they would see things that made them laugh, and perhaps make them want to say something to their neighbour. He assured them that we understood that, but also pointed out that too much of that kind of noise would make it hard to hear the story. Then Tim would stick his arm straight up in the air. (He's a tall guy – so if the room was low, he would sometimes smack his hand up against the ceiling. The kids loved that!) "When you see the hand go up," Tim would say, "then everyone needs to get quiet as quickly as possible and look straight up here."

And that was it. It seems simple, I know. Almost too simple to work! But it did. And I think it did precisely because it was so simple.

The device was just a way of giving us room to work and the opportunity to be heard in the first place. With rowdier groups, we had to reinforce it more at the start – so that they would get the idea, and understand that we really meant it. And, yes, there was the odd occasion when we did have to give in and simply carry on in spite of the noise. But 97 per cent of the time, it worked. And it worked because – just as we'd promised – the kids really were enjoying themselves.

During this time, I also learned a lot about respecting children. Tim and I often had the chance to listen to other storytellers and, sadly, some of them felt the need to adopt that sickly sweet tone of voice when talking to children. Perhaps I'm being too hard here, but it seems to me that children (older children in particular) feel that they are being "talked down to" when they hear that tone. We were determined, from the start, to talk to children in our natural voices – to just be ourselves when we were with them. I think that showed respect and that we valued them. And it was probably one of the reasons that we received their respect in return.

This approach helped to engage teachers in our stories as well. Quite often, teachers would get the kids settled for the beginning of the assembly, and then mark papers or do some other kind of work while the assembly was going on. Tim and I decided that one of our goals would be to get the teachers to put away their work and listen! Tossing in the odd adult reference or joke certainly helped, but so did the fact that we didn't talk down to the kids and made it clear that the stories we told were for "everybody".

Finally, I think I learned a lot about simplicity. Many of the schools we visited had hosted assemblies that required elaborate lighting and sets. And with certain kinds of productions, that's necessary. But it isn't with storytelling. In fact, Tim and I agreed, early on, that we would take no more into an assembly than what the two of us could carry in one trip (or that would squeeze into the back of his Honda)! That meant the obligatory cup of coffee in one hand, and a stool, or a coat rack, or a plastic dustbin full of props in the other. We took it in turns to sit on the stool. We used a few props for each programme. And the coat rack? Well, as we enjoyed explaining to the kids during the question and answer session – that was for hanging our coats on! And it gave a bit of a backdrop – a concession, I suppose to the comments we would sometimes overhear: "You mean we spent hundreds of dollars for this?!" The assumption, of course, was that a presentation without lots of fancy props and sets and lights couldn't possibly engage the children. But that assumption was wrong. Storytelling doesn't require anything but engaged imaginations. Not even coat racks and dustbins. And we proved that, time and time again.

A little girl – not more than seven or eight years old – came up to me after a session, once, and her comments say it all. "That story you told," she said – her eyes full of wonder, "I could see it! I could see everything! The old man, the mountain, the waves. I could see it!" In an age when we bombard our children with visual and aural stimulation, it's a real thrill to hear those words. Because, given half a chance, children's imaginations can run free – like they were meant to. And they can see! They really can. If only we're willing to keep things simple.

Tim and I toured for a year on our own, and then were spotted by the Schools Outreach Director of the Pittsburgh Children's Museum at a performers' showcase. She asked us to become a part of their team, representing them in schools, which we did for the next ten years. We carried on telling "Joe Magarac", but then went on to create five more storytelling programmes (none of them Bible-based, because of the separation of church and state in US government-funded schools). This took us to the magic number of six – "magic" because six is the number of grade levels in the average American elementary school. And that means that you can go back to the same school, year after year, and never have to repeat a programme with the same audience!

Here's a summary of our six programmes:

1. Joe Magarac, the traditional Pittsbugh tall tale.

2. Construct-a-Tale illustrated the basics of good story construction (character, setting, and problem) through the telling of a traditional French fairy tale, "How Johnny Pancake Did Not Marry the Princess of France".

3. "Goal tending" was so-named because Pittsburgh is a big ice-hockey town. It was based on *The One and Only Delgado Cheese*, a story about making dreams come true and one of the first books I wrote.

4. "Anderson Choose" was an original fairy tale that Tim and I wrote together. It focused on citizenship and making good choices.

5. "Folk Trails" bound together three traditional tales as a way of demonstrating how different cultures share and communicate values through story, and how similar those values often are.

6. "Tales That Tell Why" was all about science. This was a real stretch, as it wasn't exactly our strongest subject in school and we struggled to find a way to deal with science in a storytelling context. We finished up contrasting the scientific method (as illustrated by the lives of Ptolemy, Copernicus, and Galileo) with traditional stories that tried to explain how things came to be.

Looking back on it, it's strange to think that all those stories (and quite a few more, actually) were bouncing around in our heads at one time – particularly since I'm not that great at memorizing. Maybe that will be an encouragement, if that's your situation too. There's no better way to get really comfortable with a story, and plumb the depths of its power and effectiveness, than by telling it again and again and again. And I can say with confidence that we told some of those stories hundreds of times and more!

At the same time, however, we were both involved in individual pursuits. I took up writing books for children, and Tim landed better and better acting jobs, both on stage and in film. In the end, the time came when we needed to give more attention to those other pursuits. So Tim carried on with his acting, and I moved to the UK to promote my books, tell stories in schools, and teach others how to tell stories, too.

2

How Stories "Work"

M r McKee, my sixth-grade teacher, was different from any teacher I'd ever had before. For a start, he was a man, unlike most primary school teachers at that time. And then there was that other thing – the thing that happened, one Friday afternoon, early in the autumn term.

Mr McKee asked us to put away our books and pencils and papers (and let's face it, when you're eleven years old, that request, alone, is enough to make you sit up and take notice!). Then he walked slowly round the room, pulling down the blinds, one by one. Finally, he turned off a few lights so that the room was dark and cool. Everyone looked around. We couldn't imagine what would happen next! And that's when Mr McKee went to the front of the room, reached behind his desk, pulled out a copy of *The Lion, the Witch and the Wardrobe*, and began to read.

As far as I can remember, that's how every Friday afternoon went, for the rest of that term. And we listened, rapt – many of us for the first time – to the adventures of Lucy and Edmund and Peter and Susan, as they wandered through the wardrobe and into the land of Narnia. It was my first exposure to those books. And along with many of my classmates, I rushed to the library afterwards to pick up a copy for myself. But more than that, it was the first time that I ever felt what I now believe lies at the heart of every good storytelling experience. Intimacy. Community. Relationship.

Building relationships… with the teller

Before the story itself, before any "tips" and "techniques", good storytelling is all about relationships. And the first and most important relationship is the one that develops between the storyteller and the audience.

To be honest, I have struggled with the term "audience" for some time now, because it suggests a passive group of listeners who simply receive what is offered. But there is nothing passive about what happens in a good storytelling session. At the best of times, it is an occasion where the teller and the crowd build something together.

You see, storytelling is not about someone tossing out a mouthful of words for others to catch. It is about that thing that is created between them – the result of imagination and participation and eye contact and laughter and tears. Storytelling is not a presentation, it's a conversation. It's not a performance, it's a dialogue.

Therefore, the same story can be different every time you tell it – because the crowd is different, or the context is different, or the responses are different. During the course of a party, for example, you might say the same things to a number of different people. But the way you say them, the order, the emphasis, will have a lot to do with the way those people respond to you. The same thing is true of storytelling. The crowd thinks that it is watching you, listening to you. But the secret is that you are watching them, listening to them, and responding to them as well!

When my brother and I started telling stories in school assemblies, someone would inevitably try to turn the "house" lights off. I think the assumption was that the children would be quieter in the dark, as they would be in a theatre or a cinema. Well, first of all, if you've ever been in a dark cinema full of kids, you know that's not necessarily the case! But the worst thing was that Tim and I couldn't see them. And seeing them – their responses, their reactions – was essential to building a relationship with them. I have the same problem when it comes to telling stories to very large groups of people – several thousand or so. I'm not saying it can't be done. It's just harder, because the feedback is limited primarily to what I can hear. And when I can see as well, there's just that much more information. And the more information, the better, because it's all about building that relationship – seeing the crowd's reactions, hearing their responses, shaping the story to suit that particular group. Because if the relationship works, then the story will too.

So how do you build a relationship with a group of people? I think you do it in the same way you would with an individual.

Be yourself. As I said in chapter 1, resist the temptation to use that "sickly sweet" voice with children or the "pious" voice when you're telling Bible stories. Just be honest about who you are. If you're big and loud and noisy, then your storytelling will probably reflect that. But if you're quieter, then don't try to be something you're not – let your stories reflect that, too.

Be confident. Even if you're shaking inside! Kids, in particular, can smell the fear and the uncertainty. But even with adult groups, everyone feels more comfortable when the person "up front" seems comfortable, too.

Be friendly. Smile as you introduce yourself, or set down the ground rules for the kids. Let them know, right from the start, that this is going to be a good experience, and that everyone is going to have fun.

Be smart. Choose your first story carefully. If I'm doing a half-hour or forty-five minute session, I seldom just do one long story. I do lots of little ones, because that gives me the chance to learn something about the group. I usually start with a story that I know really well, partly because of the "confidence" thing, but more importantly because it gives me the freedom to watch and listen to the crowd. If I'm not thinking about how the story goes or what comes next, I'm free to gauge their responses. Is there a particular kind of humour that they like? Are there a few who are really getting into it? I'll keep my eye on them, and look for a little support, in case things get shaky later! And as for the ones who look as if they want to leave – I remind myself to try something different with them in the next story, because it takes longer for some people to warm to you than others (it's that relationship thing again!). And what if some people never warm to you? Well, stop looking at them and focus instead on the ones who are really enjoying your stuff!

Be fun! Start with something funny – or at least something fun. It's been my experience that most people would rather laugh than cry. So save the serious stuff for later – for just the right moment. It will go down so much better when it comes as a surprise.

"Hang on a minute!" I hear you say. "It's all right for you. You go to lots of different venues and do the same stories each time. What about me? I have to do a different Bible story each week for my school assembly, or Sunday school class, or Bible club. What do I do?"

Well, you have a different set of advantages. You do have to prepare a new story each week, that's true. And in that case, it is more difficult to get really comfortable with the story, as you would with one that you had told a dozen times. But you do have the advantage of knowing your group a lot better than an occasional visitor like me ever will. You know the kind of stories they like, the kind of participation activities they most enjoy. You know who will be up for a bit of "acting along" with you (and who might get totally carried away!). It's the relationship thing again, so use that longer-term relationship – the fact that you really know your group – to your advantage.

I still think it's best to focus on stories that are fun or exciting. That will earn you the right and respect to do that quieter, more serious, tale from time to time. And be honest, in that case; there's nothing wrong with saying something like, "Usually we have a bit of a laugh at story time, but this week, we're going to do a really sad or serious story." And then maybe just give them a question to be considering as they listen to you tell it.

Building relationships… with the characters

There is another relationship that is important to storytelling. This is the one that develops between those who hear the story and the characters in the story itself. Think of your favourite story. Which character do you like the best? With whom do you identify? One of my clearest childhood memories has to do with a picture book we had of "The Three Little Pigs". I can remember getting very upset every time the Big Bad Wolf fell down the chimney and landed in the boiling stew pot. I'm not sure what it says about me, but I liked the Big Bad Wolf! (Hey, he worked hard, he stuck to it, he was just doing what wolves do! And that brick-house pig always looked so smug!)

It's this "identification with characters" that makes any good narrative work. Think of your favourite film, your favourite soap opera, your favourite drama or situation comedy. The best ones are always character-driven, because it's the relationship that develops between you and those characters that keeps you watching. And it's true for storytelling, as well. It's like that moment at the end of a good book when you turn over the last page and wish that you could spend just a little more time with those characters. If you have told the story well, then your audience will have identified with one character or another. And better than that, some of them will have accompanied that character on his or her journey and maybe even experienced some sense of discovery or transformation along with that character. And that can be a very powerful experience, indeed.

In his book, *Peace Child*, Don Richardson describes his efforts to tell the story of Jesus to the Sawi tribe in Papua New Guinea. The tribe was known for its cannibalism and its treachery, so when the people in the tribe heard the Gospel narrative, the character they most related to was Judas! As you can imagine, this was a real problem for the missionary, who wanted them to understand what Jesus had done and that Jesus was the real hero of the story. Fortunately, the Sawi also had a tradition which they used to deal with the treachery. One tribe would offer another tribe one of its own children to be raised by that tribe, and that exchange would bring the treachery to an end. That child was called the peace child, and when Richardson explained that Jesus was God's peace child to make things right between him and his world, the Sawi understood. All because they were now able to relate to that character!

I am convinced that storytelling has the power to shape and change lives. It really can lead to new discoveries – new ways of thinking and acting. And that brings us to the third significant relationship in storytelling – the relationship of storytelling to a particular community.

Building relationships... with one another

Traditionally, storytelling was the means by which values, histories, and cultural expectations were passed from one generation to another. Whether the storyteller was a priest or a bard, the point of the story was not simply to entertain, but also to shape and to teach – to define what was good and bad, what was acceptable and unacceptable. Jesus used his parables, for example, to challenge deeply held cultural values and assumptions among the religious establishment of his time.

I always have a little chuckle when I hear filmmakers argue that cinema has no direct effect on the way that people behave. Either they have no understanding of what they are doing, or they hope that we don't. Film and television are one of the chief means that our modern culture uses to access stories. And stories shape cultures. The proof lies in the enormous amount of money that corporations are willing to invest in all those little stories we call advertisements. Do you think for a minute that they would go on spending that kind of money if they weren't confident that those little stories had the power to change what we buy? Storytelling is powerful precisely because it is subtle and subversive, because it can sneak up on you and surprise you. And that's why it needs to be used responsibly – as a means of building community and not destroying it.

Several years ago, my brother and I told a story about self-sacrifice to a class of eleven-year-olds in a Pittsburgh city school. It was a story we had told successfully on a number of occasions, about a rabbit who gives up his life for a field mouse. When the story was finished, the kids just stared at us for a minute, looks of shock and disbelief on their faces.

"That was stupid!" one of them said, at last. "Why would that bunny die for a field mouse?"

"Yeah," echoed several others in the class. "It doesn't make any sense!"

We tried our best to explain that giving up something you wanted for the good of someone else could be worthwhile. Tim even slipped in a little Bible quote (without referencing it, of course!). "Haven't you ever heard the saying – the best thing someone can do is to give up his life for a friend?" They hadn't.

The fact is, they just didn't "get it". Maybe it was the way we told the story. Maybe it was just that particular group of kids. But we came away from that experience determined to make sure that more of our audiences heard more of those kinds of stories – so that there would be some balance to the "take-what-you-can-get-and kill-as-many-people-along-the-way" kinds of stories that seem to find their way into too many children's lives.

We quickly discovered that schools were really hungry for that kind of story, because it provides a way of talking about all those "citizenship" and "values" issues that teachers sometimes struggle to communicate, particularly in a way that doesn't sound like they're "preaching". So if you think there's too much violence, intolerance, and hatred in your community, there's something you can do about it. You can tell stories – stories that are just as powerful, just as exciting, and just as much fun as all those violent tales – but stories that are about gentleness, forgiveness, peace, and love.

And that most definitely includes stories from the Bible!

At every children's ministry event I have ever attended, someone has inevitably quoted Psalm 78, and with good reason. The early part of this psalm says exactly what I have been saying here – people are shaped by the stories they hear. So we have a responsibility to pass on the best stories, particularly those that deal with the relationship between God and his people. Have a look:

My people, hear my teaching;
  listen to the words of my mouth.

I will open my mouth with a parable,
  I will utter hidden things, things from of old –

things we have heard and known,
  things our ancestors have told us.

We will not hide them from their descendents;
  we will tell the next generation
the praiseworthy deeds of the Lord,
  his power, and the wonders he has done.

He decreed statutes for Jacob
  and established the law in Israel,
which he commanded our ancestors
  to teach their children,

so the next generation would know them,
  even the children yet to be born,
  and they in turn would tell their children.

Then they would put their trust in God
  and would not forget his deeds
  but would keep his commands.

They would not be like their ancestors –
  a stubborn and rebellious generation,
whose hearts were not loyal to God,
  whose spirits were not faithful to him.
Psalm 78:1–8 (NIV)

Do you see it? Not only does the psalmist tell us to pass God's story on to the next generation, he tells us why we should do it. So they will keep his commands – and not mess up like some have done! This is all about shaping a generation, shaping a culture. And there's no point arguing that we have no right to do that. Someone will do that, inevitably – either intentionally or as a by-product. For as long as there are stories, stories will shape cultures. So why not tell the best ones? The ones God himself has given us.

And with that, I feel obliged to take at least some space to mention a group of people who have been doing a splendid job of that in the UK, over the last twenty years. There is lots of excellent work being done in this regard, across the nation – many groups committed to passing God's story on to the next generation and making sure that it continues to be, at the very least, a part of our collective cultural consciousness. My favourite group among these is Open the Book. All right, I confess, I'm biased. They use my *Lion Storyteller Bible* as the core source of the stories they tell in schools. And they did ask me to be a patron. But, honestly, I'd be excited about their work if neither of these things had happened – because of the history of their ministry and the way they have gone about putting that Psalm 78 mandate into effect.

Originally, Open the Book was never meant to be a national initiative. A small group of Christians in Bedford felt led to tell the story of the Bible, in order, from Genesis to Acts, to the children in their local schools, over the course of one year. They trained small groups of storytellers, two to three per group, comprised mostly of mums, schools workers, vicars, and pensioners – folks who were available during the day. They learned the stories. They made costumes. They built props (sometimes quite elaborate ones!). And in the first year, they told their stories to children in ten local schools. They didn't preach or even do much unpacking. They just told the stories, and the schools were so pleased with what they did that, the following year, fifteen more schools wanted Open the Book groups. So they recruited more volunteers and trained more storytellers, and word started to get around. I think I can probably take some responsibility for that. Whenever I visited a conference or did a storyteller training, I mentioned what these folks were doing and passed on details for contacting them. And, amazingly, people did. It was such a simple idea – and such a good one – particularly that bit about doing the stories in order. I'm convinced that, even in churches, many Christians don't know the "Big Story" – the overall narrative sweep of the Bible. So they don't know how the individual stories fit in, how they connect to one another, and how they relate. The genius of Open the Book is that the children in their audiences get the story in order, so it's less like *Aesop's Fables* ("Oh, here's a lovely story, children with a lovely message") and more like one big adventure. Which, of course, it is!

The other beautiful thing about the programme is that it has re-energized many people who thought their time for ministry had passed. I think the oldest Open the Book member I have come across was in her nineties (if there's anyone older out there, please do let me know). The wonderful thing (the divinely inspired thing, I think) is that those folks come from a generation where the story was passed on, through vibrant Sunday school programmes – so they know the stories, are passionate about the stories, and are keen for this chance to make a difference in a generation several steps down the line.

Christians across the country began to recognize all of this, and started Open the Book groups in their communities, as well. For the greater part of that time, there was no national organization, no website, no budget (apart from what people raised and gave in their own cities and towns and villages). But the thing kept growing. And at the time of writing this book, there are something like 17,000 storytellers in the programme, telling Bible stories in over 3,000 schools, reaching over 800,000 children. There is no question in my mind that this "flood" of Bible stories is making a difference in those schools and communities. The fact that schools themselves are now approaching Open the Book groups and asking them to come to them shows that they recognize the value. And in the best cases (and there are plenty of examples) this simple passing on of Bible stories has brought schools and churches and communities together. Telling stories makes a difference!

Stories not only have the power to shape communities, they are also a means by which we can build a sense of community. A lot of communication, these days, requires only a face in front of a screen. But storytelling is all about a face in front of a face – faces together, in fact, sharing laughter and tears, surprise and joy. And today that's not a common experience for many children – or adults, for that matter. True, it's more threatening in some ways than sitting alone in front of your television. You might laugh out loud at the wrong time, or have to wipe a tear from an eye. But it's ultimately more rewarding, for it's a chance to discover (or perhaps rediscover!) what happens when people experience a story together.

I have had many experiences over the years that have brought this to light. I was in a school several years ago, telling a story about a bunch of animals that each had different talents. At the end of the story, I asked the children what their talents were. And in the midst of those answers, one boy simply blurted out, "I'm no good at anything!"

I wasn't sure what to do. I didn't know that boy, but there was someone there who did – a teacher, on the other side of the room. She said, "Liam, I've just graded the maths test, and you did better than anyone in the class!" And, boy, did Liam's expression change, because right there, in that little community that had been brought together by a story, he had the chance to admit something really painful and also to find an answer to that pain.

It's almost like the story is a kind of boat. We climb in together – and yeah, the storyteller steers or mans the sails or whatever needs to happen to get the journey started. But in the best situations, everyone gets to contribute to the journey, each in his or her own way – and we go somewhere together.

It can happen in churches, and in classrooms too when teachers can find some room in the straightjacket of the National Curriculum (don't get me started!) to sit down and relax with their class around a book. It's also happening in other storytelling groups that are springing up all around the country. And, I'm told, there are still places where storytelling happens in pubs on a regular basis. But why not in hospitals and old people's homes and corporate headquarters, as well? Why shouldn't storytelling have a place wherever people come together? For as we let the stories we hear touch our own stories, we become a part of *each other's* stories. We understand, we sympathize. And hopefully, we experience a deeper sense of community.

Building relationships… with God

When it comes to biblical storytelling, there is one more relationship to take into consideration. And that's the relationship with God himself. For God reveals himself through story.

If you were to ask an ancient Israelite to tell you about God, it is unlikely that he would share some abstract philosophy with you. He might recite a psalm. He might show you a few rules. He might quote you a proverb. But it's most likely that he would tell you a story: "My father Abraham was a wandering Aramean. God called him and promised him that if he would follow him, God would give him a land of his own and descendants to outnumber the stars in the sky or the sands in the sea."

Or she might say: "My people were slaves in Egypt. But God set them free and led them to a land flowing with milk and honey!"

The God of Israel is revealed in the story of Israel. We discover who he is by watching how he deals with his people. God's creative power, his passion for justice, and his patient, steadfast love are all revealed in that story.

And when he chose to reveal himself fully what did God do? Did he drop an essay down from heaven? Did he pass out a theological tract? No, he came in the person of one man – Jesus – who was not just a good storyteller, but who was, himself, The Story. So that by watching what he did, and listening to what he said, we could understand what God was like. Between "once upon a time" and "happily ever after", between "the beginning" and "the end" – that's where we find the Alpha and the Omega – for God is revealed in story.

That means that biblical storytelling is quite sacred stuff. And quite powerful, too! It's not just a matter of standing in front of a group of kids and hoping to survive the following fifteen minutes. No, that Sunday school room, that school hall, that slot in the middle of the family service – that is sacred ground! For it is an opportunity for God to do what he has done from the start of his relationship with his people – to reveal himself, to show who he is and what he can do – through the story that you tell!

3

Retelling the Story

Find A Way "In"

If storytelling really is more a dialogue than a monologue, then someone has to get the conversation started. And that is why it is so important for the storyteller to decide how he or she is going to tell the story.

You mean you don't start with "once upon a time" and finish with "and they all lived happily ever after"? Not necessarily. In fact, one of the great challenges of storytelling is finding a way "in" to the story – that "hook", that "device", that "gimmick" if you like, that pulls the listener in and makes the experience memorable. Some of the people in the group may have heard your story before. This is particularly true with biblical storytelling, where preachers, Sunday school teachers and RE co-ordinators alike are faced with the annual task of finding an inventive way "in" to the Christmas and Easter narratives (not to mention Noah, Jonah, and David and Goliath). The last thing you want is to encounter that groaning, been-there-done-that look. And even if the story you are telling is new to the audience, it is still better to tell that story as creatively as possible – so they hear it at its best, the very first time.

So what do you do? You can start by just "playing around" with the story. Many years ago, I was asked to write a book about angels. The subject was all the rage at the time, and I didn't want to write a book that was just like all the rest. So I took a close look at the Bible stories about angels and asked a couple of questions: What if God created angels in the same way that he made us? Not white, winged clones, but unique individuals, suited to particular tasks. What if an angel's appearance had something to do with the job it was called to do? I tried to answer those questions in the book, and that is why, in *Angels, Angels All Around*, the angel who is sent to make a meal for Elijah in the desert bears a striking resemblance to a TV chef. The angel who leads Peter out of prison is a clever little Puck of a fellow. And the angel who rescues Daniel from the lions' den looks a bit like a lion himself and plays through the night with the beasts so their attention is diverted from their dinner! Was I reading between the lines?

Certainly. But I believe that asking questions of the story is one means of finding a unique way into it.

Another way "in" is to alter the point of view from which the story is told. In my book *Bible Baddies*, for example, I have retold familiar Bible stories from the point of view of the villains. The message of the story remains the same (and, in fact, sometimes becomes even clearer!), but the fresh approach really grabs an audience's attention. This works well with other kinds of stories too. In "The Wolf Who Cried Boy", I simply reversed the roles of the traditional story. It's the wolf (a little wolf, in this case, who is fed up with his mother's cooking) who does the fibbing. And the boy (the promised treat to relieve the tedium of his mother's meals!) who provides the occasion for the lie! And in "The Three Billy Goats' Stuff", I set the story in a school playground and made the troll the school bully. He was always threatening to beat up the smaller students, unless they gave him their "stuff", but is thwarted, at last, by the three new "kids" in school. The possibilities are endless, and it can make a well-known story really riveting, once again, because the listeners are always wondering whether the ending will be same, and how you'll get there, having started from an unfamiliar place. And more than anything else, it's just good fun!

The trick is to surprise and to delight your listeners, because it's when they're enjoying themselves that they are truly open to the power of the story itself. It's much as Aesop suggested in his fable about the sun and the wind – whimsy, humour, joy and delight are more effective paths to discovering truth and experiencing change than any heavy-handed approach. Granted, you will be called upon to tell stories that are, by their very nature, more serious. But even there, finding an original way "in" to the story, and surprising your audience, will open that story up – even to those who have heard it a hundred times before.

When it comes to biblical storytelling, there is another good reason for finding an original and inspiring way "in" to the story. It makes the story shine anew for the teller, as well.

Several years ago, I was taking an RE class at the school across the street from the church I pastored. My remit was to talk with the class about the reasons Christians behave the way they do – how they decide what is right and what is wrong. I told them that Christians are people who follow Jesus. So they try to do the things he did. I asked them if they knew any good things that Jesus did.

One girl said that he healed people. A boy said that he fed people who were hungry. So we talked about the ways that we could do those things now. And then a little boy at the back put up his hand.

"Didn't Jesus die by being crushed under a big rock?" he asked.

I thought about that for a moment.

"No," I said. "He did die, but he didn't die that way." And then I explained how Jesus actually died.

"You might be thinking about what happened three days after he died," I continued. "Do you know what happened next?" I asked. The little boy shook his head.

"Well," I went on, "When Jesus died, they buried him in a tomb, a grave, and rolled a big stone in front of it. And three days later, when the stone was rolled away, Jesus wasn't there any more. Jesus was alive."

The little boy looked at me, and I promise you, this is what he did. His mouth hung open and all he said was "Wow!"

I could have been the apostle Paul, in the first century, speaking to an audience in Corinth or Athens – because, just like those people, the boy had never heard that story. His reaction – wonder, amazement, awe – said it all.

That little boy is not alone. Our schools and communities and, sadly, yes, even our churches are filled with people who do not know the story. Not that story, perhaps – but lots of other ones. And when they hear it, they are knocked out by it, excited, thrilled. One of my favourite retellings is the story of the stilling of the storm. And when I do it in schools, without fail, the audience gets dead quiet when Jesus stands up in the boat – and you can hear a pin drop when he tells the wind to "be quiet now" and the waves to "settle down". And it's all because almost no one knows what's going to happen next. And there's the disconnect. Because if you have been a Christian for a while and you are familiar with the story, then sometimes that "wonder" is missing. "Yes, of course, Jesus fed 5,000 people and made the blind see and even raised the dead," you think, but the wonder – that initial amazement – is gone, or at least much diminished. This isn't a criticism, it's just what happens when anyone becomes familiar with a story (even an incredible one like the story of Jesus). It's easy to take it for granted.

The problem is that if you tell it in that been-there-done-that way, if the excitement isn't there for you, then it won't be there for those who hear the story either. And you will be doing both them and the story a disservice.

I always say that what Christians need to do is to rediscover the "shine" in the story – the thing that makes that story amazing for them. And the interesting thing is that the very process you use to rediscover the "shine" is the same process you use to retell a Bible story.

It begins with what may seem to you the most obvious, logical, and sensible step. But it's a step that too often gets missed:

If you want to retell a story from the Bible, the first thing you need to do is to read it in the Bible.

See? Obvious! You'd think so, anyway. But the reality is that many people retell retellings, or work from a shaky and inexact memory, or just "wing it". And that just won't do. Not for retelling and particularly not for finding that shiny thing that makes it work for you.

I've been there myself, so I know what I'm talking about here. When I sat down to retell the story of the battle of Jericho for *The Lion Storyteller Bible*, I didn't look at the text at all. I figured I knew that story inside out. I went to Sunday school and Bible college and seminary. Of course I knew the story of Jericho! And then I thought, well, maybe I should just have a peep – to make sure. And sure enough, when I actually read the text, I discovered something I'd never seen or heard before. An Angel! An angel of the Lord, with a sword, encouraging Joshua on. Well, I got excited about that angel and stuck him in the story and he's been a unique part of that retelling ever since – a surprise to other people who thought they also knew all there was to know about that story.

Reading the text first gives you the chance to discover those interesting little details that will bring the story alive again for you. Sure, you can always use someone else's retelling. And as an author of loads of Bible retellings, it's in my interest that you do so. But I have to be honest with you too – the best retellings are the ones that spring from something interesting, exciting, or novel that you yourself have found in the text.

The other reason for reading the text first is that it gives you the chance to ask questions of the text – questions your audience might well have and questions that you can find the answers to ahead of time. I do the same kind of preparation for a retelling as I would do for a sermon. If I stumble across something I don't understand, I consult a commentary or talk to someone who might know the answer. You can do the same. Talk to your pastor or priest. Ask for some good reference material. There is a lot of joy in that process and the discoveries that result from it. I was retelling the story of Jesus' first sermon in Nazareth, the one that's recorded in Luke 4. It's the one where the congregation seizes him at the end and tries to throw him off a cliff! I got to wondering about Nazareth – how big was it? How many people lived there? So I did a little research (OK, I googled it!) and it turns out that Nazareth had a population of only about 120 people at that time. One hundred and twenty, that's nothing! So most of those people would have known Jesus' family – no question. Which makes their reaction to his message even more extraordinary. This wasn't some stranger they were tossing into the valley – it was someone they knew, someone from their tiny little corner of the world – which made his claims even more ridiculous, blasphemous, and audacious.

Or there's the parable of the friend who has a visitor at midnight. He doesn't have any food in his house, so he bangs on another friend's door until that friend relents and gives him some bread. It's Jesus' way of talking about persistence in prayer.

But did you ever wonder – what was that man doing, arriving at midnight? It's not as if there were lighted roads in those days. Wouldn't it have been dangerous? Well, no. I was in the Middle East a few years ago and had to catch a plane home at midnight. As we drove to the airport, we passed crowds of people on the road. In fact, we passed families having picnics. At midnight!

"Why are they out so late?" I asked my host.

And he looked at me as if I was stupid. "Because it's too hot to be out in the day!"

Makes sense, doesn't it? And it certainly helps to make sense of Jesus' story.

So start by reading the text. Then ask questions of the text. Oh, and if you're doing a Gospel story, read all three (or four) versions from the different Gospels. One version might suit your needs better than another.

When I read the passage from the Bible, there are three main elements I am looking for – the three elements that are a part of every story – character, setting, and problem. We have already discussed the importance of characters in a story and will look at that again. Suffice it to say that you need to read the text with an eye on the details it reveals about each main character as a way of then bringing those characters to life in your retelling. And you need to do the same with the setting and the problem.

What is the Setting?

What is the setting of the story? That's the question you have to ask next. Many stories are utterly dependent on the audience knowing what the setting is. Imagine the Three Little Pigs without their houses, the Troll without his bridge, or Cinderella without a fancy ballroom. And in the case of Bible stories, there are so many that we know by their settings – The Woman at the Well, The Fiery Furnace, The Storm at Sea.

And those settings are varied and interesting and fun! People who have been Christians for a while have those pictures of what I call "generic Bible land", where every setting is made up of a house with a flat roof, a palm tree on either side, and a camel! But there is so much more to biblical settings than that. And your audience needs to know where they are!

Now, there's no need for a lengthy, flowery description. That may have worked, once upon a time, but these days I think it can unnecessarily slow down the pace of the story. It's the problem that drives the story – remember – and a lot of descriptive language can clog up the traffic! So keep the descriptions simple and clear. Trust me (or if not me, then all the editors I've ever worked with!) – a few well-chosen words can be more accurate and poetic than a paragraph's-worth of bad ones. Better still, you can sometimes even give your audience the chance to "be" the setting. This won't work with every story, obviously, but it can be very effective with some.

When I tell the story about Jesus calming the storm, I ask the audience to rock gently back and forth. They become the waves on the sea. They become the setting. And not only do they hear about Jesus' power to still storms, but they experience it as well!

You can find hooks in settings, as well, that will help you to shape the story. As I read through the story of Joshua and the Battle of Jericho, the thing that jumped out at me was the fact that they had to march around the walls. So the phrase "round and round" became the hook to tie the story together. The walls go "round and round" the city. Joshua's thoughts spin "round and round" in his head. The angel's sword swings "round and round" his head. The soldiers gather "round and round" to hear the plan. And, last of all, the people, at last, march "round and round" until the walls come tumbling down. It's simple, I know! But as I've suggested many times already, it's usually the simplest ideas that are the best. And when they are connected to the setting, they also help, I think, to make the story more real, more concrete.

What is the Problem?

Every story has one central problem. And it is the problem that drives the story – that makes the listener stay with the story to the end to discover how that problem is resolved. Will Cinderella get to the ball? Will Red Riding Hood escape the wolf? Will the tortoise win the race, or will the hare? Those are the problems that push these stories along. So the problem needs to be stated early and then used to build the tension throughout the story.

The difficulty is that, unlike finding the characters or the setting, finding the main problem is sometimes a little more tricky.

With some stories, there is more than one central problem to choose from. Is the story of Zacchaeus about a bad man who needs forgiveness, a lonely man who needs acceptance, a short man who can't see, or a town that needs to understand Jesus' priorities regarding the company he keeps? The main problem could be any of these, but it can't really be all of them – not in one story, anyway. You have to choose which problem *you* want to drive the story, right from the start, because the way you tell the story (the point of view you choose, the participation exercises you use – everything in fact) will depend upon the problem you want to resolve.

You could say the same thing about the problem in the prodigal son. The problem could be, "Will my dad take me back?" The problem could be "Will my son come back?" The problem could be "Why did my dad take my brother back?"

There is a sense in which the problem you choose depends partly on your own preference, and partly on the needs of the group for whom you are preparing the story. But you still have to choose.

There's another potential difficulty. It's not uncommon for stories to have too many problems to solve in one sitting. The story of Joseph, extremely familiar now because of *Joseph and the Amazing Technicolor Dreamcoat*, is a good example of that. The story comes to us in several episodes: Joseph the dreamer, Joseph the slave, Joseph the servant of Potiphar, Joseph the prisoner, Joseph the ruler, and Joseph the saviour of his people. Each of those episodes has its own driving problem. So it might be best to tell it in several sittings, or at least as several episodes.

Finally, the problem you choose to drive a story might have something to do with the age and maturity of your audience.

The story of Jonah is a good case in point. When children are very small, we sometimes just tell them about a man who was swallowed by a big fish (or a whale). As they get older we tend to focus on Jonah's disobedience as the main problem. But a closer inspection (particularly of that bit at the end) reveals that the problem in "Jonah" is actually all about racism. That's right – racism! Jonah's disobedience is due to the fact that he hates the people of Nineveh and does not want God to save them. That's why he sits on the hill, at the end, and watches over the city. He's waiting – waiting for them to fall back into their evil ways, in the hope that God will destroy them after all. So what does God do? He grows a tree to give Jonah shade. And then he sends a worm to kill the tree. And when Jonah complains that the tree is dead, God brings him face to face with his upside-down priorities.

"You care about this tree," God sighs, "but you care nothing for a city full of people who do not know their right hand from their left." And that's where the story ends! We never even get to hear Jonah's response. Why? Because the original storyteller – the person who wrote the book of Jonah – wanted the reader, wanted the hearer, to provide his or her own response. Will we love those whom God loves (even though they are different, even though they are our enemies)? Or will we continue in our prejudice and hate?

It's a powerful story, Jonah. But it's even more powerful (and surely more appropriate to our day and age) when you understand the true nature of its problem.

So, choose your problem – that's the key thing – for it will affect everything else you do.

4

Storytelling Tips and Techniques

The Place of Play

When I was a boy, I had lots of little plastic dinosaurs and farm animals and toy soldiers and cars and trucks. On the days that we couldn't go outside, my two brothers and I would take all of those little plastic toys, dump them into a pile on the middle of the floor, and spend ages choosing which ones we wanted on our "team". Then, when all the choosing was done, we'd act out little adventures with those toys. We'd visit each other's "houses", and drive around in the cars, and at some point a battle would inevitably break out, and somebody's toys would go flying down the stairs!

What were we doing? We were playing. And when it comes down to it, I believe that's what storytelling is all about. It's play – a verbal kind of play. So whenever I prepare to stand before a crowd, the first thing I do is to go to the "place of play". I'm not sure where that is, exactly. It's in my head, and in my memories, and in my heart, all at once. But I know when I'm there. And I think that the children I share the stories with know that too. It's like they can see it in my eyes, sense it in my voice, pick up on it as we build that all-important relationship. It's a place they're familiar with, you see. And a place where adults seldom go. So when they see an adult in the place of play, it makes a difference – it really does. They lean forward, they listen, and they smile. And they want to see what is going to happen next!

Good storytelling begins with being in the place of play. Why? Because kids love it when adults go there. If you're a parent or a grandparent or a teacher, you know exactly what I mean. When you take the time to get down on your hands and knees and join your children in play, they are surprised and delighted all at once. And I think that's because, for just a short while, we crawl into their world – with their rules and expectations –instead of forcing them into our world. Frankly, I think the same thing applies to storytelling with adults. One of the reasons they enjoy it is because they get to "play", to be children again, for a while, to go to some Never-Never Land, some once-upon-a-time place, and be in touch with the best kinds of childhood memories. I know that's true, not only because of what I see in the expressions of the adults who enjoy a good story, but also because of what I have seen in the eyes of those who try their hardest to resist it. I've told lots of stories in all-age family services over the years, and there are always a few adults in every church who really struggle with that experience. For some reason – maybe because their own childhood wasn't a happy time – they just don't want to go to that place of play. And they know that's where a story will take them.

Being in the place of play simply makes it easier to be a good storyteller. When I'm in the place of play, I'm relaxed, I'm looking forward to what will happen next, it's easier to respond to the unexpected, and I'm in the mood to have fun (which is even possible with quite serious stories). When I'm not in the place of play – when I'm tired, maybe, or just not happy to be in front of a crowd on that day – I can feel the difference, I really can. I'm tense, I'm more nervous, I'm less likely to pick up on those little things that happen in the audience and help to make the stories come alive. It's simply harder to build that all-important relationship. I don't see or hear the audience as clearly as usual. I get frustrated more easily if things go wrong. It's a bit like sports, I guess. When a football player or a tennis player is relaxed and into the game, then there's a flow, an energy to what they do that can turn even the biggest mistake into something good. For a storyteller – that "zone" is the place of play.

The place of play is also a place of commitment. When children play, they rarely do it half-heartedly. They throw themselves into it – doing whatever the game, the scenario, situation demands. When I was a kid, I can't ever remember saying to my friends, "Sorry, it's a bit embarrassing to have to pretend I'm a monster today." Yes, we'd argue about who had to play what role, but that was always because there were some roles that were just plain better – usually because they were more, rather than less, outrageous. Children can tell if you're in the place of play by your willingness to "go for it" – to set aside the normal adult inhibitions and act in the joyful, unrestrained way that they do. And when you're in the place of play, you're more likely to want to go there, yourself.

"But what about the other adults in the room?" people often ask me. "I'm all right when I'm on my own with the kids," they say, "but I don't want to look a fool in front of my friends or workmates or the other people in my church." All I can suggest is this. Your willingness to go to the place of play and look like a fool will not only bring joy to the children in your audience (and get them on "your side"), it will bring a little joy into the lives of your friends and colleagues, as well! And what could be wrong with that? And I don't just mean that in a "laugh at you and not with you" kind of way. The silliness, the goofiness, the joyful surprises, or the honest tears that are a part of the best kind of storytelling – those simple and basic emotions – are the very ones that get suffocated as we become older and more sophisticated. Storytelling can set them free, and set a part of us free along with them.

There are some groups, however, who are not that keen on going to the place of play, and they make the hardest audiences. Adolescents, particularly, can be difficult (although I have even experienced this among younger children), especially in settings where groups from one or more schools have come together. There's a fear about not appearing "cool" in front of their peers, which often makes them very quiet and unresponsive. These groups require a slightly different approach.

It starts with remembering that "relationship" thing again. Your goal is not to embarrass your audience (well, not until you know them, anyway!), so you do the best you can do and start with a story that's pitched where you think they are. If they're sitting back, arms folded, with that "too-cool-for-storytelling" look in their eyes, don't start with something that's too young, too silly, or requires too much participation. Give them something you're confident with, so that you can watch their reactions and find out what they like. Test the waters with a little participation. Will anyone volunteer? How do the others react? Try several different kinds of humour as well. Do they laugh the hardest at slapstick, wordplay, or sarcasm? Find out what works and go with that. If, for some reason, you're committed to a serious story, then be real with it – give it everything you've got. I've discovered that teenagers, in particular, can really get into a serious story, partly I think because it shows that you're taking them seriously. You're not treating them like children, but like the adults they consider themselves to be. Whatever you do – keep watching them. Get your energy from those who are responding positively. Ignore, for a while at least, those who insist on training their eyes on the ceiling. They will come along as more of the others do. You can count on it. And by the end of the session (this is my experience, anyway), they'll be "playing" along with the rest of the audience – although they'd be horrified if you were to call it that!

Bringing characters to life

One of my all-time favourite stories is "Aunt Mabel's Table". It's one of the first ones I ever wrote and I've told it hundreds and hundreds of times. So many times, in fact, that when the marketing and sales people at my publisher accompany me to promotional events, they run screaming from the room at the first words of the introduction! Every storyteller has a few stories like "Aunt Mabel's Table" – stories that work so well, and they enjoy telling so much, that they can hardly keep themselves from doing it!

"Aunt Mabel" works for a couple of reasons, I think. It has an interesting problem (that's what drives the story – remember?). Five dinner guests. Five cans of food. You have to eat whatever is in the can you choose. But none of the cans has a label. It's like a culinary version of Russian roulette!

But what really makes the story work is the variety of characters around the table. There is Aunt Mabel, for a start, who has invented this little "game". At one point in the story, she is described as being "a little different from other people". There is her husband, Uncle Joe, who has allergic reactions to just about everything. There are her children, Sue (who is probably the least eccentric of the lot), and Tom, who got dog food the last time they played the game! And then there is Alexander – the visiting nephew – from whose point of view the story is told. These characters are talking constantly – guessing what is in each can and commenting on the contents –so it's important that the audience can easily distinguish one from the other. That's the challenge of bringing a character to life.

When I first told this story, I took a hard at look at each of the characters and found a couple of adjectives to describe each one. Then I tried to find a voice, a set of expressions, and a posture to "portray" each character.

Aunt Mabel stands up straight and tall, her hands folded in front of her. Her voice is high and posh, with just a hint of barely disguised eccentricity! She smiles almost all the time – because she loves her strange little game.

Uncle Joe, on the other hand, hates the game. He's stooped over. He's grumpy. And he's loud! "That sounds like the lumpy meat spread you always buy!" he shouts. "The kind that makes me burp!"

Alexander's cousin Sue doesn't like the game either. But she knows it's not going away, so her voice suggests a sense of sad resignation.

Cousin Tom is a bit of a geek. He's got a nasal voice and a buck-toothed expression that I use to convey his hope that he won't end up with yet another can of dog food.

And Alexander? He's confused and nervous and just a little frightened by this curious dining experience. So I make his voice and actions small and tentative.

I develop my characters in the same way in my retelling of the story of Daniel in the Lions' Den. This first appeared in *Angels, Angels All Around*, and then it was turned into a stand-alone picture book, *Dinner in the Lions' Den*, complete with some amazing illustrations by Tim Raglin.

I usually tell the story on my own, so once again it's key that the audience knows the difference between the characters. Daniel was quite old when he was chucked into the lions' den, so I walk with a stoop and give him a croaky old-timer's voice. Father Lion gets a deep, growly voice, Mother Lion a high-pitched ladylike voice. The cubs sound like the little kids they are. And the angel is boomy and Brian Blessed-like. With the lions, I adopt a crouching kind of posture, while the angel stands tall – again simply to suggest a difference and to make sure the audience knows who is speaking.

The idea is to make the characters interesting, funny, and distinct, and to do it as simply as possible, so that the change from one character to another doesn't interrupt the smooth flow of the story. That's why I have a problem with using lots of props and costumes. If I'm telling the story on my own, then the time that it takes to change hats or wigs or shirts or whatever usually distracts the audience from the story itself. The trick is to keep it simple – to find just the right "face" or just the right "posture" so that the character can be recognized immediately. Try them out in front of a mirror. That's one of the easiest ways to see if your expressions or postures work. If they make you laugh, then they will probably make your audience laugh, as well. When my brother Tim was a kid, he used to spend hours in the bathroom. We thought he had digestive problems, but it turns out that he was just practising his silly faces! I'm sure that's one of the reasons he's so good at doing them now. And you will find better faces, too, if you try them out and work at them (and are part of a family with really strong bladders!). So think about your characters, try out a few faces and postures, and keep the characterization clear but simple.

And that brings us to character voices. Lots of aspiring storytellers have told me that they struggle creating voices, but I'm convinced that most people can do voices – five, at the very least! Let's take a look at each one:

> The "high and squeaky" voice is one that most people can do – a voice that would suit a little child, or a fairy, or a baby bird type character. I find that this voice works particularly well if you're a big guy. Kids love the humour that comes from that kind of contrast. So have a go. Why not try it out, right now! Take the first couple of lines of "Twinkle, twinkle little star" and say them in the highest and squeakiest and funniest voice you can do. If you do, you'll notice that that little voice is echoing around somewhere at the top of your throat, right smack in the middle.

> The "high, scratchy" voice is made by just moving the "high and squeaky" voice to the back of your throat. This voice is great for squirrels and rabbits and hedgehogs and the like. It's cheekier than the pure high voice and works well with really mischievous characters. So go on. Try the "Twinkle, twinkle" thing again with that voice. It's at the top and the back of your throat.

> The "big, deep, and boomy" voice comes from right at the bottom of your throat, but back in that echoey middle part again. It's great for kings and giants. That's right – go on and try it. "Twinkle, twinkle" would be all right again – but you might want to use "Fee-fi-fo-fum" this time to get just the right idea!

> The "rough, growly" voice comes from deep in the back of your throat again. This one works for angry giants or lions or tigers or anything really that's meant to be big and scary. A little warning, though – this one will make you want to clear your throat afterwards, and even cough sometimes – and so might interrupt the flow of the story. Someone also told me once that this voice is not particularly good for your throat and could cause damage if used too

much. So use it sparingly. That will make it even more effective! Go on and try it, just to see how it works for you.

The "nasal" voice is initially created by pinching your nose, just below the bridge, and speaking. This voice is great for those geeky characters. Practise this for a while and you'll find that it won't be long before you can do it without the "pinching" bit.

So you see, there are five voices that anyone can do. And when you add your own voice – there are six! The fact of the matter is that you probably won't need any more than that in the average story. But if you want to add some variation from story to story, you can always play around with whatever regional accents you can do. The UK is blessed with a wonderful variety of regional accents that can make for some very interesting characters and really bring stories to life.

I would encourage you to use accents, with a couple of warnings. First, you need to feel pretty confident about your accent before you use it. There's nothing better than when the audience recognizes and laughs along with a really good accent. And nothing worse than when the audience gives you that puzzled look that shows they can't figure out what it is you're trying to do! So it's probably best not to "try out" an accent in the place from which that accent comes! Developing your Geordie accent in Swansea might go down just fine. But don't work on your Welsh one there!

It might also be sensible to avoid purely ethnic accents. There's a fine line here, I know. And it changes from culture to culture. But as a white Westerner, I would feel uncomfortable doing an Asian, middle-eastern, or "black" voice. It's too easy to stereotype. And, yes, I know that you could say the same thing about regional accents – but there doesn't seem to be the same risk of offence with those. And for some reason that I can't quite get my head around, everyone seems to laugh at a bad French accent (except, presumably, the French! Who knows? Maybe they get their laughs from bad English accents!). Anyway, try to be sensitive; the bottom line is that it's tough to build a good storytelling relationship with an audience you've already offended.

As with faces and postures, it's important that you find a voice that's appropriate to your character. Sometimes it can be fun to work against type. A giant with a little squeaky voice can be funnier than one with a big loud voice, for example. What you don't want to do, though, is to work against the problem in your story. If the giant is meant to be evil, it's probably best not to make him funny (unless you're going for a camp kind of evil). Or if you have a character who is meant to have something quite sombre to say in the story, it might be better not to give him or her a silly voice. All you will get then are laughs when you are trying to be serious. This can be a particular problem in biblical storytelling when it comes to choosing a voice for God or for Jesus. I always go for some variation of my "normal" voice for Jesus, and I work hard to erase any trace of that breathless, pious, "religious" tone (particularly since Jesus spent a lot of his time fighting against that very thing!). As far as the voice of God goes, the temptation is always to turn up the reverb and do the deep and boomy voice. I think that works sometimes, but that it's also helpful to remember that, as in the Old Testament story of the prophet Elijah, God sometimes speaks in a "still, small voice" as well!

Repetition

Here's a little quiz! When you think of the story of the Three Little Pigs, what phrase comes to mind? "I'll huff and I'll puff and I'll blow your house down"? Or maybe "Little Pig, Little Pig, let me come in" and "Not by the hair of my chinny-chin-chin". And how about the phrase that you connect with the Three Bears? "Who's been sleeping in my bed?" right? And Jack and the Beanstalk? "Fee-Fi-Fo-Fum, I smell the blood of an Englishman!" Of course! And what is the reason that you remember those phrases? It's because they are repeated, over and over again throughout those much-loved stories.

When I say to my grandchildren "Little Pig, Little Pig, let me come in!", they know exactly how to respond. Because repetition works! It's a very important part of traditional storytelling. And here's why. First of all, repetition helps the storyteller to remember the story! Once upon a time, stories were not written down. They were passed on, orally, from teller to teller. Repetitive devices helped to keep the story anchored in the teller's head. That's why repetition often takes place at the transition points in stories – to conclude one section or set up another. It saves the teller from having to think about how to get into the next part. It's there, in the mind, as a kind of breathing space.

Similarly, repetition also helps to make the story more memorable for the audience. Tim and I would go back to the same schools, year after year, and invariably we would be greeted by kids shouting out a repetitive phrase from the year before (and sometimes even four or five years before). The phrases stuck – and so did the story along with them.

Repetition also helps to build tension in a story. The audience soon catches on to the fact that certain phrases or actions will happen again and again. Then they look forward to the repetition, expect it, anticipate it, and enjoy it when it comes round again. So if that repetitive device is linked to the problem in some way (as it often is), then it serves to create the kind of tension that every story needs on its way to a resolution.

Finally, repetition encourages participation. There is a wonderful Puerto Rican tale about a grandmother struggling to put her grandson to bed. The bedroom door is squeaky and every time she shuts it, it wakes him up. So she fills his bed with a variety of pets to keep him company. The sounds of the door and the boy and the animals are repeated over and over again. And I find that I don't even have to tell the audience to make those sounds along with me. After I have repeated them a time or two, they catch on to how the story works and jump right in. That kind of spontaneous participation is a wonderful thing, but it happens in that particular story only because of the repetition.

What this story also demonstrates is that repetition is particularly effective with younger children. I think it has something to do with the confidence that comes from catching on to the pattern of the story. It's similar, in a way, to what happens in the television series, *Teletubbies*. There is that moment, in every episode, where the audience sees a short film on one of the Teletubbies' bellies. And when the film is over, what do all the Teletubbies say? That's right, "Again, again!" Yes, that bit is repetitive as well – but that's not the bit I'm referring to. Adults don't need to see that short film again. And most of them don't want to. But for the target audience, seeing the film again is just the right thing. Because the second time round, they've got it! There are no surprises. Nothing to be scared by, if you are so inclined. They know what's going to happen. They have caught on. They get it! And in a world where there's lots they don't yet get, that inspires a certain amount of confidence and security and they can enjoy it even more the second time.

So when I retell stories for very young children, I make sure that I include lots of repetition. Because they like it *and* they need it.

I still include repetition for older audiences (for all the reasons I have stated above) and because even adults enjoy a bit of repetition. You see it when you hear your favourite song, and the guitarist hits that chord to kick off the chorus, and you start singing along!

Some of the stories that you tell will already have those repetitive devices built into them and I encourage you to use them. But if those devices are not there already, it's not that hard to come up with repetition of your own.

Once again, keep it simple – a phrase, a response, an action (something that's easy to catch on to and fun to do) will keep your audience with you, right through to the end.

At the end of this section, you will find a number of retellings that depend totally on repetition – stories that are simply a series of "verses" (only this isn't poetry), each comprising two repeated lines. There are two reasons why I wrote them this way. The first is that they "work". Repeating the first line three times gives the teller the opportunity to milk the maximum meaning out of the line – to emphasize one part of the sentence the first time it is said and different parts on the subsequent times.

I always teach all the actions at the start – because it's fun and it sets the mood for the story. But I know, just as the audience does, that without a bit of prompting along the way through the story, they won't remember what those actions are. Doing the second line three times, first reminds them of the action and then gives them the chance to catch up with and enjoy what they have been given to do.

That's the "official" reason for structuring the stories in that way. The "historical" reason is that I was once given a nine-minute slot to tell a story, but only had three minutes'-worth of material in the piece – so I figured that if I just did everything three times... well, you do the maths!

Participation

Now to what is, in my opinion, the most important storytelling device of them all. If storytelling is truly a dialogue, then someone needs to get the conversation started. If storytelling is really just a verbal form of play, then it's no fun to play alone. Participation is the icebreaker that starts the conversation, the invitation for everyone to get down on their hands and knees and play.

Participation comes in many forms. At its simplest, a participation device is something that everyone in the group does together. Maybe it's an action that everyone does on cue. Maybe it's a line that everyone echoes back to the storyteller. Maybe it's a response that everyone makes when a certain word is spoken. Sometimes it's helpful to start the story by telling the crowd what they need to do at a certain point. And sometimes it works just as well to ask them to do it when you get there. The important thing, though, is that the participation device should be easy to catch on to (that simple thing again!), and fun to do.

A participation activity that's too difficult is a bit like that part of the wedding ceremony where the bride and groom have to say their vows, and the vicar gives them those long wordy chunks to repeat. Everyone feels bad when the couple stumble and fumble and mispronounce the words. And the same thing can happen in a story.

But it can be just as bad when the participation activity is simply not interesting. There's nothing better than being involved in a story where everyone is doing something together that's fun. And there's nothing worse than going through the motions to get through an activity that's not.

So how do you tell the difference? Well, you have your own experience to start with. Does a particular phrase, action, or response feel like it's fun to you? If not, then find something else. Certain things almost always work – silly noises (body noises particularly – but your repertoire really needs to extend beyond fitting raspberries somewhere into every story!), funny faces, and, for some reason, elephant and monkey impersonations. Exaggeration of any kind, in fact, will usually work – as long as you're comfortable exaggerating, yourself, and having fun with it too. That's the key, really. If you introduce an activity as if it's the best thing in the world, and the group sees that you're enjoying yourself, they are more likely to enjoy it too. And more willing to have a go in the first place.

Participation activities where everyone is doing the same thing are probably the easiest kind to initiate. There's more security for each individual if everyone looks foolish, and so you're likely to get more of the crowd involved. If some folks are not participating, however, don't harangue them.

A little gentle encouragement is all right. Something like "OK, everybody now!" But singling out non-participants will not win you many friends. Some are more shy than others. Some might be struggling to do the activity or repeat the words – no matter how simple. Some might have certain disabilities, even, that make the activity more difficult for them. And some people just don't like to participate! So be gentle. Continue having fun with those who are joining in. And hope that those who aren't will catch the spirit of the thing and join in later. It's that relationship thing again. It will take longer for some folks to feel secure with you than for others. Give them time. Don't rush the relationship. And more often than not you will find them getting involved a story or two later.

A word or two about very small children, here. Many little children are frightened by loud noises. They can't stand them – they really can't. On the other hand, there are other small children who love to make loud noises!

What do you do if that's one of your participation activities? You warn them, that's what. You say something like, "We're going to make a really loud noise, and if you don't like loud noises, now is the time to hold your hands over your ears!" That won't spoil things for the kids who like to make the noises. In fact, it will give them time to take a really big breath! But it will prepare the kids who don't like them. And surprisingly, it will give them the chance to make the noise too – but in a safe and secure environment. I can't tell you how many little children I've seen – hands held tight over their ears and shouting for all they're worth!

Here's another thing you might want to keep in mind, when it comes to small children and participation. I learned this the hard way, actually. When I started storytelling, I worked mainly with primary school children. But then my sister, who worked in a pre-school, asked me to tell some stories to her class. When the time came for participation, I did the kind of thing I normally did with older children – I asked three of the kids to come up front and play different parts. They were simple parts and the children did very well, but just as soon as the story had finished, the other children began to shout "Again! Can we do it again?" (It was that Teletubby thing, again – see above.) You see, everybody wanted the chance to play those three parts! But in order to make that happen, I would have had to tell the story fifteen times at least! So now, when I tell stories to very small children, I give everybody the chance to do everything. And then we don't need to do everything again!

(Having said that, there is no reason that you can't repeat a story in a session, if the audience really wants you to. As a matter of fact, it happened just the other day during a story-building session with a brilliant class of Year 7s! It's the ultimate compliment, I suppose – that a group should enjoy a story so much that they want to repeat the experience.)

The final thing I need to say about participation and very small children is that they should not be put into situations where they feel too vulnerable or insecure. I was telling the story of David and Goliath, once, and chose a four-year-old girl for the part of David. Unfortunately, I left David on her own for too long, while I dealt with King Saul and Goliath. And it wasn't long before I felt someone tugging on the leg of my jeans. I looked down, and David was about to burst into tears. "What am I supposed to do, now?" she whimpered, the panic building. I tried to calm her down. "It's OK!" I said. "You're doing fine." But she still looked really nervous. At one time I would have simply asked her if she wanted someone else to play the part. But that can be harmful too. It wasn't her fault that I'd left her on her own for so long. So, instead, I asked her if she wanted someone else to come up and help her. As it happened, there were red-headed twin girls sitting right near the front. They were a little older than her but they were obviously her friends, so she asked if they could come up and play David too. So, suddenly, David was not one girl, but three! Not historically accurate, but it worked. As a matter of fact, it worked incredibly well! She regained her confidence, her friends supported her, and when they repeated David's lines in unison, it was brilliant!

It was that relationship thing again. The story is important, yes. You want to tell it and tell it well. But the people who participate in the story are more important, still. So if you have to stop things, or alter things, or even have a three-headed King of Israel, to make somebody feel better – then that's what you do: because participation creates possibilities that go beyond the power of the story itself.

I have seen this happen many times, but one occasion stands out in particular. It happened near the end of a storytelling session. I needed a boy to come to the front and act out a part, and I chose a little guy sitting right at the back. The teachers gasped a little when I pointed to him. (I get that a lot, actually. The cheeky attitude that can cause so much trouble in class is often perfect when it comes to picking someone to play a part. I don't know how many times that teachers have told me afterwards, "You picked the naughtiest kid in the school!") Anyway, I pointed to this child, the teachers gasped, and then he came up and did a great job. And then, during lunch, the teachers told me this boy's story. It turns out that reason they gasped was not because he was naughty, but because he was terrified of standing in front of a crowd. He had cried right through the school Christmas play, and they were worried that being up front during the story would have the same effect. Well, it didn't. And I would like to think that the secure and joyous environment that we were all a part of in that storytelling event had helped that little boy to find a way past his fears. Yes, participation is great. It makes any story better. But if it can help make somebody in the audience feel better, too – then that's the best thing of all!

So how do you choose a volunteer, when the participation activity requires an individual and not the whole group doing the same thing together? As I said earlier, you start by looking for that cheeky expression or that smiling face. Ideally, you want a volunteer who really wants to be in front of the crowd – someone who will enjoy the moment and help others enjoy it, too. Sometimes the crowd itself gives you a clue. One child will have her hand up and others around her will be pointing at her, as well. That's often a good choice, because the others think she's funny, or popular, and want to see her up there. This is especially true when it comes to choosing teachers as volunteers. When Tim and I did our assembly programmes, we always built a place into the story where we would need a teacher to come up to the front. Kids love to see their teachers doing silly, ridiculous things. But you have to be careful. We made sure that our teacher participation time was somewhere in the middle of the story. That gave us time to look around – to see which teachers were really enjoying themselves – because we wanted to go for someone who was a good sport. Again, the children would often make the choice for us. We'd ask for a teacher's help and all fingers would point to one man or one woman in particular. It's not that the kids wanted to see someone humiliated. They seldom knew what was coming, anyway. Instead, they knew who would be fun! They knew who made them laugh. And that's who they wanted to see up front.

What if no one volunteers? Then you do a little coaxing, have a little fun, assure the crowd that the activity won't be difficult. And if you're still stuck, you can ask two people to do one job (like our little David who needed that added security), offer to do it yourself, or just take a chance and pick someone who's been smiling all along (even if their hand's not in the air!).

Sometimes you get lucky and that little extra coaxing does the trick. And then, of course, once the rest of the audience sees that the volunteers are having fun, you have much less trouble getting someone next time round!

Have I made some bad choices through the years? Sure, it's inevitable. There have been the odd occasions (some truly odd!), where volunteers have refused to do certain things, or frozen, or been so wild and over the top that it was difficult to control them. And then there was that teacher – just the one, amazingly – who told me exactly what I could do with my participation activity! But, remember, this was over a twelve-year period, in front of hundreds of thousands of people. And in most of those stories, the participation went very well indeed. Sure, using volunteers is a risk. But it's one I'd take any day, because when it works (and it usually does), it brings an element of freshness and variety and surprise into the stories that would not otherwise be there. And, as I think I have demonstrated, it has the potential to do so many positive things for the participants, themselves.

Finally, here are a few more participation "tips" you might find helpful. Always be friendly and encouraging. I like to ask the name of the person who has come to the front and shake his or her hand. It helps to make that person feel more comfortable, I think, and lets him know that he is more than a moving "prop". It also makes it easier to refer to that person by name if something unusually fun happens, or you want to remark on the "performance" in one way or another. And I do think that each "performance" should elicit some remark – a clap at the very least, a "well done", or something more, if what happened was really special. Sometimes you find that you really relate well to the volunteer, and she feels free to comment, and you do too – and a little repartee develops. That's fine, as long as the rest of the audience isn't left out – as long as it continues to serve the story. It's back to the basics again – relationships and playing. If that's what's going on up front with the volunteers, then everyone will have a better time.

The same rule applies to individuals as it does to groups – make sure that the participation is simple and interesting. If there are "lines" to repeat, break them into little chunks – make them easy. Most of the time, I just say the line, myself, at that point in the story, and then have the volunteer repeat it after me. That way, we both get to enjoy ourselves as we say it, and the volunteer doesn't have to stand there worrying about whether or not she'll get the words right. If it's an action, make it clear what you want the volunteer to do. And if there is any difficulty, put the volunteer first. Always give that person the chance to step down gracefully if he doesn't feel comfortable.

Part Two

The Stories

The Old Testament

1

The Whole Story

I'm convinced that it's not only people outside of the church, but those within, as well, who don't have a clear picture of the "Big Story". And without that picture, the individual stories lack context and meaning. There is an overarching narrative in the Bible – a story arc into which each individual narrative fits. And this reading is an attempt to tell that Big Story as simply and concisely as possible. I have used it in churches and schools and training events, and each time I have seen the light bulbs go on and heard the "Ahas!" and the "So that's how it fits together!"

Without this story, all that follows is at risk of being turned into a collection of moral tales and fables. In fact, I would argue that what I call the "Aesopization" of the Bible is to blame for much of the misunderstanding that people, Christian and non-Christian alike, have about this amazing book. So let's start here, with the Big Story, and let that story set the context for the stories to come.

Telling tips

Most of the actions are done with the teller's hands. I have put them in parentheses after each line to help you along the way (I've almost done this piece enough times to remember what goes where, but I still find it helpful to have the cues). It's important that you teach the "chorus" to everyone first and run through it a couple of times with them. And make sure that you eyeball them the first couple of times you want them to come in, so they know how it works. And, yes, feel free to change or add to the actions.

Chorus

Worship God (*hands raised in praise*).
Respect yourselves (*hands on chest*).

Love one another (*hands clasped*).
Make good use of the world (*make shape of world*).

So God made the world,
And his voice was like a pair of hands (*put finger to mouth, then hold out hands*).

Day One (*one finger*): Light and Dark (*use hands to make two spaces*).
    Day Two (two fingers): Sea (wavy motion), Sky (make big arc with hand above), and Space (higher arc).
    Day Three (*three fingers*): Earth, hard as Rock (*fist*), and from the earth, green growing things (*with other hand, grow plant from behind*).
    Day Four (four fingers): Sun (sunburst with one hand), Moon (make crescent shape with two hands), and Stars (pick out stars with fingers).
    Day Five (*five fingers*): Sea Animals (*fish motion*) and Sky Animals (*bird motion*).
    Day Six (*six fingers*): Land Animals (*bunny*). And finally, and best of all, Man and Woman (*a finger for each – one on each hand*), Adam and Eve, made in God's image.

And God looked at it all and saw that it was GOOD *(thumbs up)*.
    And he said:

Worship God,
Respect yourself,
Love one another,
Make good use of the world.

And on Day Seven, God rested *(head on hands)*.

But then the serpent, a sly and crafty creature *(wiggly finger on one hand)*, spoke to Eve *(upright finger on other hand)*.
    "So God told you not to eat that fruit? Well, I say, take a bite – and you will be just like him."
    So Eve took a bite (upright finger on one hand bites hand shaped like apple – fist with thumb sticking out the top).
    And Adam did, too (do the same – reversing hands).

And suddenly everything was mixed up *(mixed-up hands)*.
    They were ashamed of themselves (finger on each hand – look at each other and run from each other).

They used each other (*fingers fight*).

They worshipped the world (fingers bow – power, wealth, fame, shoes! gag).

And when God came calling, they did not worship him, they ran from him and hid (*fingers run and hide*).

So God came up with a plan – a plan for his hands – to make things like they were, and maybe even better, so that once again all would be good (*thumbs up*).

> Worship God,
> Respect yourself,
> Love one another,
> Make good use of the world.

He chose a man (*single finger*), a man named Abraham, and took him from his home to another land (*grab finger with other hand and move it*). "I will bless the world through your family," God promised.

And he gave him a son called Isaac (*another finger joins first one*).

He gave Isaac two sons, Jacob and Esau (*two more fingers join*).

He gave Jacob twelve sons (hands and toes gag: count Abraham's kin up to that point on your fingers – one man, then his one son, then his two sons, then you come to twelve sons – so you start counting on fingers, run out, then lift a foot in the air as if you are adding with toes).

And when a famine came, he took one son and then the whole family to Egypt (*make a "Walk Like an Egyptian" shape*), so they would be safe.

And there the family grew – grew so large that Pharaoh became frightened and turned them into slaves (*hands holding bars*).

So God used his strong hand (*raised fist*) to set them free.

He made a way through the Red Sea (*parting motion with hands*).

He watered them (hands water garden – watering pot)

And fed them (hands like feeding a child)

And led them through the desert with Fire (*flame motion*) and Cloud (*make puffy cloud shape with hands*).

And he gave them rules to live by. Rules that said:

> Worship God,
> Respect yourself,
> Love one another,
> Make good use of the world.

And finally he brought them back to the land he gave to Abraham (*move finger with other hand again*), where everything should have been good (*thumbs up*)!

But because they were also children of Adam and Eve, things got all mixed up again (*repeat mixed-up motion*):

And they did things to shame themselves (*as before*)

And they used each other (*as before*)

And they worshipped the world (turn gag round: start with woman – fame, wealth, power – then man – Ferrari!)

And they ran from God and hid (*as before*).

So God called upon his "right-hand men" (*hold right hand high*):

Judges (*bring down gavel motion*) like Gideon and Samson,

Good Kings (*crown of two hands on head*) like David and Hezekiah,

Prophets (*hand from lips – outward*) like Elijah, Isaiah, and Jeremiah,

To lead them back to him.

But the more he reached out to his people (*one hand reaches*), the more they ran away (*the other moves away*).

And finally he had to let them go off to slavery again (*hands on bars again*) – off to Babylon – for seventy long years.

He brought them back, at last (one hand brings back the other).

And then God went quiet (*"Shhh!" motion – finger to lips*), very quiet, for 400 years. It takes time to make a plan – a good plan, that is – and this one was a doozie!

If his people wouldn't come to him, then he would go to them.

So he put on hands (*pretend to put on hands – like gloves*). The hands of a man called Jesus.

And he spoke through those hands and reached out through those hands.

And those hands were just like a voice (*finger from lips outward again*).

"Worship God," he said. And his hands cleansed the temple of injustice and greed (*pushing-away motion*).

"Respect yourself," he said. And his hands welcomed the outcast (*pulling-in, welcoming motion*).

"Love one another," he said. And his hands healed the sick (*gentle touch*) and forgave the sinner (*holding motion*) and brought enemies together (*clasp hands*).

"Make good use of the world," he said. And his hands stilled the storm *(violent hands, then still)* and turned water into wine *(pouring motion, then glass raised)*.

His people should have been happy. Everything should have been good *(thumbs up)*.

But because they were children of Adam and Eve, everything got mixed up again *(mixed-up motion)*.

And they took those hands

And bound those hands *(hands crossed)*

And drove nails through those hands (finger in each palm – or hammering motion)

And pinned them to a cross (hands held out in crucifixion position).

Where they took hold of and then cast away every wrong thing anyone would ever do.

And when those hands were quiet and still, they folded those hands *(fold hands)* and put them in a tomb *(roll stone in front)*.

One day passed, then two, then three *(count with fingers – 1, 2, 3)*.

And because they were God's hands, no tomb could hold them. No power could still them forever.

So they rolled the stone away *(roll stone away)*, and burst out of the tomb *(bursting motion with hands)*.

And when he went to see his friends, Jesus said, "Don't be afraid, it's me. Look, see the nail-prints" *(show nail-prints – 1, 2)*. "These are my hands" *(hold out hands)*.

And before he left them, before he waved goodbye *(wave)*, he put his message in their hands *(finger to lips to hands)*. "Go," he said, "go tell everyone:

> Worship God,
> Respect yourself,
> Love one another,
> Make good use of the world."

And so they did,

From Judea

To Samaria,

To the ends of the earth (point to a spot, then one further away, then one further still),

To you and me (point to audience and then to self).

And now we are his hands *(hold out hands)*
To do his work.

And one day, when he returns, he will wipe away all that is mixed up *(mixed-up motion)*, and every tear with it *(wipe tear from cheek)*.

And the work of his hands *(hand held high)* and the work of our hands *(hand held low)* will make a new heaven *(two hands held high coming down)* and a new earth *(make shape of world)*.

And we will worship him
And respect ourselves
And love one another
And make good use of that world forever.

Give yourself a hand! *(Applaud.)*

2

The Fourth Vulture

Genesis 21:8–21

Here's a story from Angels, Angels All Around. *Hagar is in the desert, sent away by Abraham, and the vultures are circling. It's those vultures, high in the sky, one then two then three then four, which chart the progress of the story and move it along. It's a simple device, but it builds the tension until the fourth vulture swoops down in Hagar's direction.*

Telling tips

I have nothing special to suggest because I think that participation could spoil the mood. Just tell it dramatically on your own.

One Vulture.
Hagar saw him out of the corner of her eye as she raised the water pouch to her son's cracked lips.

Empty. The water was all gone.

And the vulture celebrated with a shrill cry and a lazy loop-the-loop.

Two vultures.
Their wings beat slow and heavy, like hot wind against a tent flap.

Hagar heard them as she picked up little Ishmael and laid him in the scraggly shadow of a desert bush. The bread was gone too. And with it any hope for survival. Hagar cradled her son's head and stroked one sunken cheek.

"Quiet now," she said. "Sleep now."

And in no time, the exhausted boy was off. Hagar gave him a dry kiss, eased his head onto a rolled-up blanket, and sat down a short distance away. She could not bear to watch him die, but she could shield him from the sun's hot stare. And she could chase away the vultures.

Three vultures.

Hagar cursed them, shaking her fist at the sky. But they took no notice. They just chased each other, tracing circles round the face of the sun.

Hagar cursed the sun, too. And the desert – this dry and empty place she was forced to wander.

And then she cursed the day that had brought her here – that day so long ago when everything seemed simple.

She had been a servant girl. And Sarah was her mistress. Sarah, the wife of Abraham – leader of the tribe. Abraham, who left the comforts of city life to find a new land, a land that God had promised to show him.

God had made another promise, too, so they said. Abraham and Sarah would have a son who would be the first child of a mighty new nation. But Abraham and Sarah weren't getting any younger. Indeed, Sarah was already well past her childbearing years.

And that's where Hagar came in.

"Go to my husband," Sarah had ordered her, "and bear his child. I am too old. God's promise is surely not for me. But perhaps through you, Abraham will see the promise come true."

Hagar had obeyed her mistress. She had given birth to Ishmael. And, for a time, everyone had been happy. Then, several years later, Sarah miraculously became pregnant too, and gave birth to a son she called Isaac. From that moment, Hagar's happiness had begun to flicker and fade, till it finally disappeared like some desert mirage.

Sarah's jealousy was the problem. She feared that Ishmael and not Isaac would receive Abraham's inheritance, because he had been born first. So she made life miserable for Hagar and Ishmael, and finally persuaded Abraham to send them away into the desert.

So now, along with the desert and the vultures and the sun, Hagar cursed Sarah, her jealous mistress. She nearly cursed Abraham too. Abraham, her master and the father of her son. But then she remembered that look in his eyes as he sent them away.

The look that said, "I don't want to do this."

The look that said, "I can't find any other way."

The look that said, "I believe things will be all right."

Were those looks real, Hagar wondered. Or were they just mirages? Were those tears in the old man's eyes, or just a reflection of the desert sun?

Four vultures.

And the fourth bigger than the rest.

What did it matter anyway? thought Hagar. In a short time, both she and Ishmael would be dead. The vultures would get their dinner. Sarah would get her way. And Abraham would still get what his God had promised – a son, a family, a mighty nation.

Abraham's God had been good to him. Oh, that he would be so good to her.

And yet there had been a time, Hagar remembered, a time when God had been good to her. A time shortly before her son had been born, when Sarah's jealousy was just beginning to brew. A time when she had fled, afraid of Sarah's evil temper.

Then God had sent an angel to comfort her. "Call your son Ishmael," the angel had told her. "The name means 'God has heard.'"

Ishmael was moaning. She could hear him crying out in his sleep. Would his name hold true? Hagar wondered. Would God hear him now?

One vulture.

At the sound of the boy's cry, the fourth vulture cried back – long and hard and fierce. And instead of descending on their victim, the other three vultures flew away.

Hagar ran to Ishmael, ran to the bush, ran to rescue him from the great dark bird that still remained. She threw herself over her son, wrapped herself around him, buried her head, shut her eyes and waited.

The fourth vulture dropped lower, in ever shrinking circles. It grew larger and larger the closer it got, until it was a huge winged shadow, blocking out the scorching eye of the sun. It hovered over Hagar and Ishmael, hung low in the air. And then the vulture spoke!

"Don't be afraid," it said. "God has heard the cries of your son. See, I have chased away the vultures. I have shielded you from the sun. And now I have something to show you."

Slowly, Hagar lifted her head and looked up.

Round, dark eyes.

Black, feathery hair.

And a sharp beak of a nose.

The face that greeted her looked much like a bird's. But the kindness and love in that face could only have come from somewhere far beyond the sky. And she knew in a moment that the wings beating above her were angel wings.

Like a mother cradling twin children, the angel lifted Hagar and Ishmael into its wings, and then onto its back. They flew straight for the sun, high above the desert, until they could see for miles in every direction.

The angel turned to the north. "There is Abraham's camp, the place from which you came."

Then it turned to the south. "There is an oasis – with food and water, where you can rest and live!"

Finally, it turned to the east. "And there – do you see it? All that land and the land beyond? That is the land that will one day belong to your son Ishmael and to his sons after him."

And then the angel dived straight for the oasis. And the swiftness of the dive startled Hagar, sent her hair whipping round her head, and made her clutch tightly the soft feathers that surrounded her. But even the speed of the descent could not shake the smile that now rested on Hagar's face.

When they reached the shimmering pool, Hagar filled her water pouch until it wanted to burst. Then she poured the water into Ishmael's mouth and over his face, and into her mouth too. And when she had drunk her fill, she turned to thank the angel.

But it was gone. The sky was empty. The sun had begun to set – no longer the burning eye of an enemy, but the warm, watchful gaze of a friend.

And that's when Hagar gave thanks to God.

For one angel.

One promise.

And no more vultures.

3

A Wife for Isaac

Genesis 24

Introduction

I love "counting" stories! And kids seem to like them, too. So the repetition built into this story is a counting kind of repetition. The counting serves to break the story up into sections and effectively announces transitions in the narrative. But it also serves to remind the hearer of the main problem.

Telling tips

Break your group up into three sections. Teach the first section: "Ten Camels, Nine Camels, Camel Number Eight". Teach the second section: "Seven Camels, Six Camels, Five Camels, Four". And then last section: "Three Camels, Two Camels, Camel Number One". Don't teach them the last line in each of their sections, mainly because one of those lines changes at the end and you will need to say that. So, for example, let them do the counting in each section, "Ten Camels, Nine Camels, Camel Number Eight", and then you finish off with the final line – "He waited at the well outside the city gate."

Ten Camels
Nine Camels
Camel Number Eight
He waited at the well outside the city gate.

Seven Camels
Six Camels
Five Camels
Four
The servant waited at the city of Nahor.

Three Camels
Two Camels
Camel Number One
He was looking for a wife for his master's son.

Abraham could not have been more clear:

"I do not want my son Isaac to marry a Caananite girl. So go to the land I came from, to the city of Nahor, and find a wife for him there. Then bring her back here.

"Do not take my son with you, or let him go to fetch his bride. He needs to stay here, in the land that God has promised us.

"You must bring her back for him."

Ten Camels
Nine Camels
Camel Number Eight
He waited at the well outside the city gate.

Seven Camels
Six Camels
Five Camels
Four
The servant waited at the city of Nahor.

Three Camels
Two Camels
Camel Number One
He was looking for a wife for his master's son.

The task seemed impossible! Who should he choose? How would he know? And how could he persuade her family to let her return with him?

"An angel." That's what his master had said. "God will send an angel ahead to prepare the way."

But as far as he could tell, there wasn't an angel in sight. Just a well. And his ten camels. And a parade of beautiful potential wives.

Ten Camels
Nine Camels
Camel Number Eight
He waited at the well outside the city gate.

Seven Camels
Six Camels
Five Camels
Four

The servant waited at the city of Nahor.

Three Camels
Two Camels
Camel Number One
He was looking for a wife for his master's son.

So the servant prayed:
"God of my master Abraham, help me. Use me to fulfil the promise you made to my master, when you said that his descendants would fill the land where you led him. Show me the woman you have chosen to wed his son."
And then he paused. And then he continued:
"Here's what I'm going to do. I'm going to ask each woman for a drink from her water jar. And if one of them offers to give water to my camels, as well, I will know that she's the one!"

Ten Camels
Nine Camels
Camel Number Eight
He waited near the well outside the city gate.

Seven Camels
Six Camels
Five Camels
Four
The servant waited at the city of Nahor.

Three Camels
Two Camels
Camel Number One
He was looking for a wife for his master's son.

Before the servant had even finished praying, a beautiful young woman called Rebecca arrived with a water jar.
She went to the well. She filled her jar. And the servant ran after her and asked her for a drink.
"Of course," she said. And when he had drunk his fill, she asked, "Can I bring some water for your camels too?|
And at once he knew. She was the one!

Ten Camels
Nine Camels
Camel Number Eight

He waited at the well outside the city gate.

Seven Camels
Six Camels
Five Camels
Four
The servant waited at the city of Nahor.

Three Camels
Two Camels
Camel Number One
He was looking for a wife for his master's son.

So, as he prayed a little prayer of thanks, the servant produced two gold bracelets and a gold nose ring and gave them to the girl. He asked her to take him (and his ten camels) to her father's house, where he told them all about his master and his mission and his hopes that she would marry his master's son.

More gifts were given – to Rebecca and to her family, too. And finally she agreed to go with the servant and meet Isaac.

So off they went – the bride-to-be, the servant, and the ten camels – to meet his master's son.

Ten Camels
Nine Camels
Camel Number Eight
He waited at the well outside the city gate.

Seven Camels
Six Camels
Five Camels
Four
The servant waited at the city of Nahor.

Three Camels
Two Camels
Camel Number One
The servant found a wife for his master's son.

4

I Hear Them Crying

Exodus 3

This is the first of a series of four Moses stories I performed at a Christian festival a while ago. I was asked to tell the stories not from Moses' point of view, but from God's. And so, in this first story, we crawl behind the bush and see the story unfold from God's perspective. I think it's important to share that with your crowd, because that point of view is critical to the participation activity you will be asking them to contribute to the story. I think this reading (and the three that follow) would work nicely for adults as an introduction to a sermon series on Moses. They could also be used in all-age services, and in Sunday school – particularly for children aged eight and up.

Telling tips

Divide the group into two. Have one group put their hands to their ears and join you in saying "I hear them crying". Have the other group shield their eyes as if they are looking for something, and join you in saying "I see them suffering". Start small and quiet with this, and, as the reading moves along, lead the group in making this louder and more intense. If you are simply going to deal with the Moses story, you might want to finish before the alternative ending, but if you want to bring the point a bit closer to home, then fill in whatever current issues you think are appropriate and carry on until the end.

At the top of a mountain, behind the mask of a burning bush, God watched the old shepherd creep closer and closer. He looked an unlikely choice. Unlikely like Abraham. Unlikely like Isaac. Unlikely like Jacob, before him. But the old shepherd was God's choice. And now it was time to say hello.

"Moses!" God called. 'Don't come any closer. Take off your shoes. For I am the God of your ancestors, Abraham, Isaac, and Jacob. And this is a special place."

Terrified, the old shepherd did as he was told. He slipped off his sandals and covered his eyes. Who wouldn't? And then God spoke again:

"My people are slaves in the land of Egypt.
I hear them crying, I see them suffering.
They work long hours for nothing at all.
I hear them crying, I see them suffering.
Their masters whip them, and beat them, and bruise them.
I hear them crying, I see them suffering.
Their children are taken and murdered in front of them.
I hear them crying, I see them suffering.
I care for my people, I hurt when they do.
I hear them crying, I see them suffering.
And now I have come down to save them.
For I hear them crying, I see them suffering."

And then God paused. And then God waited. The bush burned dim and low, for God had something else to say. Something sure to send the old shepherd shaking. Something scarier than anything that had happened so far.

"And Moses," God said at last. "Moses, you are going to help me."

Possible ending

There was an item in the paper about starving children.
I hear them crying, I see them suffering.
There was something on the TV about a deadly disease.
I hear them crying, I see them suffering.
They want to pass a law to kill even more unborn babies.
I hear them crying, I see them suffering.
The council won't give permission to house refugees.
I hear them crying, I see them suffering.

And Moses, I know you're an unlikely choice.
And Moses, I know that sometimes you're scared.
But Moses, the bush is burning – like God's passion for
a world in need.
And the holy place is any place where those needs are met.

So Moses, won't you hear?
Moses, won't you see?
Moses, won't you care?
And Moses, when God comes to save,
Moses, won't you be his helper too?

5

A Thousand Bricks a Day

Exodus 5

I like this reading a lot, because I think it helps bring home, through the participation and repetition, the hopelessness the Israelites must have felt.

Telling tips

Teach the chorus before you start, and help your group to really get into it. A pile of straw – use two hands to make the shape of a pile. A lump of clay – one hand throwing a lump of clay, as onto a potter's wheel. A thousand bricks a day – two hands building a brick wall, brick by brick. The grunt – at the end is essential, particularly for a younger audience.

The key is to get the idea of the drudgery across in the way you say it, but also to have a bit of fun with the actions.

> A pile of straw,
> a lump of clay,
> a thousand bricks a day (grunt).

The people of God worked hard for their masters. Every day. All day. And if they did not make as many bricks as they were meant to, the slave-drivers would whip them and beat them and bruise them.

> A pile of straw,
> a lump of clay,
> a thousand bricks a day (grunt).

God felt sorry for his people. So he spoke to his helper, Moses. "I have decided to rescue my people," he said. "To lead them out of the land of Egypt. But we must take this one step at a time. Tell Pharaoh, the king of Egypt, that my people must go into the desert to worship me for three days."

> A pile of straw,
> a lump of clay,
> a thousand bricks a day (grunt).

So Moses did what God said. But when Pharaoh heard, he just laughed. "The god of your people?" he chuckled. "Sorry, I don't think we've met. And if I've never heard of such a god, why should I listen to him, or let you leave to worship him?"
"You're lazy, that's all. You and your people! Now get back to work!"

> A pile of straw,
> a lump of clay,
> a thousand bricks a day (grunt).

But later that day, Pharaoh spoke to the slave-drivers. "Our slaves have asked for a little holiday," he sneered, "to worship some god or other. Obviously, they have too much time on their hands. So I think we shall teach them a lesson. Up till now, we have given them the straw they need. But from now on, they will have to find their own straw. And they will still have to make the same number of bricks each day!"

> A pile of straw,
> a lump of clay,
> a thousand bricks a day (grunt).

So the people of God went to find their own straw. They gathered what little they could from the fields. But with so much gathering to do, there was no way they could make as many bricks.

> A pile of straw,
> a lump of clay,
> a thousand bricks a day (grunt).

And because they failed to meet their goals, the slave-drivers whipped them and beat them and bruised them even more. "This is not fair!" they cried to Pharaoh. "This is your fault!" they cried to Moses. "You told us you came to help. But now you have made things worse!"

> A pile of straw,
> a lump of clay,
> a thousand bricks a day (grunt).

So Moses went to God and told him what the people said. "I know it looks bad now," God answered. "But trust me, Moses, when Pharaoh sees my power, everything will change. There is hope. There will be justice. And, one day soon, my people will no longer sing:

> A pile of straw,
> a lump of clay,
> a thousand bricks a day (grunt)."

6

But Pharaoh Would Not Listen

Exodus 7–14

The trick with this reading is to create a sense of excitement (and even a little humour) as the plagues progress, while also communicating the seriousness of the story. The audience will follow your lead, so it's up to you to make that change of tone obvious – getting very solemn, in particular, as you do the actions about the death of the firstborn. You might even want to say "And Pharaoh would not listen" at that point, with a touch of sadness and regret.

Telling tips

Because there are so many actions and sounds for this story, I have included the tips at the appropriate places in the text. Before you begin the story, you will need to teach your group the Pharaoh line ("Nyah, nyah, nyah, nyah, nyah!" – and make it really big – like a child in the playground!) and also the wave UP and wave DOWN for the end. Otherwise, tell them you will show them what to do along the way, and then give them time to do the actions/sounds themselves after you. It might be helpful to have an assistant or two up front, so the crowd can follow them – it will help with the timing and the enthusiasm, and with knowing when to bring each action to an end. Don't pull a volunteer from the crowd for this. Use someone you have had a chance to practise with!

"Moses," God said, "I want you to pass a message on for me. Go to see Pharaoh, the king of all Egypt. Tell him it's time to set my people free. And warn him that if he does not listen, some terrible things will happen."

So Moses did as he was told. He went to see Pharaoh and passed on God's message. But Pharaoh would not listen. (*Everyone cover their ears and shout "Nyah, nyah, nyah, nyah, nyah!"*)

So God filled the rivers of Egypt with blood. (*Make waves with hands – ick!*) God filled the houses of Egypt with frogs. (*Jump and/or make frog sounds.*)

God filled the skies of Egypt with gnats. (*Make a buzzing sound and wave arms about.*)

But Pharaoh would not listen. (Everyone cover their ears and shout "Nyah, nyah, nyah, nyah, nyah!")

So God struck the land of Egypt with flies. (*Slap arms and neck.*)

God struck the animals of Egypt and they died. (Make sad "moo" or "baa" sound.)

God struck the people of Egypt with sores. (Stroke arms.)

But Pharaoh would not listen. (Everyone cover their ears and shout "Nyah, nyah, nyah, nyah, nyah!")

So God sent hail to crush the crops of Egypt. (*Make falling/pelting sounds.*)

God sent locusts to eat up whatever was left. (*Make gobbling sounds.*)

God sent darkness to blot out the days of Egypt. (Look around as if they can't see – hands in front, feeling.)

But Pharaoh would not listen. (Everyone cover their ears and shout "Nyah, nyah, nyah, nyah, nyah!")

So God sent an angel to kill the sons of Egypt – the firstborn son in every house. (*Pretend to hold dying child in arms – solemn.*)

And when Pharaoh's son died along with the rest, finally Pharaoh listened. "Go!" he said to Moses. "Go and take your people with you."

But as soon as they had gone, Pharaoh changed his mind.

Still he would not listen. (Everyone covers their ears and shout "Nyah, nyah, nyah, nyah, nyah!")

He leaped into his chariot and sent his army after them.

Soon the sea stretched out before God's people, and Pharaoh's army rushed, like a wave, behind them. What could they do?

"Raise your special walking stick," God whispered to Moses.

And Moses listened. Moses listened! He did what God told him, and the sea split in two before him (*do a wave UP and hold it there*) – leaving a path right down the middle.

God's people hurried to the farther shore, the Egyptian army close behind. And when the last of God's people had reached the shore, God spoke again.

"Lower your stick now, Moses."

And when Moses did, the waters rushed back again. (*Do the wave DOWN.*)

God's people were free at last. (*Cheer!*)

But the army of Egypt was swept away. Because God had spoken – and Pharaoh would not listen.

7

The Tyrant's Tale

Exodus 7–14

Here's part of the big story that an Ancient Hebrew (assuming you could find one) would tell if you asked him about his God. It's taken from Bible Baddies. *And it's one of my grandma's favourites. So there, lots of boxes ticked – and an interesting retelling to boot.*

Telling tips

You need to get into the heads of the characters in this one – the magicians and Pharaoh himself – to bring them to life.

At first it was almost amusing.

"Did you see those two old men?" Pharaoh chuckled to his magicians. "They looked like a couple of goats, dragged out of the desert."

"Desert goats!" agreed the first magician.

"Moses and A-a-a-ron," baa-ed the second.

Pharaoh laughed out loud. "And did you hear what they wanted?"

"LET MY PEOPLE GO!" mocked the first magician in a deep and booming voice.

"OR YOU'LL BE IN BIG TROUBLE!" boomed the second.

"THE GOD OF THE HEBREWS DEMANDS IT!" boomed Pharaoh too. And they all laughed together.

Pharaoh wiped his eyes. "I suppose I should cut off their heads," he chuckled. "But everyone needs a good laugh, now and then. And I've got to admit it, two desert tramps demanding that I, the supreme ruler of all Egypt, release some stupid Hebrew slaves is the funniest thing I've heard in a long time!"

"Ridiculous!" agreed the first magician.

"The craziest thing I ever heard!" added the second.

No one was laughing the next day, however, when Moses and Aaron walked up to Pharaoh as he strolled along the River Nile.

"Not you again!" Pharaoh sighed.

And his two magicians sighed with him.

"The Lord God has sent us," Aaron explained. "You refused to let his people go and so now, by his power, I will turn the waters of Egypt to blood!"

The magicians couldn't help it. They grinned, they chuckled, they burst into laughter. But when Aaron touched his staff to the river, the smiles dropped from their faces, for the water was blood red.

"How did he do that?" Pharaoh whispered to his magicians.

"It's a… a… trick," stuttered the first magician.

"A-anyone can do it," explained the second.

"Then show me," Pharaoh growled.

The magicians hurried off and managed to find a bowl of clear water. Then they walked slowly back to their master, careful not to spill a single drop. They said their secret words. They shook their sacred sticks. And the water in the bowl turned to blood, as well.

"See," said a more confident Pharaoh to Moses and Aaron. "Anyone can do it!"

"Anyone," agreed the first magician, with a relieved sigh.

"Anyone at all!" boasted the second.

"And so," Pharaoh concluded. "You can tell your god that I will not let his people go."

Seven days later, however, Moses and Aaron came to visit Pharaoh once again.

"This is starting to annoy me," he muttered.

"And me, as well," agreed the first magician.

"Peeved, that's what I am," added magician number two.

But all Aaron said was "Frogs."

"Frogs?" repeated a puzzled Pharaoh.

"Frogs?" echoed his two magicians.

"Frogs," said Aaron once again. "Because you would not let his people go, our God will send frogs. Frogs in your houses. Frogs in your streets. Frogs all over your land." And with that, Aaron waved his staff over the Nile and walked away.

Pharaoh glanced around. "I don't see any frogs," he grunted.

"No frogs here," shrugged the first magician.

But the second magician simply said, "Ribbit."

"That's not funny," Pharaoh growled.

"It wasn't me – honest," the second magician pleaded. Then he lifted up his robe and pointed to his feet. "It was him!"

The frog hopped slowly away. And then, all at once, an army of frogs poured out of the Nile to join him.

Pharaoh and his magicians ran as fast as they could – away from the river, away from the frogs. But when they hurried into the palace, the frogs were there as well. Frogs on the floor, frogs on the furniture, frogs in the cups and plates and bowls!

"A simple trick," panted the first magician.

"We can make frogs too," added the second.

"I'm so pleased to hear it," Pharaoh grumbled. "But can you make them go away?"

The magicians looked at one another, and then sadly shook their heads.

"Then fetch me Moses and Aaron," Pharaoh sighed. "I think it's time to give them what they want."

So Pharaoh told Moses and Aaron that he would set the Hebrews – God's chosen people – free. Aaron smiled and raised his staff and the frogs all died.

But once they were gone, Pharaoh went back on his word, and refused to let the Hebrews go.

So that is why the plagues continued, each one worse than the one before. And that is also why the magicians came to Pharaoh, at last, with a message they knew he would not want to hear.

"Your Majesty," the first magician began, "these plagues can only be the work of some very powerful god. You must stop the suffering. You must let the Hebrews go."

"First there were the gnats," moaned the second magician. "In our eyes and in our ears and up our noses!"

"And then there were the flies," added the first magician. "In our food and in our clothes and in our beds."

"And then the animals died," sniffled the second magician. "The camels and the horses and the cows."

"And now these boils!" groaned the first magician.

"Stop your whingeing!" shouted Pharaoh, as he struggled to his feet. "Do you think that I am blind? That my family and I have not suffered as well? We, too, have swatted gnats and flies. We, too, have watched our animals die. And we, too, are now covered with these crippling sores. But if you think for a minute that I am going to give in to the Hebrews and their god, then you can think again. For I am Pharaoh, king of all Egypt, and no one – no one in heaven and no one on earth – is going to tell me what to do!"

The magicians hurried away.

Pharaoh stood his ground.

And so the plagues continued.

Hail rained down on Pharaoh's fields and crushed all Egypt's crops. Then anything left growing was devoured by hungry locusts. Finally, darkness covered the whole of the land. And when the magicians had grown tired of bumping into the furniture and having nothing to eat, they took their empty stomachs and their skinned knees one last time into Pharaoh's palace.

They found him sitting… alone. He was no longer frustrated, no longer annoyed. No longer angry, no longer enraged. No, he just sat there, quietly brooding, with his teeth clenched tight and his knuckles white around the arm of his throne.

"What do you want?" he muttered, barely looking at his magicians.

"We want you to give up," urged the first magician.

"Please!" begged the second. "Please let the Hebrews go!"

"No one will think less of you," the first magician argued. "You have done all you could."

"But the Hebrew god is just too strong!" added the second. "And besides, we have heard. We have heard what the next plague will be."

Pharaoh slowly raised his eyes and stared at his magicians. "The death of the firstborn," he said softly. "Your son, and your son," he pointed. "And mine as well."

"Please, Your Majesty," the first magician pleaded. "My wife and I – we could not think of losing him!"

"We love our sons. And we know you love yours," the second magician continued. "And you have the power to save their lives!"

"Power?" sighed Pharaoh. "What power? The god of the Hebrews controls the wind and the rain and the light. But I am just a king. And yet. And yet…" And here the king smiled a hard and cruel smile. "And yet there is still one power that remains. The power to say 'No'."

"But the children," the magicians pleaded. "The children will die!"

The king's smile turned into a hard and cruel stare. "Sometimes," he answered coldly, "a leader has to harden his heart to the sufferings of his people for the sake of his people's good."

"For his people's good," sighed the first magician.

"Or for the sake of his own pride," muttered the second.

"Out!" Pharaoh commanded. "Get out!" he shouted again. "And if you want to keep your heads, you will never return to this place!"

One week later, the magicians stood solemnly together and stared out over the Red Sea.

"So he let them go, after all," the first magician sighed.

"The weeping. The wailing," sighed the second magician in return. "They say he tried hard to shut it out. But then his own son died – and that was too much, even for him."

"So he let them go. And then he changed his mind – again!"

"I suppose he thought he had them trapped. Perhaps it never occurred to him that a god who could send locusts and hail and turn the Nile to blood could quite easily divide a sea, as well."

"And so the Hebrews crossed on dry ground. And our own army? What about the soldiers sent after them?"

"Drowned. Drowned as they tried to follow. Drowned as the divided sea washed back over them."

"So our suffering was for...?"

"Nothing. Nothing at all."

"And what about Pharaoh?" asked the first magician. "What do you hear of him?"

The second magician shook his head. "One of his servants told me that he has forbidden anyone in the palace to even speak about this event. And he has ordered the court historians to make no record of it whatsoever."

"A proud man," muttered the first magician.

"Proud to the end," agreed the second.

And the two magicians turned away from the sea and walked sadly home.

8

I Will Be Your God

Exodus 16–20

The themes of this story are "celebration" and "covenant". God has rescued his people from slavery and now, as they celebrate their newfound freedom, they enter into a very specific relationship with him. The way you tell the story needs to reflect this – both the joy (which comes through the fun and funny bits) and also the commitment (as the crowd look at the cross near the end, and embrace each other in the chorus).

Telling tips

The chorus can be done in a variety of ways, depending on your crowd. If folks know each other well, you can break them into pairs, with one member of the pair saying (with outstretched arms), "I will be your God" and the other replying, "We will be your people" and embracing the first person. You might like to have a pair at the front to model this, with you (or you and a partner) leading everyone else in saying the lines. The advantage of this is that it has a real tactile appeal – and speaks the message of the text into the body. If folks know each other less well, then you can divide the whole group into two groups – one side of the room and the other – then just have them face each other during the chorus and lead them in their lines. As a final option, you might like to say the first line and have the rest of the crowd respond. As previous stories, I have placed the rest of the actions in the body of the text. The easiest thing for the crowd would be for you to divide them into five groups and have each group do the actions in their respective sections. Or you could just teach the actions first and have everyone do everything. There's a greater chance that they'll forget that way – but you can have fun with that too! By the way, make sure that you have fun doing the actions. That's the best way to guarantee that they will as well. And I don't mind if you can come up with something that's more appropriate for your group (or just funnier!).

Now that I have set you free, and saved you from your enemies...

> I will be your God.
> We will be your people!

I'll lead you through the desert to a land of milk and honey. I'll be a cloud by day (*look up and say, "Ooh, puffy!"*), and a fire by night (*make siren sounds*).

> I will be your God.
> We will be your people!

I'll feed you when you're hungry; you can count on me. Quail from the sky (*flap wings and make bird sounds*) and manna from the earth (*you can say "MMM!"*).

> I will be your God.
> We will be your people!

I'll lead you to fresh water; you can count on me. Water from a rock (*make strong pose and grunt*) in the middle of a desert.

> I will be your God.
> We will be your people!

I'll help you build a tent. I'll give you all the plans. A special place to worship me (*hold hands in the air*), a special place to meet with me (*then turn to neighbour and hold upraised hands together to make the shape of a tent*).

> I will be your God.
> We will be your people!

And I'll give you rules to live by – to treat each other well. No thieving, no killing, no wanting your neighbour's donkey (*hee-haw!*) or his wife (*ooh la la!*).

> I will be your God.
> We will be your people!

And together we will wait for a prophet just like Moses, who will welcome (*reader stretches arms wide in shape of a cross*) all the world to join with our community.

> I will be your God.
> We will be your people!

And lions (*everyone roars*) and lambs (*everyone baas*) will lie down together and the kingdom of heaven will come to earth.

> I will be your God.
> We will be your people!
> I will be your God.
> We will be your people!
> I will be your God.
> We will be your people!

9

The Donkey and the Sword

Numbers 22–24

This has always been one of my favourite Bible stories. And seeing as the most remarkable thing about it is the talking donkey, why not tell it from that donkey's perspective?

There were so many things the old donkey wanted to say:
"Could you brush a little harder?"
"Do you mind if we stop and rest now?"
"Barley cakes again?"

So many things. But donkeys were donkeys. And people were people. So she had to rely on sneezing and snorting, bucking and stalling, and the occasional huffy hee-haw, to tell her master what she wanted.

Balaam had been a good master, really. They'd been together since they were boy and foal, dashing around father Beor's yard till the sweat dripped off his forehead and lathered up on her sides.

Who could have guessed that Balaam would grow up to be so important?

He was doing some important thing now – meeting with important people. Well, at least their horses were important. She know that much. Tall, white stallions pawing the ground not a double donkey's length away from her. Neighing and whinnying to each other in high and horsey tones.

They were obviously not interested in talking with her, so she clip-clopped up to a window to see what her master was doing. There were three other men with him, one for each horse. She couldn't understand what they were saying. But if she could have, she would have known that the men were princes, and she would have heard their very generous offer.

"Balaam, son of Beor," said the first man, "we bring you greeting from the king of Moab. The people of Israel have come into our land, licking up all that is around them like an ox licks up grass. They have already defeated our neighbours, and we fear that they will destroy us next."

"And so we beg you," continued the second man, "to come with us and curse them. For we have heard that you are a great prophet, and whoever you curse stays cursed, and whoever you bless stays blessed."

"Look, here is silver! Here is gold!" said the third man. "And our king promises that you may have whatever else you want, if you will only come and curse these people."

Balaam looked at the three princes, and he looked at the gold. This was not the first time the king of Moab had made such an offer. Each time Balaam had looked to God for advice. And each time, God had plainly told him not to curse the people of Israel. They were special to God.

Still, thought Balaam, all that gold... A new house. A new wardrobe. A new horse! His old grey donkey had grown awfully slow. Hmmm... he wondered... perhaps God had changed his mind.

"Gentlemen," Balaam announced. "Stay with me tonight. I will speak with God, and in the morning you shall have my decision."

The donkey watched the princes leave her master's room. She watched her master pace the floor. She watched him sit down, lift up his hands and talk to the ceiling. Then she nodded off to sleep, her chin on the windowsill.

As it happened, God was watching Balaam, too. And God could see a battle going on in Balaam's heart – a battle between Balaam's desire to do what was right and his desire for gold. God could also see that Balaam was determined to go with the princes. So God spoke.

"All right, Balaam," he said. "You may go with the princes tomorrow. But you must say only what I tell you. No more. No less."

The next morning Balaam was in a dreadful mood. He had not slept at all well. And the battle was still raging in her heart. The donkey could tell that her master was upset by the way he kept digging his heels into her side and prodding her along. She wanted to tell him that she was moving as fast as she could. She wanted to say that she didn't care about keeping up with those show-off stallions. She wanted to say that years of loyal service were worth far more than a flashy mane and a little extra speed.

But donkeys were donkeys, and people were people. So she just shook her long eyes and clip-clopped along at a donkey's pace until the three horses and their princes were almost out of sight. And that's when the battle in Balaam's heart came to an end.

I am a great prophet, he told himself. Whoever I curse stays cursed. Whoever I bless stays blessed. Everyone says so. So why shouldn't I be wearing beautiful clothes? And why shouldn't I be riding a strong stallion – instead of this plodding old donkey?

I will do as the king asks, he decided. I will curse the Israelites. Surely God won't mind, just this once?

But God did mind. For God still had his eye on Balaam's heart, and he could see it sparkle and shine with thoughts of gold. So God sent an angel to warn Balaam and to win back his greedy heart.

The donkey saw the angel right away. It was standing in front of her and blocking the road. It was three donkeys high and two donkeys wide. And it was waving a sword that could chip-chop any clip-clopping creature in half.

She didn't know what this thing was after, and she didn't take time to ask. After all, donkeys were donkeys and this thing was… well, whatever it was, it didn't look happy. So she turned off the road and ran into a vineyard to hide.

Balaam, on the other hand, could not see the angel. And he was angry. First his old donkey couldn't keep up, and now she was dashing off on some detour. "Get back!" he shouted through a mouthful of grape leaves. "Get back on the road!" And he pulled hard on the donkey's reins and kicked even harder into her sides.

This kind of language the donkey understood. But she decided that if there was ever a time for her to be donkey-stubborn, this was it. So she ignored her master's commands and headed for a path at the far end of the vineyard – away from that thing with the sword.

But all of a sudden, the enormous angel was blocking her path once again.

"Stand still, donkey," the angel commanded in a voice that made a hee-haw sound like a whisper. "It's not you I want. It's Balaam, your master." Then it raised the sword as if it was going to strike.

Perhaps the donkey felt a sudden streak of loyalty to her master. Or maybe she was just too terrified to stand still. In any case, when she saw the sword above her head, the old donkey bolted through the narrow gap between the angel and the stone wall of the vineyard.

But in the process, she also managed to crush Balaam's foot against the wall's rough stones. And because Balaam still could not see the angel, he was furious.

"Stupid animal! Worthless beast!" he bellowed. "Stop!" And he struck her fiercely across the neck.

There was no time to stop, the donkey decided. There was time only to run. And run she did. But the path grew narrower and the walls on either side grew closer. And then the donkey once more found herself face to face with the angel. This time there was no gap to slip through – not so much as a bridle's breadth.

And so the donkey came to a sudden stop and dropped to her knees. Balaam tumbled over her head and landed right at the feet of the angel.

When he reached for his staff, the donkey thought he might – wonder of wonders – fight the enormous thing. What she didn't know was that Balaam still could not see the angel. What she didn't expect was what happened next.

Balaam struck *her* with the staff. Hard and cruel, as he'd never struck her before.

The donkey was hurt and angry. If only she could talk. Now, more than ever before, she wanted her master to know how she felt. But donkeys were donkeys. And people were people. So she sneezed and snorted and shook her head and got ready to let out the loudest angriest hee-haw she knew. But when she opened her mouth, this came out instead:

"What have I done to you to make you hit me?"

"What have you done?" Balaam spluttered and roared. "You've made me look like a fool in front of some very important people – that's what. And you've probably broken my foot as well. And if I could afford a sword instead of this ridiculous staff, I'd kill you here and now."

"Kill me?" howled the donkey. "But why? We've been together all these years. We've shared roads and deserts and mountains and streams. And in all those miles, have I ever let you down?"

"Well... no," huffed Balaam.

And then he stopped. And he stared at his donkey.

And his donkey stared back.

And no words, donkey or human, could describe their expressions or express the surprise they felt.

"We're talking!" said the donkey. "But that can't be. After all, donkeys are donkeys, and people are people."

"And sometimes people are donkeys, too," said another voice – a deep, rumbling voice.

It was the angel with the sword. The angel the donkey had seen all along. The angel that Balaam could finally see, too. And both the donkey and Balaam fell down in terror at the angel's feet.

"Take your master Balaam, for example," explained the angel to the donkey. "He decides to do what he knows will displease God. I come to warn him, to frighten him, to stop him from cursing God's people. You do everything you can to save him from my sword, donkey. And what is your reward? The same thanks he gives to his God – abuse and scorn. He's a stubborn man, your master. More stubborn than any donkey."

"I – I am sorry now," Balaam stammered. "I didn't see you... didn't know you were there." His voice was little more than a whisper. "And if you want me to, I'll go back home right away."

The angel lowered its sword and shook its head. "No, Balaam. God wants you to go with the princes. He has a surprise for the king of Moab. But you must do as God commanded – say only what he tells you to say. No more. And no less."

And then, before the angel disappeared, it waved the sword over Balaam's head one last time, just to make sure he got the point.

Balaam clambered aboard his donkey. As best they could, they raced after the princes, catching them finally as night fell. When they met the king of Moab, Balaam remembered to do exactly what God had commanded him. Every time the king asked Balaam to curse the people of Israel, God whispered a blessing from him to say instead. And since everybody knows that what Balaam blesses stays blessed, the people of Israel enjoyed happiness and prosperity for a long, long time.

The king was furious, of course. In fact, Balaam was lucky to return home with his life – much less any gold and silver.

As for the donkey, she never spoke again. But then, she never felt the need to. For, from that time on, Balaam could not have been a more grateful or caring master.

After all, donkeys are donkeys. And people are people. And as long as they understand each other, there isn't much left to say.

10

The Walls Fall Down

Joshua 6

This is a story that I use in workshops when I want to give an example of using the setting as the basis for finding a way into the story.

Telling tips

Divide the audience into three groups: one to your left (the people of Jericho), one in the middle (the wall) and one to your right (the Israelites). Ask the group in the middle to stand in a line, side by side, facing the Israelite group – you may need more than one row, depending on the number in this group – or you could just start by making this group a bit smaller than the others. Also choose someone to play an angel and give them something sharp to wave about. I usually use a pen (one that clicks or has a top is best – because you can cover the point if your volunteer looks a bit overactive!). Then tell the story and encourage everyone to play along. I usually just read the lines of the angel out loud and then get the angel volunteer to shout them after me. I do the same with the people of Jericho when they make fun of the Israelites.

The walls of Jericho went round and round. Round and round the whole city. The walls were tall. The walls were thick. How would God's people ever get in?

Joshua's thoughts went round and round. Round and round inside his head. He was the leader of God's people now that Moses was dead. But how could he lead them into Jericho?

The sword of the Lord swung round and round. Round and round the angel's head. "God will lead you into Jericho," said the angel to Joshua. "He has a secret plan. All you have to do is trust him."

The soldiers of Israel gathered round and round. Round and round their leader, Joshua. He told them the angel's plan. He didn't leave out one bit. The soldiers were amazed!

So the army of Israel marched round and round. Round and round the walls of Jericho. Once round each day. Six days in a row. And the people of Jericho laughed.

"Why are they marching round and round? Round and round the walls of Jericho? Is this a parade? Is it some kind of trick? They'll never beat us this way!"

But still the army marched round and round, round and round, on the seventh day – they marched round once, they marched round twice. They marched round Jericho seven times. Then they raised their voices. They blew their trumpets. And the walls came crashing down!

The people of Israel danced round and round. Round and round the ruins of Jericho. "God is our helper!" they sang and they shouted. "He will never let us down!"

11

Ehud and Eglon

Judges 3:12–30

Right then, this is the story where my "gap management" may well have gone astray. I'll leave it to you to decide.

Telling tips

Like the other former *Bible Baddies* pieces (Old Testament, chapter 7), this one needs to be read or told dramatically.

Every night it was the same. For eighteen years, the same. Ehud would wake up, suddenly, cold and sweating and afraid. And that face, the face in the dream, would be laughing at him all over again.

Shouting, that's how the dream began.

"The Moabites are coming! They've crossed the river and they're heading towards the village!"

What followed next was a mad, rushing blur – a spinning haze of colour and fear and sound. His father's hand. His sister's screams. His mother's long black hair. Goats and pots and tables, running and flying and falling down.

And then, suddenly, everything would slow down again, to half its normal speed. And that's when the man would appear. The laughing man. The fat man. Eglon, king of Moab.

He would climb down from his horse, every bit of his big body wobbling. And with his soldiers all around, hacking and slicing and kicking and killing, he would walk up to Ehud's family, each step beating in time with the little boy's heart.

His father, Gera, would fall to his knees. His mother, as well, with his sister in her arms. And then the big man, laughing still, would raise his sword and plunge it first into his father, and then through his mother and his sister too.

Finally, the laughing man would raise his bloodied sword and turn to Ehud, five-year-old Ehud. But before the king could strike, there would come a sound, a call, from somewhere off in the distance. The king would turn his head, look away for just a second, and Ehud would start to run – run between the burning buildings, run past his dying neighbours, run till the nightmare was over, run… until he awoke.

Every night, for eighteen years – that's how long the dream had followed Ehud. But tonight, he promised himself, tonight the dream would come to an end. For today, King Eglon of Moab, the fat man, the laughing man, the man who had murdered his family, would come to an end, as well.

Ehud thanked God for his family, and particularly for his father, and for the gift that his father had passed on to him. It was a gift that not even the Moabites could take away, a gift that made him the perfect candidate for the job he was about to do – the gift of a good left hand.

Most soldiers were right-handed. They wore their swords hanging from the left side of the body, and then reached across the body to draw them from their sheaths. That was what the enemy looked for, that's what the enemy watched – the right hand. For the slightest twitch, the smallest movement of that hand might signal that a fight was about to begin. So, a left-handed man enjoyed a certain advantage, particularly if his sword was hidden.

Ehud rubbed his eyes, rolled off his sleeping mat and reached for his sword – the special sword that he had designed just for this mission.

It was only eighteen inches long – far too short for battle, but just the right size for strapping to his thigh and hiding under his robes. And it was sharpened on two edges, so he could cut in both directions. He'd wipe the smile from the fat man's face, all right!

He'd waited for this day for eighteen years. And for those same eighteen years, the nation of Israel had been paying tribute to King Eglon. For the invasion which had destroyed Ehud's village had also swept across the land and resulted in Israel's surrender to Moab. And so, every year, great quantities of treasure and produce and livestock had to be delivered to the royal palace and presented to Eglon himself, as a sign of Israel's submission.

Today was the day – Tribute Day. And the man chosen to lead Israel's procession, chosen by God himself to walk right into the presence of the king, was none other than Ehud, the left-handed man, the man with the sword strapped to his thigh, the man who was finally in a position to set both himself and his people free.

Ehud thought he would be nervous, but instead he was overcome with a sense of calm and purpose. He led the procession, according to plan, out of Israel and across the Jordan river, past the stone statues of Gilgal and into the palace of the king.

He had imagined this moment for years – face-to-face, finally, with the man he hated most in all the world. *What will I feel?* he had often wondered. Hatred? Disgust? The overwhelming urge to reach out and strike Eglon where he stood? All those feelings, he knew, he had to overcome if the plan was to succeed. He must be submissive, polite, and reverential if he was to win the trust of this tyrant. But when Eglon, at last, appeared, Ehud was shocked by what he actually felt.

The king was still a big man – now far heavier than Ehud had remembered. So heavy, in fact, that his attendants had to help support his weight as he staggered towards his throne. But as for laughter, there was none at all, not even a chuckle – just a hard and constant wheeze as the man struggled to move.

Pity. That's what Ehud felt. And he couldn't believe it. Pity, and the surprising sense that, somehow, he had been robbed. This was not the man he'd dreamed of – the fat man, the laughing man, the nightmare man. No, this was a sad and pathetic man, crippled by excess and by power, and unable to raise a sword even if he had wanted to.

Still, Ehud reminded himself, there was the mission – the job he believed God had sent him to do. And pity or not, for the sake of his people, he would do it.

And so he bowed and he scraped and he uttered the obligatory words:

"Noble Potentate, Ruler of all You survey, Great and Mighty One."

Then he stepped aside as, one by one, the gifts were laid before the king. Eglon, however, hardly paid attention. He nodded, almost imperceptibly, and acknowledged each part of the tribute with the slightest wave of his hand. It looked to Ehud as if he was bored with the whole affair, or just too old and tired to care.

When the formalities had finished, Ehud sent his entourage away, then turned to the king and said, "I have a secret message for you, Your Majesty."

For the first time, Eglon looked interested. His dull eyes showed some spark of life as they focused on Ehud.

"Silence!" the king wheezed at his attendants. "This man has something to tell me."

Ehud looked around, nervously. "It's for your ears only," he whispered. "Perhaps if we could meet somewhere... alone?"

The king considered this, and then nodded. "Very well," he agreed. "Meet me upstairs, in my roof chamber. It's cooler there, anyway. Oh," and here he glanced at the sword that hung from Ehud's side, the long sword, the decoy sword, "you will, of course, leave your weapon outside."

Ehud smiled and bowed, "Of course!"

That smile never left Ehud's face – not once, while he waited for the king to be helped up to his chamber. For the plan was working perfectly, as all the spies had said it would. Eglon loved secrets; they had assured him. Dealing and double-dealing, they explained, were how he had hung onto his throne. And that made this plan all the more sweet. For Ehud's robe concealed a secret that the king would never expect!

Finally, the guards called Ehud up to the roof chamber. They looked at him suspiciously. They took away the sword that hung at his side. Then they sent him in to the king.

Ehud bowed again. And the king waved him forward.

"So who is this message from?" asked Eglon, and the cruelly calculating look in his eyes reminded Ehud, at last, of the man he saw each night in his dreams.

"From one of your commanders?" the king continued.

"Or from one of your spies?" he went on.

"Or perhaps the sight of all that treasure has convinced you to speak for yourself – to betray your own people?" And with that, the king began to laugh. A little, choked and wheezing laugh, but it was enough – enough to rekindle Ehud's ebbing wrath, enough to force him to play his secret hand.

"No," he answered firmly. "The message is neither mine nor my commander's. The message I have for you is from God himself." And he reached his left hand under his robe and drew his sword.

Three times – that is how he had always planned it. Once for his father, once for his mother, once for his poor murdered sister. But the first blow was so fierce that the sword plunged all the way in, swallowed up past its hilt in the fatty folds of Eglon's stomach. And even though Ehud tried to retrieve it, all he got was a fistful of entrails and blood.

Ehud locked the chamber doors to buy himself some time, then he hurried out down the servants' staircase. A part of him wanted to savour this moment – to stand and gloat over Eglon's bloated corpse. But if he was to avoid a similar fate, he needed to run. And he thanked God for the escape route the spies had plotted out for him.

Down from the roof chamber and along the quiet corridors of the private quarters – that was the plan. And, sure enough, he passed no one but a startled maid. He rehearsed it as he went: one more turn, one more hallway and he would be out. But as he dashed around the final corner, he stumbled over something, and fell in a sprawling heap onto the floor.

It was a boy. A little boy. "And he's not hurt," thought Ehud, relieved.

"Who are you?" the little boy asked, as he picked himself up and flashed a friendly smile.

"I'm... umm... it's not important," Ehud stammered. "I have to be going."

"Well, if you see my grandfather," the boy said, "will you tell him I'm looking for him? He said he would tell me a story."

"Your grandfather?" asked Ehud.

"The king, silly!" the little boy grinned. "Everybody knows that!" And Ehud just stood there, frozen.

He could hear the chamber doors crashing down. He could hear the shouts of the attendants, and their cries, "The king, the king is dead! Someone has murdered the king!"

He had to go. He had so little time. But all he could do was stand there. And look at the boy. And look at his own bloodied hand. And look at the boy again. And watch as the smile evaporated from his innocent five-year-old face.

And then Ehud ran. Ran as he ran in his dream. Out of the palace and past the stone statues to the hills of Seirah. The army of Israel was waiting there – waiting for his return. And as soon as he shouted, "King Eglon is dead!", the army swooped down to the valley below.

Ten thousand died that day. Moab was defeated. Israel was freed. And Ehud had his revenge, at last. And finally, after much carousing and shouting and celebrating, he rolled, exhausted, onto his mat, looking forward to his first full night's sleep in eighteen years.

But unlike Ehud's enemies, the dream would not be so easily defeated. For as the night wore on, it returned – more real than ever.

There was the little boy. There was the shouting. There was the slashing and the screaming and the dying. Ehud trembled and shook just as he had for eighteen years. But when he looked, at last, into the eyes of the man with the bloodied sword, Ehud awoke with a start. For the man with the sword was left-handed. And the killer's face was his own.

12

Chariot Wheels

Judges 4–5

This is a perfect example of what can happen when you go back to the text and, as I have suggested, read the whole story. In this case, that had to do with moving beyond the narrative description of the life of Deborah (in Judges 4) and on to the Song of Deborah (in Judges 5). There at the end of the poem is the poignant depiction of Sisera's mother, peering through the latticework, waiting for her son to come home. It's a familiar picture, particularly in light of the numbers of wars raging across the globe at the moment. And even though Sisera is the "bad guy" in this piece, no mother ever looks at her son that way: when he is off to war, he is always fighting on the right side, and all she wants is for him to come home. It's that feeling that I have attempted to bring out in the piece, while still telling the story. And as a result, it demanded that I tell the story, at least in part, from one specific character's point of view.

Telling tips

You could do this with another person – alternating voices between the sections that describe what Sisera's mum is experiencing (a woman's voice would be best here) and the sections that describe Sisera himself.

The old woman looked out the window
   "What can be keeping him?" she wondered as she watched for the rising dust and listened hard to catch the clatter of iron wheels.
   And then the wondering spilled out into words.
   "Why is his chariot so long in coming?" she whispered. And then comforted herself with the knowledge that her son commanded 900 of those chariots.
   Her son. Her warrior. Sisera, leader of the army of King Jabin of Hazor.
   She peered through the latticework. Nothing.

That's how he had described the army he would face that day.

Israelites. Ants. Crushed under his iron wheels for twenty years now. Destined to be crushed again.

So why was she worried? And why did her hand shake so?

Her lady-in-waiting tiptoed quietly from behind and looked out the window as well.

"I suspect they are still dividing the spoils," she said. "It can take some time to find them."

And if she had known, and if she could have peered, across the miles – the fields and rivers and hills – she would have seen that Sisera was, indeed, in search of something. But it wasn't the spoils of war. No, with his army routed and his soldiers corpses, he was looking for a place to hide.

"A girl or two for each man," said the lady-in-waiting. "That's what they'll find." And she might have been a prophet.

Bloodied and bruised, Sisera stumbled to the tent of Heber, and found Heber's wife, Jael, standing there.

"I'm thirsty. I'm bleeding. I'm cold," he cried.

So she welcomed him into the tent. She covered him with a blanket and gave him milk to drink.

"Beautiful garments," said the lady-in-waiting. "That's what they'll find. Embroidered clothes for us all."

"I'm exhausted," said Sisera to Jael. "Wait by the door. Let me get just a little rest. And if anyone should come by, tell them there is no one here."

Then he curled up under the blanket and soon was fast asleep.

Sisera's mother looked out the window. She looked again, in vain.

Jael looked, as well, and she found what she needed straightaway.

A tent peg.

A hammer.

And when she struck the blow, the peg went straight through his temple and, for just a second, he opened his eyes. Like he was looking for something.

"Beautiful clothes," said the lady-in-waiting. "Plunder. The spoils of war, my lady. Just you wait and see."

So the old woman waited.

And the old woman watched.

And listened for the clatter of chariot wheels.

13

The Fleece on the Floor

Judges 6

The important thing in this story is to communicate Gideon's uncertainty – reflected in the weakness of his support troops and in his need to ask for confirmation through the "fleece" – not once, but twice!

Telling tips

Divide your crowd into three groups and teach them the chorus. Manasseh should have a high, squeaky voice; Asher a nerd-like voice; and Zebulun and Naphtali (one group for both) an old man's voice. The idea is that they are not the ideal fighting force! In the second line, and in the same voice, Manasseh says "We'll choke you"; Asher says, "provoke you"; and the Zebulun and Naphtali group says, "and try to poke you in the eye!" You also need a volunteer (wearing a fleece!) to play the fleece. This person sits on a chair, and several other volunteers sit on the floor. They are the ground. Give one of them a squirty bottle (or water pistol) filled with water (be careful whom you choose here!). That person squirts the fleece at the appropriate time in the story. Don't tell them at the start that the roles will soon be reversed. If they don't know the story, just let them be surprised! Give the squirty bottle to the "fleece" person after Gideon begs for a second test – and let the revenge begin!

The Midianites and their allies crossed the River Jordan and camped in the Valley of Jezreel. It looked as if they were about to take over for good. So Gideon blew his trumpet and gathered soldiers from four of the tribes of Israel.

We're Manasseh/Asher/Zebulun and Naphtali
We'll choke you/provoke you/and try to poke you in the eye!

Now Gideon was no warrior, but even he could see that this was not a promising start. So he asked the Lord for some help. "Lord," he prayed, "you said you would use me to save your people. But look what I have to work with!"

> We're Manasseh/Asher/Zebulun and Naphtali
> We'll choke you/provoke you/and try to poke you in the eye!

"If you really mean what you've said, if you're really going to help, could you possibly, maybe, give me a sign? Here's what I had in mind. I'll take a fleece, an ordinary fleece, and lay it on the threshing floor. And if, tomorrow morning, the fleece is wet but the ground around it is dry, then I'll know for sure that I can count on you." So Gideon laid the fleece on the floor (*fleece person sits down*). And, sure enough, when he returned the next morning, the fleece was wet (*shoot fleece with water bottle/pistol*), but the ground around it was dry! Gideon felt much better. And then he had another look at his army

> We're Manasseh/Asher/Zebulun and Naphtali
> We'll choke you/provoke you/and try to poke you in the eye!

So Gideon went back to the Lord. "Lord," he prayed, "please don't be angry, but is there any chance that I could have just one more sign? How about this? I'll put the fleece on the ground again, and this time, could you keep the fleece dry and wet the ground around it?

So Gideon put the fleece on the ground, and sure enough, the next morning, the fleece was dry, but the ground around it was soaking wet. (*Fleece person sprays everyone else!*) "Thank you, Lord," prayed Gideon. "Now I know that you will be with us, no matter how impossible this seems."

And so Gideon, and his army...

> We're Manasseh/Asher/Zebulun and Naphtali
> We'll choke you/provoke you/and try to poke you in the eye!

... went off to face the Midianites

14

A Tale of Two Families

1 Samuel 1–2

A few years ago, I had to prepare a worship service based on the first couple of chapters of the first book of Samuel, and the difference between these two families – the opposite directions that resulted from changing circumstances – really jumped out at me. It's all down to that Overweight-Diva-Winding-Up-the-Wagner thing, isn't it? You just can't tell what's going to happen until the story ends. And because God is at work in this story, there's a lesson for us all about assuming too much, too soon.

Telling tips

Either you can do this one on your own, or, to emphasize the difference between the stories, you might want to read one half and have someone else read the second half. And then split the last line between you.

Hannah

Hannah was barren. And in the time and the place that Hannah lived, to be barren was to be cursed.

But things are not always what they look like.

Situations are not always what they seem.

And God has a way of taking one thing and turning it into something completely different.

Hannah was married to Elkanah – a man of means who could afford a second wife – Peninnah. And Peninnah, as it happens, was not barren at all. She had a brood of children, whom she stood before Hannah, at every opportunity, to make her curse even worse.

Elkanah was a good man. He saw, he understood, he longed to ease Hannah's pain. So when the family trooped from their home in Ramah to the holy place at Shiloh each year, and when they sat down to eat a portion of the meat that had been offered as a sacrifice to God, Elkanah always made sure that Hannah got a double helping of that meat – a special treat – and, surely, the first recorded example of comfort eating.

In spite of all her children, however (and as a powerful argument for monogamy!), Peninnah was jealous of this simple act of kindness. And she did all she could to make that a curse, as well.

"It is God who has closed your womb," she would tell Hannah, there, in the presence of God himself, in his own holy place. And she would do this, not once, not twice, but again and again and again, right up to the time of the feast. And poor Hannah would be so upset that she could not enjoy the treat her husband had planned for her. In fact, she could not eat at all.

"Eat, Hannah, eat!" Elkanah would say. He meant well, but (being a man!) he ended up saying all the things a husband should never say to his wife when she is so unhappy she can't eat.

"Why are you crying?"

"Why are you so upset?"

"You may not have any children – but you have me!"

One year, Hannah was so upset that she left the table altogether. She went to the door of the holy place, where Eli the priest was sitting. And there, through her tears, she offered up a prayer to God.

"Look at me, Lord, please! See my misery. Remember my condition. And give me a son, I pray. For if you do, then I will give him back to you, and dedicate him as your servant for all the days of his life."

These words were hard words. So hard that she could not speak them out loud. Hannah's lips moved, her tears flowed, and the old priest Eli (another man!) assumed that she was drunk.

"Sober up, woman!" he said. "This is neither the time nor the place. Take your bottle and go home!"

Hannah could not believe this. All she wanted was help, and here was another curse.

"Drunk?" she cried. "Is that what you think? I'm not drunk! In fact, I can hardly drink or eat a thing! I'm here to pray – that's all – to pour out my grief and my troubles before the Lord."

"I see," said Eli, sorry not only for her sadness but for his mistake. "Then go in peace. And may the God of Israel give you what you asked for."

It was a blessing. A blessing, at last. Hard won, to be sure. But a blessing and not a curse.

So Hannah went.

And Hannah had something to eat.

And when she saw her husband, she smiled.

And when they returned to Ramah, she lay with him and conceived and gave birth to a son and called him Samuel – a name which means "God heard me."

And when Samuel was old enough, she took him back to Shiloh, back to the old priest Eli.

And though it sounds like the act of a crazy woman, or a woman who has had too much to drink, she left her only son there to serve in the holy place.

A blessing in return for a blessing.

A blessing, not a curse.

Eli

Eli was a priest – the son of the son of the son of the son (and a few more sons!) of Moses' own brother, Aaron. And at the time that Eli lived, to be a priest – a chosen mediator between God and man – was to be blessed.

But things are not always what they look like.

Situations are not always what they seem.

And sadly we all have a way of taking one thing and making it into something completely different.

Eli had two sons – Hophni and Phinehas.

And the Bible says it about as plainly as it can be said: "Eli's sons were scoundrels; they had no regard for the Lord."

(Not the best of qualifications for the priesthood!)

They had a plan, these brothers – a clever scam – and it went something like this. When the people sacrificed their animals to God, just some of the meat was burned on the altar. Only the best bits were offered up to the Lord. To put it in contemporary terms, if you were offering God a Bourbon Crème, he would get to lick out the stuff in the middle. If you were offering him a piece of cake, he would get the corner with all the icing and the big sugar rose. Well, at the time of our story, the best bits were the fatty bits. Those bits were offered to God. And the rest of the meat was put into a pot and boiled.

During this process one of the priest's servants was supposed to plunge a fork into the pot and fish out whatever piece of meat the fork found. This piece was given to the priests to eat – a potluck way of providing for their needs.

But Hophni and Phinehas were not satisfied with this potluck blessing. They were tired of their servants hooking the odd neck and hoof and knee bone along with the choicer cuts. And what is more, without regard for their obligation to God (or to the possibility of rising cholesterol and accompanying heart disease), they were keen to add a little more fat to their diet.

So they ordered their servants to approach the worshippers before the sacrifices were made.

"The priests do not want boiled meat," they would say. "They want to choose their piece now, while the meat is raw."

And if the worshippers objected and said, "Well at least let us burn the fat for God first," then all sorts of nasty things were likely to happen to them.

Word of this spread among the people. And finally old Eli, who should have been keeping an eye on his sons, heard about it too.

To be fair, he told them off in no uncertain terms.

"If you sin against another man," he said, "God is there to intervene for you. But who will be there to help you when you sin against God himself?"

But Hophni and Phinehas were enjoying their position and its newly found privileges, and refused to change their ways.

So God sent a prophet to Eli, who gave him some unhappy news.

"You have been so blessed," the prophet said. "God has chosen you and your family to make offerings and burn incense and to be his priests. But now you have dishonoured him by taking for yourself what is rightfully his. And so the Lord says that there will no longer be old men in your family. Your sons will die together, on the same day, and the priesthood will be given to another."

And that's exactly what happened. Hophni and Phinehas were killed in a battle with the Philistines over the ark of the covenant. Killed on the same day. And when he was given the news, old Eli was so shaken that he fell off his chair, broke his neck, and died.

And what should have been a blessing – a blessing to the people, a blessing to God, a blessing to Eli and his sons – became a curse.

For while God is more than able to turn a curse into a blessing, only we can find a way to turn a blessing into a curse.

15

Goliath

1 Samuel 17:1–51a

This retelling first appeared in More Bible Baddies. *And it's here largely because I think I probably got the imaginative gap stuff right in this case. I love this retelling and hope you will, too.*

Telling tips

Once again – read it or tell it with lots of drama. A big growly voice will definitely help.

He hated little things. And maybe that was because he had never really been little himself.

He'd been a baby, once, of course. But he was the biggest baby the people of Gath had ever seen! So it was big robes and big sandals and big toys, right from the start. And "Don't push that little boy, dear." And "Careful with that pot, child." And "Don't squeeze the kitty so hard, Goliath – you'll hurt him."

Little kitties. Little puppies. Little people. The world was full of them! And it didn't take long for them to notice that he was different – and to bring it, constantly, to his attention.

Some children return teasing with humour. Others with sullen stares. But Goliath chose fear. Even the most harmless comment about his size would result in a furious beating from the big boy. Yes, he was beaten a few times by some of Gath's older lads. But he soon outgrew them all, and then no one dared challenge the boy who stood nearly seven feet tall!

His occupation was chosen for him.

"There's only one thing to do with bullies," he overheard his father say. "The army! That'll sort him out."

Given his size and his strength, he might have risen high in the ranks. But his obvious hatred for "the little generals" and "their little rules" kept him marching with the infantry. In the end, there was only one thing he was good for – frightening the enemy. And Goliath was very good at that, indeed!

He'd strap on his armour – all 125 gleaming pounds of it.

Then he'd pick up his spear – ten feet long, with a fifteen-pound iron point.

And finally he would stand at the front of the Philistine troops – a shining colossus of a man.

"A challenge!" he would roar – roar across the valley to whatever army was camped on the other side. "A challenge is what I offer! Send your best man to fight me. And if he wins (and here Goliath always had a little chuckle), we shall be your slaves."

A few men had taken up his challenge. Little men. With little swords. And Goliath always smiled when he remembered how he had crushed their little heads and left their little bodies broken and twisted and torn.

Most men, however, never even tried. His presence alone made their little hearts beat with fear and sent them retreating to their little tents.

He expected as much today. The Israelites were not just a little people, they were the littlest of them all! A few scattered tribes. A puny, ramshackle army. And if what he had heard was true – just one little god to protect them. It hardly seemed worth the trouble, but he marched out anyway, into the valley of Elah, and issued his customary challenge. He anticipated a short day's work. But he had no idea how short it would turn out to be.

The Israelites heard the challenge, as they had every day for the past forty days. And, to a man, they trembled. But someone else heard the challenge too. Someone who had never heard it before. And it made him angry.

Maybe it had to do with his feelings about his people. Maybe it had to do with his feelings about his God. Or maybe he was just tired of being little.

He was the youngest of eight brothers, after all. And no matter how much courage he had shown defending his father's flock of sheep, they all still thought of him as the "runt". Hand-me-down sandals and pass-me-down robes – that was his lot. And while his older brothers got to serve as soldiers, the best he could do was bring them lunch, and carry chunks of goat's cheese to their commanders!

"If only," David dreamed, "I could do something big, for a change."

And then he heard Goliath's challenge.

"So what do you get if you beat the giant?" he said to a soldier close by.

"A king's ransom," the soldier answered. "The king's daughter, too. Oh, and a terrific tax break for you and your family."

"Well," mused David, "I'm surprised someone hasn't accepted the challenge already."

And that's when he felt a hand – a big hand – on his shoulder. The hand belonged to his oldest brother, Eliab.

"So what are you doing here?" Eliab growled.

"Bread... umm, cheese," David muttered.

"Excuses, more like it," Eliab growled again. "Get back to the fields, where you belong!"

But David did not go back to the fields. No, he crept along the front lines, talking to one soldier after another, always about the giant. Finally, word got back to King Saul, who asked to see the boy.

The giant, meanwhile, was still waiting.

"Their little hearts are in their little throats," he chuckled, in a nasty sort of way. Then he looked down at his shield-bearer. The little man was not chuckling back. In fact, it was all he could do, in the hot noonday sun, to keep himself and the shield standing upright.

"Pathetic," Goliath muttered, and then wondered if the Israelites would ever send him a challenger.

"So you want to fight the giant?" grinned King Saul.

David had seen that look before. He got it from his big brothers, all the time. It was that "I'm-not-taking-you-seriously", "You're-just-a-little-shepherd-boy" kind of look.

So David stood as tall as he could and answered with the straightest face and the deepest voice he could manage.

"Yes, Your Majesty. I do."

"And what makes you think you can beat him?" the king continued.

David didn't even have to think.

"I have fought lions," he said. "And I have fought bears. All to save my father's sheep. And, every time, the Lord God has helped me win. I am sure he will do the same with this giant."

The king didn't know what to do. The boy had courage. The boy had faith. But if he allowed him to fight the giant, the boy would also soon be dead! Still, he needed a champion – any champion! So he made the boy an offer.

"My armour," said the king, pointing to the other side of the tent. "At least, take my armour. My shield. My sword. My breastplate. Whatever you like! You will need all the protection you can get."

David looked at the armour. He even tried a piece or two of it on. But it was much too big and much too heavy for him.

"I have all the protection I need," he said to the king, at last. "The Lord God himself will be my breastplate. He, alone, will be my shield." And he bowed and he turned, and he walked out of the tent.

Goliath, meanwhile, was tapping one big toe on the ground and humming an old Philistine folk song.

"In another minute, we're going back to camp," he said to his shield-bearer, who breathed a relieved sigh and thanked every Philistine god he could think of. But before he could finish his prayer, a cheer rang out from the Israelite camp. Someone was walking onto the battlefield.

"At last!" Goliath drooled, like a hungry man who has just been called for dinner.

The figure looked small, at first. Goliath chalked it up to the distance. But the closer he got, the smaller he seemed, until the giant realized, at last, that his challenger was no more than a boy!

"Is this some kind of joke?" he muttered to his shield-bearer. But neither the shield-bearer nor the boy were laughing.

"Or is it…" and here the giant's words turned into a snarl, "is it some kind of Israelite insult? Do they mock me? Do they make fun of me? Well, we'll see who has the last laugh!"

And then he roared – roared so the ground shook, and the shield-bearer, as well.

"Do you think I am a dog?" he roared. "That you come at me with this little stick of a boy? Send me a real challenger. Or surrender!"

"I am the real challenger," said David, in that deep voice he had used before the king. "And," (here his voice broke) "the God I serve is the real God too. And he will give me the victory this day!"

Goliath had heard enough. He grabbed his shield and raised his spear and charged. Little people and little generals and little soldiers. Little things had plagued him all his life! And now this little boy and his little army and his pathetic little god were going to pay. He'd skewer the lad and crush his little head and show them all what someone big and strong could do!

But as he rushed, enraged, towards the boy, David calmly reached into his shepherd's pouch. He placed a small stone in his sling, and he swung it round his head. Then he prayed that God would make his throw both strong and true.

The stone and the giant sped toward each other. And, at the last moment, Goliath caught a glimpse of it – a tiny speck, a minute fragment, so small it was hardly worth avoiding. But when it struck him between the eyes, he roared and he cried and fell crashing to the ground. And that little thing was the last thing that the giant ever saw!

16

Good Idea. God Idea.

2 Samuel 7

I think this reading came out of a normal weekly preaching situation. The passage from Samuel was one of the readings for the week, and it seemed like a good idea (or maybe even a God idea!) to focus on the difference between what we dream up and what God has in mind for us.

Telling tips

I'm pretty sure I just read the text myself when I did it, but to further emphasize the "Oh", you might want to ask your group to join you in saying it. Or even split the group in two and have one group do the "calling" kind of "Oh" as in "Oh, Nathan" and the other group do the "discovery" kind of "Oh" as in "Oh, I see". And, to further emphasize the point (or maybe just beat it to death!), you could put "Good Idea. God Idea." up on the screen at the end.

"Oh Nathan!" said King David to the prophet one day. "I've got a good idea! I live in this very nice palace, with cedar walls and cedar sofas and every modern cedar convenience. But the Lord God has to make do with that tiny little tent we call a tabernacle. Why don't we build him a house?"

"Oh, what a good idea!" said the prophet Nathan to King David. "You live in this very nice palace, with cedar floors and cedar panelling and that lovely cedar cooker. But the Lord God has to make do with that tatty little tent. Why don't you build him a house?"

But that night, the Lord God spoke to the prophet Nathan.

"Oh Nathan," he said. "I hear that the king has a good idea. He wants to build me a house. I don't mean to sound ungrateful, but I have just one question: When did I say I wanted a house?"

"Compared to the king's cedar palace, my tent is indeed tiny, and getting a little tatty too. But it has served me well for many years, and it let me move with my people – from the wilderness to this lovely promised land."

"Oh," said Nathan. "Then what shall I tell the king?"

"Oh – I know," said the Lord God. "Tell him I have a better idea. Tell him that I don't need a house, but that I would like to build him one instead! Not a house of stone or brick or cedar, but a house of people. A family that will stretch through all generations. A kingdom that will never end!"

So God built David a house – a family to last the generations. Some of them lived in palaces. Some of them lived in tents. And one of them – David's great great great great great great great great grandson – was even born in a stable!

David's palace is dust. And so is the temple his son Solomon built. But the kingdom that God made goes on for ever and ever.

Good idea. God idea.

They look almost the same. But, OH, what a difference that one little letter can make!

17

Angel Food

1 Kings 19:1–8

The premise to this story is simple – God sends an angel to feed a prophet, so maybe that angel is a chef-type of angel, gifted particularly in the culinary arts. I suppose I had Delia Smith in mind when I first wrote this, but you can tell it any way you like – so if you want to Nigella-cize the angel, knock yourself out! The story might read quite a bit differently, however!

Telling tips

There aren't really any actions for this story, and it's one you can tell on your own.

Elijah was a pretty good prophet.

With God's help, he raised a boy from the dead. With God's help, he stopped the rain from falling, as a warning to Israel's evil King Ahab. And with God's help, he defeated the false priests of the even-more-evil Queen Jezebel.

So what was he doing sitting under a bush in the middle of the desert?

He was thinking about giving up, that's what.

He was tired – tired of fighting the evil in his land, and then seeing it all come back again. He was afraid – afraid that Queen Jezebel would carry out her threat to track him down and kill him. And he was worried – worried that even God would not be able to help him this time. Worried enough to run and hide in the desert.

And so Elijah prayed a prayer, a sad and tired and frustrated prayer. "Take me away, God," he prayed.

"Take my life before Jezebel does. Kill me now. I've had enough."

And then, with bush for his blanket and a desert stone for his pillow, Elijah fell into an exhausted sleep.

God heard Elijah's prayer. God understood Elijah's fear and frustration. So God answered Elijah.

Down the secret stair from heaven, where God's surprises are stored, came an angel. A very special angel. An angel who was more like your mother than your father. An angel who was more of a "she" than a "he".

The angel pulled back a branch of the bush that covered Elijah and let one or two sunbeams land on the prophet's sleeping face. "Poor tired thing," she whispered. And she gently shook her angel head. Then she let go of the branch and rubbed her big hands together as if she was ready to get to work.

The angel reached into one big apron pocket and pulled out a flat spoon. From her other pocket, she fetched a deep, wide, wooden bowl. She set these down beside the sleeping prophet and whispered softly in his ear, "Back in a minute, pet. I've got some shopping to do."

Then she threw herself into the sky and flew north, straight for the fertile lands along the Jordan River.

The angel stopped at a threshing floor and swept a pile of freshly harvested wheat into her apron pocket. Next, she swooped low over an orchard and snatched a branch, heavy with fresh fruit, from an olive tree. Finally, the angel soared high into the hills above the river and scooped a cup of fresh, cool water from a mountain stream. Then she sailed back to Elijah – without dropping a seed or spilling a drop.

The prophet turned and shook and mumbled in his sleep.

"Just rest now, my dear," the angel whispered. "It won't be long." And then she began to hum. (A hymn from Heaven's Throne Room? A ditty from Heaven's Kitchen? Or maybe they were one and the same.)

She hummed as she dumped the wheat – *kafloosh!* – onto a flat desert rock and ground it into flour. She hummed as she clutched the olives in her big hand and – squooge! – crushed the oil out of them. She hummed as she mixed the oil and the flour together in the bowl and – bloop! – added just one long drop of the mountain water.

And then she stopped humming. And stood up. And snapped her fingers.

Eggs!

She knew she'd forgotten something. Not even an angel can make a cake without eggs.

The angel wiped her hands on her apron and cocked her head, listening to the sounds of the desert. She heard the desert wind pick up bits of sand and send them scraping against desert stones. She heard tiny desert animals skitter and slither and skip across the desert floor.

And then she heard what she was listening for – the soft, chirping song of a desert bird. A partridge.

Quick as a bird herself, the angel chased the sound and found a nest. She whispered something to the partridge, who bowed and stepped aside. And the angel bent down and listened to the nest. In two of the eggs, she heard the flutter and scratch of young bird life. But two were silent and would never be more than eggs. Those she took, with a grateful nod to the mother. Then she flew back to Elijah.

The angel mixed in the eggs and whipped up the batter until it was rich and creamy and thick. And as a final touch, she reached into her pocket and pulled out a tiny bottle of... something. (A gift from Heaven's Throne Room? A spice from Heaven's Kitchen? Or maybe they were one and the same.) She opened the bottle and sprinkled exactly seven golden flakes into the batter. Then she dipped one finger into the mix and tasted it to make sure it was just right.

Finally, she reached down deep into the hot desert sand. Down, down, down – until she found a steaming hot rock at the bottom of a boiling underground stream. She grabbed hold of that rock and yanked it right out of the ground. Then she carved a hole out of the middle of the rock and poured her batter in. Right away it started to sizzle and bubble and bake.

In no time at all, the cake was done. The angel peeled away the rocky oven as if it were the skin of an orange. Then she set the hot cake and a cup of cold mountain water by Elijah's sleepy head.

She tapped him lightly on the shoulder. "Elijah," she whispered. "Elijah, it's time to wake up."

The last time Elijah had heard those words, they were on his mother's lips. And if his aching body hadn't told him he was lying on the ground in the middle of a desert, he would have sworn that he was back at home. So who woke him up? And what was that incredible smell?

Elijah's eyes snapped open and his questions were answered in a glance. In front of him was a freshly baked cake, a cup of cold water – and an angel!

"Go on," coaxed the smiling angel. "Try some. I made it just for you."

Elijah knew he should be afraid. But he wasn't. What he was – was hungry! He tore off a chunk of the cake and gobbled it down. It was heavenly! Rich, but not sickening. Moist but not soggy. Filling but not fattening. So delicious that Elijah had to help himself to another piece. And then another. He would have finished the whole cake if the angel hadn't started humming her little tune again, and if he hadn't stretched out, tummy full, and fallen asleep all over again. And not a restless sleep this time, but a long dreamy snooze.

Quietly the angel tidied up her utensils, tucking them one by one into her pockets. And when Elijah had slept long enough, she tapped him on the shoulder again.

"Wake up, Elijah. Finish your cake. You have a long trip ahead of you. You need all the strength you can get."

Again Elijah opened his eyes. The cake was still there. But this time the angel was gone. (Gone to Heaven's Throne Room? Back to Heaven's Kitchen? Or maybe they are one and the same.)

Elijah quickly finished off the cake, licking his fingers and picking up each crumb. When he was done, he was different. He was no longer tired. The sleep had refreshed him, and the cake had filled him up so he felt as if he could walk for forty days if he had to.

And, best of all, he was no longer worried and afraid. Let Jezebel come! Let Ahab do his worst! God would take care of his prophet. Elijah was sure of that now.

Then, at that very moment, Elijah stood up and set off for Mount Horeb, the holy mountain. He was going to meet God there. He was going to find out what God wanted him to do next. And he was going to thank God for answering his prayer in a way he'd never expected – with a cup of cold mountain water and angel food cake.

18

Ahab and Jezebel – The Rotten Ruler's Tale

1 Kings 21; 2 Kings 9:30–37

Jezebel was Athalia's grandmother. Apples. Falling. Trees!

As you will see, I have tried to explore the humour in this tale (or perhaps, in memory of Grandma, simply invented it). But it does strike me that Ahab's determination to match the evil of his wife is consistent with what the Bible has to say about her leading him astray. This originally came from More Bible Baddies.

Telling tips

This story needs to be told with your tongue firmly planted in your cheek. A hint of that mad smile again wouldn't do any harm, either.

King Ahab wanted to be wicked. He wanted it in the worst kind of way! But he lacked the courage. And he lacked the imagination. And worst of all, he lacked the will – the "killer instinct" that true wickedness demands.

His queen, Jezebel, however, lacked nothing. She was, without question, the most wicked woman he had ever met. And this just made things worse. For, given her expertise at evil, her artistic flair for foul play, he could never hope to impress her with any wickedness of his own.

She sensed this, of course (even the most wicked have their compassionate side) and tried her best to cheer him up.

"Who's the wicked one, then?" she would ask playfully over breakfast.

And Ahab would blush and lower his eyes and answer coyly, "You don't mean me, do you, darling?"

"Of course I do!" she would coo. "Who betrayed his own people? Who put my god, Baal, in place of Yahweh the god of Israel? Who murdered Yahweh's prophets? And who chased his true believers into hiding? It was you, my dear – that's who. Wicked King Ahab!"

"Well, I couldn't have done it alone," he would mutter in a humble, "aw-shucks" sort of way. "I had a wonderfully wicked wife to help me."

"Nonsense!" Jezebel would blush in return. "You're quite wonderfully wicked all on your own!"

Then the conversation would turn to the weather (dry, *always* dry), or to the state of the economy (failing crops, starving cattle), and ultimately to that pesky prophet, Elijah, who had somehow managed to stop the rains from falling.

"If I ever get hold of him," Ahab would rant. "I'll murder him – right there on the spot!"

"I'll do more than that!" Jezebel would counter. "I'll torture him – slowly – and stand there and laugh as he dies!"

"I'll rip off his fingers!" Ahab would return.

"I'll tear out his hair!" Jezebel would shriek.

And on and on it would go, until the two of them would collapse in fits of evil laughter, and then set off to do their day's worth of evil deeds. It was, on the whole, a sick sort of relationship. But it seemed to work.

One morning, however, King Ahab failed to appear at the breakfast table. And when Jezebel found him – on his bed, in his room – he had a woefully *un*wicked expression on his face.

"What's the matter, dear?" Jezebel chirped. "Run out of prophets to kill?"

"No," Ahab sighed. "Something much worse than that. It's the vineyard, next door."

'Naboth's vineyard?' queried Jezebel. 'What could possibly be the problem with Naboth's vineyard?'

"It's in the way!" Ahab moaned. "That's the problem! My little garden is much too small. I want to put in some cabbages next year. And some sprouts. And two more rows of those little potatoes you like so well. But his stupid vineyard is right smack up against the property line. I've offered to buy it. I'd give him more than what it's worth. But the selfish so-and-so refuses to sell! So what can I do?'

Jezebel tried hard to hide her disappointment. There were plenty of things that Ahab could do. He was king, after all! And a wicked king (or a wicked wannabe), as well. The answer was obvious. But would telling him, straight up, snuff out the spark of true villainy she had worked so hard to ignite? Would it fracture his already brittle evil self-esteem? In the end, she decided that a simple demonstration would be the clearest (and, surely, the most compassionate) response of all.

"Leave it to me," she said quietly. Then she turned the conversation to the weather.

And, later that day, while Ahab was out digging in the garden, Jezebel sneaked into his office and picked up his pen. She wrote letters to all the elders and noblemen in Naboth's home town. She forged Ahab's signature (she'd had plenty of practice – so it was perfect!). And she stamped each letter with Ahab's special seal!

My dear friend and servant, (each letter began)

I have a favour to ask of you. Would you proclaim a day of fasting – a special, holy day – in your town? Would you be so kind as to invite my neighbour, Naboth, to this event (he has a lovely vineyard, don't you think)? Would you give him the most prominent seat at the event – some place where everyone can see him? And then would you hire two villains (I have names and references if it would be helpful) and ask them to stand up in the middle of the ceremony and accuse Naboth of some heinous crime? Blasphemy against his god, perhaps. And disloyalty to the king. And then, and I hope this is not asking too much, would you drag Naboth from that place and stone him to death?

Thanks very much for your consideration. I do hope that this will not be too much of an inconvenience. As always, my concern is for your continued health and well-being, which will be assured by your prompt response to this request.

Regards,

Ahab, King of Israel

Jezebel cackled and clapped her hands and hopped up and down in her seat. There was a joy to pure evil that never failed to delight her. Naboth would die (she had never fancied him as a neighbour anyway!). Ahab would get his vineyard. And the local noblemen would be convinced, once and for all, of her husband's utter and total depravity. She couldn't wait to see the look on his face.

Her wait lasted only a few days. Ahab appeared at breakfast, one morning – a changed man.

"I'll have two eggs for breakfast, this morning," he grinned. "And – why not, by Baal! – a few rashers of bacon, as well!"

"So what's got into you?" asked Jezebel innocently.

"Haven't you heard, my dear?" Ahab beamed. "Naboth is dead. His widow wants to sell. And now, at last, his vineyard is mine!"

"How wonderful!" said the queen. "So tell me – how did poor Naboth die?"

"It was most unusual," Ahab mumbled through a mouthful of egg. "Blasphemy. Treason. Not very neighbourly, if you ask me. But then the rumour is that the charges were trumped-up. As if..." And here the king's chewing became more deliberate. "As if someone truly wicked had it in for him." And here he stared at his queen.

Jezebel could contain herself no longer. She blushed and she nodded, like a schoolgirl caught with a love note.

"Yes, my darling, I was the one who arranged it. I thought, at first, that it might be better to leave it to you – wicked man that you are. But you were so miserable! And, in the end, I just wanted to see you happy again."

Ahab held up his hand. "Enough," he said, solemnly. There were tears in his eyes, and little yellow bits of egg on his trembling lips. "I have been blessed with the most exquisitely evil wife in the whole world. What more, I ask, could a malevolent monarch want?"

And then he gave Jezebel a big, sloppy, eggy kiss. It was, on the whole, a disgusting thing. But it seemed to work for them.

Ahab's celebration, however, was short-lived. For as he strolled through his new vineyard later that day, he was surprised by an unexpected guest.

"Elijah!" Ahab cried. "What are you doing here?"

The king's voice was shaking. Shaking with anger, as he remembered the threats he had shared with his wife. And shaking with fear, as well – for this was the man who had stopped the rain.

"I have a message for you from my God," Elijah solemnly replied. "The God who sent a drought upon this land. The God who defeated the prophets of Baal. The God who was once your God too.

"'You have sold yourself to evil,' says the Lord. 'And so, on the very spot where the dogs lapped up the blood of Naboth, they shall lap up your blood too.'"

Ahab's shaking was all fear now. "Naboth… no… you don't understand," he tried to explain. "Jezebel… it was all her doing."

"'And as for your wife, Jezebel,' the prophecy continued, 'the dogs will do even more. They will chew her to pieces and leave so little behind that even her dearest friends will not be able to recognize her!'"

Ahab wanted to be wicked. He really did. He wanted to turn his evil threats into reality. He wanted to rip off Elijah's fingers and tear out Elijah's hair and torture Elijah and murder him. But it's hard to be wicked – really hard – when what you actually feel like doing is wetting your pants!

Ahab was scared – more scared than he had ever been in his whole sorry life. So he ran from the vineyard and hid in his room and wept and wailed and hoped that Jezebel wouldn't notice.

The noise was hard to miss, however, and Jezebel was humiliated by her husband's behaviour – a feeling that turned to disgust when he told her his battle plans over breakfast, one morning.

"It looks like we have to fight the Syrians," he explained, as he lifted a dripping spoonful of porridge to his mouth. "And the prophets have told me that I will die in the battle."

"Not Elijah, again!" Jezebel moaned. "If I hear the story about the dogs one more time…"

"No, no! Not just Elijah," Ahab interrupted. "But Micaiah, as well – a prophet from Judah!" And Ahab dropped the spoon back into the bowl. "But here's the thing," he went on. "I think I have outsmarted them. And it's a plan so devious that I am sure you will approve. When I go into battle, tomorrow, I will not be dressed as Ahab, king of Israel. I will wear a disguise! The Syrians will try to kill some other poor fool and I shall escape unharmed!"

Jezebel was appalled. And so upset that she thought she would lose her breakfast, right then and there. After all her work, all her training, all her coaxing and encouraging and example setting, had it come down to this? Her husband was not evil. Her husband was not wicked. He was a nasty little man, at best. And a coward, to boot!

"All right, my dear," she said, very quietly. "Whatever you think is best." But inwardly she hoped that she would never have to look at that face again.

Her wish came true, of course. Ahab disguised himself, just as he said he would. But a stray arrow struck him, anyway. He bled to death in his chariot, and when his servants washed the chariot down, they did so at the same spot where Naboth had died. So just as Elijah had predicted, the dogs lapped up Ahab's blood.

A civil war broke out in Israel. The king's heirs and the king's commanders fought for control of the country, and in the end it was a man named Jehu who was victorious. He rode to Jezebel's house one morning, even before she had breakfast.

She knew he was coming. It was inevitable. So she put on her best clothes and make-up. "He's a ruthless man," she thought. "Perhaps I can win him over and make him more ruthless still."

But Jehu was plenty ruthless, already. When he saw her in the window, he called out to her servants and demanded that any who were loyal to him should seize her and throw her out of the window to the ground.

There were plenty of volunteers, and while Jehu went into the house and had something to eat, the dogs breakfasted on the body of the dead queen.

"Someone had better bury that woman," he said to one of his servants. But when the servant went out in the street, there was nothing left to do. Elijah's prophecy had come true again – there was nothing left of Jezebel but her skull and her feet and the palms of her hands!

19

Water and Fire and Sky

2 Kings 2

Again, the repetition in this story is meant to summarize the story as a whole, in a sense, by focusing on the chief elements in the setting.

Water and Fire and Sky.

The days of Elijah were coming to an end. So he chose a successor from the school of the prophets.

And the prophet's name was Elisha.

Water and Fire and Sky.

"God wants me to go to Bethel," said Elijah to Elisha. "Stay here."

"I'm coming with you," said Elisha to Elijah

"I will not leave you on your own."

Water and Fire and Sky.

So Elisha followed Elijah to Bethel.

And when he got there, the other prophets said to him, "The Lord is going to take your master today."

"I know," said Elisha. "But I'd rather not talk about it."

Water and Fire and Sky.
  "Now God wants me to go to Jericho," said Elijah. "Stay here."
  "No, I'm coming with you," said Elisha again.
  "I will not leave you on your own."

Water and Fire and Sky.
  So Elisha followed Elijah to Jericho.
  And when he got there, the other prophets said to him, "The Lord is going to take your master today."
  "I know," Elisha nodded. "But I'd rather not talk about it."

Water and Fire and Sky.
  "The Lord has sent me to Jordan," said Elijah, at last. "Stay here."
  Elisha shook his head. "I'm coming. You know that.
  "I will not leave you on your own."

Water and Fire and Sky.
  So Elisha followed Elijah to the River Jordan.
  Fifty prophets stood and watched as Elijah took off his cloak and rolled it up and touched the water with it.
  Fifty prophets stood and watched as the river parted from right to left, parted right down the middle!

Water and Fire and Sky.
  Elisha followed Elijah across the river. Followed him on dry ground.
  And when they got to other side, Elijah said, "The Lord is taking me today. What can I do for you before I go?"

Water and Fire and Sky.
  Elisha said to Elijah, "Give me a double portion of your spirit – the power that God has given you."
  "That's a hard one," said Elijah. "But I'll tell you what, if you see me when I go, you can have what your heart desires."

Water and Fire and Sky.

And all of a sudden, there was fire. Horses of fire! A chariot of fire! And as Elisha watched, Elijah was carried off by the chariot in a whirlwind up to heaven. And only his cloak was left behind.

Water and Fire and Sky.

Elisha looked into the sky. His master was gone. So he tore his clothes in grief and then picked up his master's cloak and walked back slowly to the river.

Water and Fire and Sky.

When he got to the river, the cloak in his hands, he asked a simple question, "Where now is the God of Elijah?"

And when he struck the water with the cloak, just as he'd seen his master do, he had his answer.

For the river parted again, just as it had before, and Elisha walked across on dry ground.

Water and Fire and Sky.

When he returned, the fifty prophets were waiting, amazed.

"The spirit of Elijah now rests on Elisha," they proclaimed. And they bowed before him.

"There are fifty of us," said the prophets. "Let us go and search for Elijah. Perhaps the Lord has set him down again on a mountain somewhere."

Water and Fire and Sky.

But Elisha knew better.

"No," he said. "There's no point."

But they persisted, and when they had looked for three days, they found nothing.

"I told you not to go."

20

Jars

2 Kings 4:1–7

One of the tricks of any retelling is the choice of "point of view". In this case, I didn't invent the children – they were already there. But I did name them, flesh them out, and give them a lot more to do, largely because I thought that seeing much of the story from their perspective would help draw other children in. And also because the wonder of the miracle – following all the hard work of the gathering and dropping of jars, simply seemed more wonderful – more miraculous – when seen through their eyes. Finally, I think that taking the time to make them real people in a real family makes the miracle and their rescue more meaningful.

Telling tips

There are no special tips for telling this one – unless you have lots of children in front of you, lots of jars, and a "bottomless" jug of oil – to demonstrate.

Daniel peeped out of the window. He was only six, and just tall enough to stand on his tiptoes and stick his nose up over the sill.

His little brother, David, was only four, and he wanted to see, as well. So he pulled a stool to his brother's side and, rocking back and forth as he went, clambered up on it.

"Watch out!" Daniel complained.

"But I want to see too!" moaned David. "I want to see mum!" And he stuck his nose over the sill, as well, with a "What's she doing?"

"She's talking to that man," explained Daniel. "She said his name is Elisha. He's a prophet – like Dad was."

"What are they saying?" asked David.

"Can't tell," Daniel shrugged. "Too far away."

And so they were. In fact, as Daniel and David's mother had planned, they were just close enough so the boys could keep an eye on her, and just far enough away so they could not hear what she was saying.

"Nathan had debts," she sighed, wiping a tear away with her sleeve.

And the prophet nodded, as if he knew.

"The thing is…" she continued, and it was all she could do to keep from bursting into tears. "The thing is, now that he is dead, his creditors want to collect from me what he owed."

"And?" asked Elisha.

"And," she sighed even harder. "I have nothing to give them. Nothing at all. So they have told me that they will take the boys and sell them into slavery to pay the debt."

Now Elisha sighed, looking past the desperate mother to the two clumps of curly black hair that kept bobbing up and down at the bottom of her window.

"Do they know?" he whispered.

She shook her head. "No, of course not. How could I tell them? They just know things are bad. We have so little to eat. They miss their father."

"So there's literally nothing left?" asked the prophet?

"A bit of oil." The woman shrugged. "That's all."

"Oil, you say?" The prophet grinned. "The sign of God's presence." And then he nodded. "That will do nicely."

"I told you to stop rocking!" Daniel shouted. "I told you you'd fall down!"

"I'm OK," grunted David, picking himself up off the floor and rubbing one elbow.

"But you broke the stool!" Daniel shouted again. "Mum is going to be really angry!"

And just at that moment, she burst back into the house.

"Boys!" she announced. "I've got something for you to do. Now!"

"David broke the stool!" shouted Daniel.

And David started to cry.

"It's all right," she said, giving him a hug. "Really. There's something very important I need you to do. And you have to do it quickly."

"What is it?" asked David.

"You have to borrow jars," she said. "Empty jars. As many as you can get. From everyone in the village."

"But why?" asked Daniel.

"Because Elisha said so," she nodded. "Now, go!"

So they went – one brother up the street and the other down, banging on doors, borrowing jars, and juggling them in their arms all the way back home.

David dropped a couple on the way. And Daniel sighed and shook his head. But, several trips later, when by they had begged and bothered and pestered every neighbour, their house was filled with jars.

David and Daniel's mum shut the door.

"It's what the prophet said to do," she explained. Then she took what little oil she had and poured it into one of the jars. She poured and she poured, until the jar filled up.

"I don't get it," said Daniel. "There wasn't enough oil to do that."

"I know," said his mum. "But the prophet told me to keep on pouring."

So she did. And before they knew it, the second jar was full! And the one after that!

"This is fun!" chirruped David, replacing the full jar with an empty one. "Let's see if we can fill them all."

And, believe it or not, they did! One by one, they filled every jar in that house. The jars on the floor and on the chairs and on the table; the jars in the corner of the floor and the middle of the floor. Every jar everywhere!

"What do we do now?" asked Daniel, tiptoeing round the jars.

"We sell what we can and we keep what's left for ourselves," answered his mum. "That's what the prophet said. And I think that should be enough to pay all our debts and take care of us for a long time."

"And to buy a new stool?" asked David sheepishly.

"Maybe even two," his mother grinned.

And she hugged them both and held them tight.

"One for each of my boys."

21

See!

---

2 Kings 6:8–23

"See" and other words relating to sight tie this story together.

The king of Aram went to war against God's people. He set up his camp, intent on surprising them.

But the surprise was on him, for God showed his prophet, Elisha, exactly where the Arameans were camped, and he warned the king of Israel.

"See!" said Elisha. "The king of Aram is camped here. You might want to avoid that spot."

And when the Arameans moved, God showed him again.

"See!" said Elijah. "The king of Aram has moved his army over here now."

Time after time this happened, and the king of Aram was furious.

"There is a spy in our camp!" he shouted at his commanders. "Who is it? Tell me now!"

"There is no spy," said one of his officers. "Elisha the prophet is to blame. Somehow, he sees everything we do."

"Then find him!" roared the king. "And when you do, bring him to me. See to it. Now!"

So spies were sent to look for Elisha, and when they found him, in Dothan, an army followed and surrounded the city by night.

When Elisha's servant woke the next morning and looked out of the window, he ran to his master in a panic.

"Come and see!" he cried. "The army of Aram has us surrounded. Horses and chariots and soldiers; more than I can count."

The prophet looked as well. But he saw something else.

"Don't be afraid," he said to his servant. "Those who are with us are more than those who are with them."

The servant looked again and shook his head. "What do you mean?" he cried. "I see an army outside the city walls and not one soldier within. We're helpless. We're doomed."

So Elisha prayed.

"Open his eyes, Lord, so he sees what I see."

And when the servant looked again, he began to tremble, not out of fear but for wonder and joy.

"Tell me what you see," said Elisha.

"Horses," whispered the servant. "Thousands of them, all over the hills. Horses. And chariots of fire!"

"See," grinned Elisha. "It is just as I said. God is with us. And not a moment too soon, for here come the Arameans."

At that moment, the army attacked. And Elisha prayed again.

"Blind them, Lord," he prayed, "so they cannot find me."

And so God did.

"We can't see! We can't see!" cried the soldiers, stumbling into one another and falling from their chariots.

So Elisha offered to help them.

"You're looking for the prophet, aren't you?" he asked them.

"Yes! Yes!" they answered. "But we can't see! How can we possibly find him now?"

"I know where he is," said Elisha, and it was all he could do not to laugh. "Follow my voice, and I'll lead you to him."

So climbing down from their chariot and picking their way slowly along the road, the soldiers followed Elisha, listening for his voice.

And Elisha led them straight to Samaria, the capital of Israel, and into the presence of his king.

And then the prophet prayed again.

"Open their eyes, Lord, so they can see."

And when they looked. And when they saw. They were surrounded by the army of Israel!

The king of Israel was delighted!

"Shall I kill them?" he asked the prophet.

"Kill them?" cried Elisha. "Of course not. Don't you see? If you treat them well, they will go back to their master with news of your mercy and of the power of God. And perhaps that will put an end to this war."

And so it did. The king of Israel prepared a feast for his prisoners, and then set them free. And when they told their story to the king of Aram, the fighting stopped.

See!

"I don't believe it!" said the prophet's servant.
"It worked!" said the prophet's king.
And the prophet just grinned and said "See!"

22

Athalia – The Wicked Granny's Tale

2 Chronicles: 22–23

This is an obscure story, to be sure. In fact, when I mention it in churches, I often get blank stares. But it's one that my Grandma Brosi told a lot, which is strange in a way, since it's all about a grandmother who murders her grandchildren so she can become queen of Judah! Frankly, I'm just happy that I never had anything my grandma wanted.

Telling tips

Just enter into the spirit of the thing – that's what Grandma would have done: a mad smile on her face as Athalia's wickedness is revealed, and an even madder one at her comeuppance.

Sweet and gentle. Wise and kind. Kitchens rich with the smell of fresh-baked treats. That's what grannies are like!

But Athalia was not your typical granny.

She was cruel and ambitious, deceitful and sly. And she had never baked a biscuit in her life! Evil plots were her speciality, and she cooked one up the moment she heard that her son, the king, was dead.

She gathered her guards around her. She whispered the recipe in their ears. And even though they were used to violence and to war, they could not hide the horror in their eyes.

"Yes, I know they're my grandsons," Athalia sneered. "But I want you to kill them, so that I, and I alone, will inherit the throne!"

Athalia was not your typical granny. And she hadn't been much of a mother either. So perhaps that is why her daughter, Jehosheba, was not surprised when she peeped into the hallway and saw soldiers marching, swords drawn, towards the nursery door.

Jehosheba had a choice. She could rush to the nursery and throw herself in front of her little nephews – and be killed along with them, more likely than not. Or she could creep back into the room from which she'd come and try to save the king's youngest son – the baby she'd been playing with when she'd heard the soldiers pass.

The cries from the nursery answered her question. She was already too late, and she cursed the palace guards for their speed and efficiency. Speed was what she needed, as well, for she could hear the guards' voices coming her way.

"Did we get them all?"

"We'd better get them all?"

"The queen will have our heads if we've missed one."

And so they burst into each room, one by one, down the long palace hall, and Jehosheba had time – barely enough time – to wrap her hand round the baby's mouth and duck into a cupboard.

"Don't cry," she prayed, as the soldiers grunted and shuffled around the room. "Please don't cry."

"No one here," someone said at last. But Jehosheba stayed in that cupboard, as still as a statue, long after they had left the room. Then she wrapped up the baby in an old blanket and bundled him off to her home in the temple precincts.

Athalia stared sternly at her soldiers.

"So you killed them? Every last one?" she asked.

"Every last one," they grunted back. And Athalia's stare turned into an evil grin.

"Then tell me about it," she ordered. "And don't leave out one tiny detail."

When the guards had finished their story, Athalia sent them out of the room, and then she tossed back her head and cackled.

"At last. At last! AT LAST! Queen of Judah. Mother of the nation. That has a nice ring to it. And my parents... my parents would be so proud!"

Jehosheba's husband, Jehoiada, however, had a very different reaction.

"Well, what did you expect?" he fumed, when Jehosheba told him about the murder of their nephews. "With a father like Ahab and a mother like Jezebel... well, the apple doesn't fall far from the tree!"

"But I'm HER daughter!" Jehosheba protested. "You don't mean to say..."

"No. NO!" Jehoiada assured his wife, as he wrapped his arms around her. "I didn't mean that at all. You are a wonderful mother – a good woman who knows the One True God. And because of your love and courage little Joash, here, is still alive."

"The true ruler of Judah," Jehosheba added. "If only the people knew. You're the high priest. Perhaps you could tell them..."

"Even if they knew, they would do nothing," Jehoiada sighed. "Athalia is much too powerful, and they are still entranced by the false gods she worships. No, we must wait – wait until they have seen through her evil ways. And then, and only then, dare we show this little fellow to them. Meanwhile, we shall hide him here, in the high priest's quarters, in the temple of the One True God. For this is the last place your wicked mother will want to visit."

One year passed. And while little Joash learned to crawl and then to walk, his evil grandmother was busy murdering anyone who dared to take a step against her.

Two years passed. And as Joash spoke his first words and toddled around the temple, Athalia sang the praises of the false god Baal and offered him the blood of human sacrifice.

Three years, four years, five years passed. And as Joash grew into a little boy, the people of Judah grew tired of Athalia's evil ways.

Six years passed, then seven. And when Joash was finally old enough to understand who he was, Jehoiada decided that the time had come to tell the nation, as well.

"We must be very careful," he explained to his wife. "The palace guards are finally on our side, but your mother still has some support among the people. We mustn't show our hand too soon."

"So how will you do it?" Jehosheba asked.

"On the sabbath, it is the usual custom for two thirds of the palace guard to stay at the temple while the others return to the palace to protect the queen. Tomorrow, however, the bodyguards will leave as expected, but they will not go to the palace. Instead they will return to the temple by another route and help to protect young Joash, should anything happen."

"Ah!" Jehosheba smiled. "So Joash will be surrounded by the entire palace guard – while my mother will be left with no soldiers to do her bidding!"

"Exactly!" Jehoiada grinned back.

When the sabbath came, the people gathered in the temple, as usual, to worship the One True God. But there was nothing usual about what happened at the end of the service. Jehoiada, the high priest, led a little boy out in front of the crowd. Then he placed a crown on that little boy's head. And while the palace guard gathered round the child, the high priest shouted:

"Behold, people of Judah! Behold your true king! Behold Joash, son of Ahaziah!"

All was silent for a moment and then someone cheered. Someone else joined in and soon the cheering filled the temple and echoed from there to the palace, where Athalia was waiting, wondering what had happened to her guards.

She was old and frail now, but as wicked and as stubborn as ever!

"What's going on? What's all the noise about?" she muttered as she hobbled out of the palace and across to the temple.

"Out of my way! Get out of my way!" she ordered. And the crowd parted before her. And that's when something caught her eye – a glint, a gleaming from the little king's crown.

"What's the meaning of this?" she glared. "This looks like treason to me!"

"Not treason, Athalia," said the high priest. "But the true king of Judah restored to his rightful throne – Joash, your grandson!"

"My grandson?" Athalia shuddered. "But I thought… I mean… my soldiers… they told me…"

"That they had murdered them all?" asked Jehoiada. "Is that what you meant to say? Well, in their haste to fulfil your wicked ambition, they missed one – the one who stands before you now. The true king of Judah!"

"Treason!" shouted the old woman again, but her words were stifled by the palace guard that quickly surrounded her.

"Where are we going? What are you doing?" she demanded to know as they led her away. "I'm an old woman – a grandmother – don't push me!"

"Don't worry, granny," one of the guards whispered in her ear. "This won't take long. Remember what you had us do to your grandsons all those years ago? Well we're going to do the same thing to you now!"

Athalia shrieked, but only the guards heard her final cry, for the crowds were still cheering – cheering for Athalia's grandson and for the end of her wicked reign.

23

Everything but You

Ecclesiastes 3

This is a piece that I wrote in the middle of a conference. I really do love the thrill of writing from the moment – of trying to capture what's going on in a particular time and place. There's a power in it that comes from the immediacy, I think. I suppose it may make the reading less useful in another context, but I don't think that's true of this one. I like to think it's what might have happened if the preacher who wrote Ecclesiastes had met the preacher who was Paul.

Telling tips

I read it on my own, with music playing in the background, as I recall, as a kind of meditative interlude between two worship songs. But it would work just as well with two or even three readers, alternating verses – and maybe working together as a chorus on the "Everything keeps on changing. Everything but you" lines.

Yeah, everything keeps on changing
And everything has its place.
And everything keeps on changing,
Everything but you.

We greet our newborn children
And say goodbye to our dying parents;
We settle into the new neighbourhood
And move away from our old friends.

And everything keeps on changing
Everything but you.

We kill off our rivals and our passions and our dreams
And try to put a plaster on the pain.
We wreck the ones we care for
And erect a monument to our ambitions on the ruins.

And everything keeps on changing
Everything but you.

We weep like drunks for what love we have lost
And laugh like drunks for what love we have found.
We weep and we mourn,
We laugh and we dance.

And everything keeps on changing
Everything but you.

And we throw away what we later stoop to gather,
Embracing the sacred stones of wisdom that dropped from our hands in
youth.

And everything keeps on changing
Everything but you.

And we look and we look and we look and we look
For purpose and value and meaning
Until we're too weary and worn out and wasted
To want to look any more.

And everything keeps on changing
Everything but you.

And we keep what's precious
And dispose of what's not,
Except for those of us
With big attics or garages or sheds,
Because surely we'll find a use for it someday,
Mending what's torn up and broken.

And everything keeps on changing
Everything but you.

And sometimes we just have to be silent
And stare
At the face of a lover
At the place of wonder
At the grave of the one who is gone.

And sometimes we just have to speak
And say
I love you
I praise you
I miss you.

And everything keeps on changing
Everything but you.

And we love and we hate
And we fight and make peace
With our friends
And our neighbours
And our husbands
And our wives
And our parents
And our children
And our churches.

Because everything has its time
And everything has its place,
And everything keeps on changing, Lord,
Everything but you.

24

The Passion

Isaiah 53:5

Several years ago, there was a controversy among evangelicals in England over the nature of the atonement. Preachers and teachers and theologians weighed in with their opinions, and, on the whole, I found it helpful to hear and to read what they had to say. But, at the end of it all, I wondered if there might be a simpler way to talk about what God did through Jesus when he died on the cross. And this little piece was the result. As you will see, it doesn't explain any of the "mechanics", mainly because I'm not entirely convinced that the "mechanics" can be explained. Or even that there are "mechanics"! I think the atonement is a lot more personal than that – and the result of God doing, in his way, what we see around us every day.

Telling tips

This is one to read on your own. Or, if you like, you can have someone else read the italicized bits for emphasis.

When I was six, I spilled my milk. And it poured over my plate, and onto my lap and down to the floor. So my mother soaked up the milk, and mopped up the floor, and stopped me from crying and popped me into a fresh set of clothes. And when she finally got back to the table, her dinner was cold.

When the milk gets spilled, somebody needs to clean it up.
And cleaning up means giving up something for someone else.

I turned on the evening news and there was a house on fire. No one knew how the fire started. Arson? Faulty wiring? A stray, smouldering cigarette? But everyone knew that there was an old woman trapped in that house. So a fireman went in and carried her out. And there he sat, sooty and sweaty and sucking down oxygen.

When the milk gets spilled, somebody needs to clean it up.
When the fire burns, somebody needs to put it out.
And putting it out means putting yourself at risk for someone else.

I watched *The Passion of the Christ* when it first came out. I sat through two hours of violence and pain. And I asked myself, "Why? Why did Jesus have to die that way?"

Then I thought about my mother. And I thought about the fireman. And I thought about this world of ours, where people get knocked down and blood gets spilled and hatred burns. And I wondered, if it takes the sacrifice of a mum to mop up milk, and the sacrifice of a fireman to put out a fire, maybe, just maybe, nothing less than the sacrifice of God himself is adequate to clean up the whole of this mess of a world.

When the milk gets spilled, somebody needs to clean it up.
When the fire burns, somebody needs to put it out.
When the world goes wrong, somebody needs to fix it.
And fixing it up means God giving himself up for us.

25

Some Things I Just Don't Understand

Jeremiah 1:5

Quite honestly, I have never understood it. I really haven't. And I suppose I wrote this as a way of expressing that in as succinct a manner as possible. Either an unborn child is a baby, or she's not. And surely the worst scenario is that she should be a baby only if we decide she is. And a collection of cells – worthy of even less consideration than a fox in a hunt – if we decide she isn't. I guess what frightens me is that we have walked down this path before. Eighty years ago, in Germany, if you were tall and blonde, you were a human being. And if you were short and dark, you weren't. We fought a war to make it clear that every human life has inherent dignity and worth – above and beyond the whims of whatever powers-that-be. So why are we choosing again? Standing in that place of power and deciding who is human and who is not? I want you – you're my baby – you can live. I don't want you – you're only a foetus – you have to die. And that's what I don't understand. I just don't understand.

Telling tips

You can do this one on your own. Or you might like to do it with someone else reading the Scripture passage when it appears. Or you could even put the passage up on a screen and have the crowd read that as a kind of response to the rest of the text.

Before I formed you in the womb I knew you,
before you were born I set you apart.... .

Here are some things I don't understand. I just don't understand.

If, among other reasons, capital punishment is immoral because there is the possibility that an innocent person might die, why is abortion acceptable? Are not all babies innocent? And even if there is just the possibility that what is growing in the womb is a person (just like the possibility that the convicted murderer is innocent), is not that possibility enough to keep us from ending the child's life?

> Before I formed you in the womb I knew you,
> before you were born I set you apart... .

If a person thinks that abortion is acceptable, what do they do when someone they know has a miscarriage? If what is in the womb is not a person – if it is just a mass of cells – how can they honestly express any grief? Is it a person who has died, or isn't it? Surely the unborn child has to be one or the other. Or is it only a person if we want it to be?

> Before I formed you in the womb I knew you,
> before you were born I set you apart... .

And why do we always say that a woman has a right to choose what she does with her body? How is the child growing inside her the same as her body? If you take a cell from the woman and a cell from the unborn child and compare the DNA, they will not be identical. The child may be "in" the woman's body, but on the basis of the best scientific evidence, it's most definitely not the same.

> Before I formed you in the womb I knew you,
> before you were born I set you apart... .

And why do we always say that abortion is about a woman's right to choose? Some men use the availability of abortion to force women to part with babies they would rather keep. When your boyfriend or your father or your husband says, "Get rid of it or you're out!" that doesn't sound like much of a choice to me.

> Before I formed you in the womb I knew you,
> before you were born I set you apart... .

And why do we spend thousands and thousands in one part of a hospital to preserve the lives of children born prematurely at twenty-three or twenty-four weeks, and then spend thousands in other parts of the same hospital bringing the lives of children of the same age to an end?

> Before I formed you in the womb I knew you,
> before you were born I set you apart... .

And why does the phrase "quality of life" always come up in this discussion? The world is full of people whose "quality of life" is inferior to ours – people who suffer enormous hardship. But we don't advocate ending their lives for that reason. I have often wondered whether it is really the unborn child's "quality of life" we are so concerned about – or our own.

> Before I formed you in the womb I knew you,
> before you were born I set you apart.... .

Maybe Jeremiah didn't really mean what he said. Maybe he didn't really think that God had plans for him, even while he was developing in his mother's womb. Maybe those words are just poetry.

Or maybe we're the ones who take the poetic licence.

"How's your baby?"

"When's the baby due?"

"Have you felt the baby kick yet?"

We know what we mean. Our language betrays us.

And that's why I don't understand. I just don't understand.

26

King Nebuchadnezzar's First Dream

Daniel 2

The detail found in the book of Daniel itself makes for a really fun retelling.

Telling tips

I think the statue is the best place to bring in audience participation, if you want to use it. Divide your crowd into six groups, one for each of the materials used in the statue.

- Have the "Gold" group look up in wonder and say "Aaah!"

- Have the "Silver" group say "Oooh!"

- Have the "Belly of Bronze" group pretend to tickle the person next to them and go "Coochie-coochie-coo!"

- Have the "Iron" group stamp their feet.

- And have the "Iron and Clay" group make a squishy, squelchy sucking sound.

- And have the "Rock" group make a great big growly roar!

Then lead them in these sounds and actions at the appropriate places in the text.

Oh, and because the "cutting up into tiny little pieces" shows up a lot as well, have everyone do a karate kick or move with you and shout "Eee-Yaaa!" when you get to those points!

King Nebuchadnezzar had a dream.
A bad dream.

A troubling dream.

A dream that kept him up all night.

So he called together all his wise men – his magicians and enchanters, his sorcerers and astrologers.

"I have had a troubling dream," he said. "And I want you to tell me what it means."

"No problem, Your Majesty," grinned the wise men. "Tell us your dream and we will tell you what it means."

"Ah, but there is a problem," said the king. "If I told you my dream, you could make up any old rubbish to explain it. How would I know you were telling me the truth? So I have decided to set you a test. Pass, and you will receive a great reward. Fail, and I will chop you up into tiny little pieces."

"And what kind of test would that be?" asked the wise men, not nearly so confident now.

"Tell me what my dream means," said the king. "But first, tell me what I dreamed!"

The wise men looked at each other and trembled. No one had ever asked them to do this before.

"Seriously, Your Majesty," they said at last, "tell us your dream, and we'll tell you what it means."

"I'm very serious," said the king. "And you're just stalling for time. You say you're wise. You say you're powerful. Then show me. Tell me what I dreamed, and then I will know for sure that you can tell me what it means."

"But Majesty," stammered the wise men, every one of them trembling now. "This is impossible. No one but the gods could do what you ask!"

King Nebuchadnezzar was furious and declared that every wise man in Babylon should be chopped up into tiny little pieces. And so it was that the king's soldiers came looking for the wise man Daniel and his three wise friends – Shadrach, Meshach, and Abednego.

Daniel did not tremble. No, he spoke to the soldier. He found out what the fuss was all about. He asked the king for just a little more time. And then he got together with his three friends – and had a prayer meeting!

They asked God to show them the king's dream. And when God did, Daniel went straight to Nebuchadnezzar.

"Do not chop the wise men into tiny little pieces," he begged, "for I can tell you what your dream means."

"But can you tell me what I dreamed?" asked the king.

"I can't," admitted Daniel. "And neither can any other wise man or magician. But there is a God in heaven who can. He has shown me your dream, King Nebuchadnezzar. And now I will tell it to you."

"You saw a statue, Your Majesty – a giant statue!
Its head was made of gold.

Its chest and arms, of silver.
Its belly and thighs were made of bronze.
Its legs, of iron.
And its feet were part iron and part clay.

"And then you saw a rock. A rock cut out of the hills, but not by human hands. The rock struck the statue on its feet of iron and clay and the statue broke into tiny little pieces that were swept away on the wind. But the rock? The rock grew into a mountain and filled the whole earth!"

Nebuchadnezzar was amazed. Daniel was right – down to the last detail. But before he could say anything, Daniel continued: "That was your dream, O King. And here is what it means.

"Your kingdom is the head of gold. The kingdom to follow will not be quite as powerful as yours. That is the arms and chest of silver. The kingdom after that – the belly and thighs of bronze – will be less powerful still. But then will come another kingdom – the legs of iron – that will crush all before it. That kingdom will divide – the feet made of iron and clay – and in the days of that kingdom, the God of heaven will set up a kingdom of his own – the rock – that will never be destroyed.

"God has shown you the future, Your Majesty – that is the meaning of your dream!"

King Nebuchadnezzar said nothing at first. He fell to the floor and bowed before Daniel. Then he exclaimed:

"Daniel, your God is the God of gods,
The Lord whose wisdom never ceases.
He showed me the meaning of my dream
And now no one shall be chopped up into tiny little pieces!"

27

The Men Who Liked to Say "NO!"

Daniel 3

You could use this as an introduction to a sermon series on Daniel.

One day, King Nebuchadnezzar's herald made an important announcement:

"All prefects and satraps,
All magistrates and judges,
All councillors and governors,
All big shots and hobnobs,
Must report immediately to the Plain of Dura.
King Nebuchadnezzar has a surprise for you!"

When the officials got there, they found a golden statue, three metres wide and thirty metres tall. It was the biggest statue they had ever seen. And gathered around the bottom of the statue was the biggest band they had ever heard.

The herald cleared his throat and took a deep breath:

"People of all nations and stations and languages,
People of all places and races and climes,
People of all landscapes and body shapes and backgrounds,

People of all time zones and hormones and kinds,
At the sound of
The trumpet, the trigon, the horn and the bagpipe,
The oboe, the zither, the harp and the lyre,
The wahoo, the farney, the honk and the oompah,
All of you must bow down and worship this golden statue.
And anyone who does not will be thrown into
A hot and humid, bright and blazing, flaming fiery furnace!"

While the herald caught his breath, King Nebuchadnezzar gave the signal and the band began to play. At once, everyone fell down and worshipped the statue.

Well, almost everyone.

For there were three officials, standing at the back, who did not bow down and who did not worship the statue. Shadrach, Meshach, and Abednego. They were all grown up now – the "*MEN* Who Liked to Say 'NO!'"

Now, most people knew King Nebuchadnezzar as the great and powerful ruler of Babylon. But anyone who knew him well, knew him simply as "The King Who Liked to Say 'GRRR!'"

And when he saw the three men standing at the back, that is exactly what he did.

"GRRR!" he snarled. "Who dares defy my order?"
"GRRR!" he growled. "Who dares insult my god?"
"GRRR!" he roared. (For he was good at this!) "Who dares? Who dares? Who dares?"

As it happened, there were several satraps and big shots and hobnobs nearby – native Babylonians, who didn't much like the idea of these foreigners from Jerusalem having such important jobs – who knew exactly who dared.

"Their names are Shadrach, Meshach, and Abednego," they told the king.

"GRRR!" snarled Nebuchadnezzar. "Bring them to me at once!"

"Well," snapped the king, when the men were brought before him, "you heard the order and failed to obey. Will you worship the statue now?"

"NO!" said Shadrach. "We will not worship your idol. Our God has told us that would be wrong."

"NO!" said Meshach. "And we will not forget our God, or his Law, or the land he gave us – the land from which we were taken."

"NO!" said Abednego, "And we believe that our God will not forget us!"

"Then off to the furnace!" roared the king.

Nebuchadnezzar GRRR-ed all the way to the furnace.

"Make it hot!" he growled. "Seven times hotter than it's been before. And tie them up tight, so there is no chance for escape!"

And so, tightly bound, The Men Who Liked to Say NO! were thrown into the furnace. But the flames were so hot that the men who threw them in died immediately!

"Charred. Sizzled. Burned to a crisp," noted the herald.

Things were different, however, for Shadrach, Meshach, and Abednego. They weren't burning. They weren't boiling. They weren't even sweating. And they weren't alone.

They could just make him out, moving through the fire. A flash of orange hair. Flaming red fingers. And a pair of burning eyes. The angel flickered like the flames before them, now red and orange, now yellow, now white. Then, one by one, he touched a finger to the ropes that bound them, and they smoked and sizzled and burned right through. But there was not so much as a blister on the skin of Shadrach, Meshach, and Abednego.

"God is with you," the angel whispered. "You have nothing to fear." And a smile ignited on one cheek and burned like a fuse across his face. Then the angel took them by the hand and led them on a walking tour of the fiery furnace. They shuffled their feet through white, hot coals. They ran their hands along red, hot walls. They filled their lungs with black, hot air. And they blew out fat smoke rings!

Meanwhile, outside the furnace, Nebuchadnezzar's lips were no longer twisted in an angry snarl. No, they hung open and limp with amazement.

"I thought we threw three men into the furnace," he said. "But, look, there are four men in there now."

The herald crept closer and looked. Then he turned to the king, his face red with the heat and dripping with sweat.

"It is an angel, your majesty. A creature from heaven. Perhaps even the god these men refused to forget. If so, he is a very powerful god indeed, for they are unharmed!"

Nebuchadnezzar leaped to his feet and ordered Shadrach, Meshach and Abednego to come out. They waded through the flames to the mouth of the furnace, kicking coals as they walked. But when they went to thank the angel, he just smiled and turned to smoke in their hands, leaving nothing but a whisper that curled around their heads, then disappeared.

"Don't forget. God is with you."

Immediately, the officials gathered round them to have a closer look.

The satraps and the prefects inspected them carefully. "Not a trace of smoke!" they noted.

The councillors and governors touched their hair. "Not even singed!" they observed.

The big shots and hobnobs smelled their clothes. "Fresh as a Babylonian spring!" they cried.

Finally, the king himself spoke up.

"Praise be to the God of Shadrach, Meshach and Abednego – the Supreme God! They did not forget him and he did not forget them – but sent his angel to save them. I therefore order that, from now on, anyone who says anything bad about this God shall be chopped up into tiny little pieces. And what is more, I shall promote Shadrach, Meshach, and Abednego to even higher positions in my kingdom."

Then he looked squarely at the three friends.

"Surely," he grinned, "you can say yes to that?"

Shadrach looked at Meshach.
Meshach looked at Abednego.
Abednego looked at Shadrach.
Then, together, they looked at the king.
"NO... problem!" they said.

28

Dinner in the Lion's Den

Daniel 6

*The different voices here really do help the crowd to tell the characters apart
– and they are fun to do!*

> **Telling tips**
>
> One to read on your own – remember to practise the voices!

King Darius did not want to dump Daniel in the lions' den. And Daniel certainly did not want to be dumped there. But a law was a law – even if the king had been tricked into making it. And Daniel had broken the law by praying to God when the law said he shouldn't.

So while Daniel's enemies were laughing and slapping each other on the back for tricking the king in the first place, two things happened.

King Darius sent up a prayer, like a little white bird, to ask Daniel's God to protect Daniel.

And Daniel sent up a little white bird of his own.

It didn't take long for God to send an answer back, but it must have seemed like ages to Daniel as he was being lowered into the lions' den.

There were four lions in the lions' den.

A huge father lion with a shaggy brown mane. A sleek mother lion with golden brown fur. And two tumbling lion cubs.

The lions looked at Daniel and drooled. Their tummies growled like only lion tummies can.

"He's skinny and scrawny and old," moaned Father Lion.

"He's tough," said Mother Lion. "But he'll be tasty."

"Dibs on the drumsticks!" said one of the cubs.

But all Daniel saw were four open mouths and four sets of sharp white teeth. And all Daniel heard was a rising, roaring chorus as the lions padded closer.

Suddenly, something like a curtain opened up between heaven and earth. God had heard Daniel's prayer, and God's answer had arrived! God's answer was an angel. A great big angel who was good with lions! An angel who looked a bit like a lion himself. A great, stocky slab-footed angel with hulking hands and a shaggy brown head of hair.

"Wait just a minute!" called the angel. "It's not time to eat yet."

"Oh?" growled Father Lion. "Then what time is it, Mr Angel?"

The angel paused for a moment and thought.

"It's scratching time," he said.

Then the angel laid one huge hand on Father Lion's head and started scratching behind his ears. Those chunky fingers felt good, and Father Lion stopped his growling, laid himself down and began to purr. With his other hand, the angel scratched Mother Lion at the base of her neck, where it met her shoulders. Soon, she was purring, too.

"Me next! Me next!" shouted the cubs. And for a long time, Daniel heard nothing but scratching and purring and mewing.

Then one of the lion's tummies started to growl again. Father Lion glared at Daniel through his mane and rolled a pink tongue across his lips and showed the end of one long white fang.

"What time is it now, Mr Angel?" he asked.

"It's belly-rubbing time, of course!" answered the angel.

Father Lion muttered a disappointed "Oh", but the other members of his family were quite excited.

"Me first!" mewed one of the cubs.

"You were first the last time," mewed the other.

"There'll be turns for everyone," said the angel as he turned over a cub with each hand. Then he smiled at Daniel and winked.

And then... you know how it is with belly rubbing. First you're rubbing bellies and then you're wrestling. If any of Daniel's enemies had found the courage to put his ear to the stone on top of the den, he would have thought that old Daniel was being torn to pieces. But it was only the lions rolling and biting and pawing at each other as they played "Trap the Tail" and "Cuff the Cub". And that great, tawny angel was playing hardest of all.

When they had finished, the lions collapsed, exhausted, on the floor of their den.

"What time is it? What time is it now, Mr Angel?" yawned Father Lion.

The angel stretched wide his arms, shook his shaggy head and yawned back, "It's sleeping time."

And the lions curled up like house cats in front of a fire and were soon fast asleep. The angel curled up with them, wrapping his long, lion-like self around them. But he kept one eye open, just in case.

The next morning everyone in the den was awakened by the crunching, scraping sound of the stone den's cover being hastily slid aside.

"Daniel!" the king's voice echoed through the den.

"Daniel! Has your God answered my prayer? Has your God saved you?"

"Yes, Your Majesty, he has indeed," Daniel's sleepy voice bounced back up into the light. "God has answered both our prayers. He sent his angel to shut the lions' mouths."

The delighted king had his servants quickly pull Daniel out of the den. Then they dropped Daniel's enemies – those laughing, backslapping tricksters – into the den instead.

The lions stretched and stood up and stared. They were wide awake now. And very hungry.

The angel stretched and stood up too. "Well, I must go now," he said. "Goodbye, lions."

And then he pulled back that mysterious curtain between heaven and earth and started to step inside.

"Wait!" growled Father Lion. "Before you go… tell me, what time is it now, Mr Angel?"

The angel looked at Daniel's enemies and the four hungry lions. And he grinned a wide cat grin. Then he drew the curtain around him, leaving only his answer and a shadow of that grin behind.

"What time is it?" said the angel. "It's dinner time!"

29

The Runaway's Tale

Jonah

And so we turn to Jonah, a Bible story in which choosing the "problem" is slightly different; it's an example of the way that the 'problem' changes, sometimes, depending on the maturity of the hearers. I have included the introduction to this retelling, originally from More Bible Baddies, *because I think that helps to make my point even more clear.*

Telling tips

As with the other longer pieces, it's best to just tell it dramatically.

There's nothing cute about the story of Jonah. I know that people think there is – that the big fish makes it the perfect story for little kids. But that's only because they don't understand what the story is about.

You see, this story is not about disobedience, even though Jonah did disobey God when he ran away from the mission God had set for him. And it's not about deliverance, either, even though Jonah is rescued from the fish and the city of Nineveh escapes destruction as a result of his message. No, the story of Jonah is all about prejudice. That's right – good old-fashioned bigotry and hate. And as far as I can tell, there's nothing cute about that.

Jonah admits as much. The people of Nineveh are not like him. They worship different gods. They are "the enemy". And he refuses to go and speak to them, not because he is afraid of what they will do to him, but because he is afraid of what God will do for them, if they respond to his message.

And that is why the story of Jonah ends so abruptly – not with an answer, but with a question. Because the author's concern is not whether Jonah laid aside his prejudices and decided to love whomever God loves. His concern is with what his readers will do. And the answer, therefore, is up to you and me.

It didn't make any sense.

The words came to him, in an instant, unexpected, like they always had. The voice was the same, unmistakable – God himself, the Maker of heaven and earth. But the message made no sense. No sense at all.

"Go to Nineveh, the great city, and speak my words against it. For I have seen its wickedness."

The first part – the part about wickedness – Jonah understood. For Nineveh was the capital of Assyria. And Assyria was Israel's greatest enemy – not only because of her powerful army, which might sweep down at any time and destroy his people, but also because of her great immorality. Idol worshippers. Pig eaters. That's what the Assyrians were. Everything they did, and everything they believed was directly opposed to the holy Law that God had given Israel – the Law that Jonah had been taught to cherish and obey. They were enemies, and pagans, intent on destroying God's chosen people, the Hebrews, and yet, God had told Jonah to go and speak to them.

And that is what Jonah did not understand. That is what made no sense. For Jonah knew his prophet's job well: Speak God's word. Deliver God's message. And hope that those who received the message would listen, and repent, and be granted God's mercy and blessing.

God's blessing on Nineveh? God's mercy – showered on the enemy of God's people? Even the possibility was unthinkable. And that is why Jonah ran away.

It didn't make any sense. Not really. Jonah couldn't run away from God, and he knew it. But he didn't want any part of the mission that God had set for him, either. So he decided that the simplest solution would be for him to get as far away from Nineveh as possible. Nineveh was east, and therefore Jonah headed west.

He went to Joppa, first – on the coast. And there he booked passage on a ship set for Tarshish, at the western end of the Great Sea. And all went well, until a storm came thundering out of nowhere.

"This doesn't make any sense!" the captain thought. Every sailor sat on his knees, praying. But the passenger was down in the hold, asleep, as if nothing in the world was wrong.

"Wake up!" the captain shouted, shaking Jonah till he stirred. "What's the matter with you? The ship is about to break in two and you are down here sleeping. Get up! Pray to your god! And maybe he will save us."

Jonah prayed. Or, at least he bowed his head. But the storm did not subside. Not even a little. So the sailors drew straws, determined to find out who was responsible for their troubles. And the short straw went to Jonah.

"Who are you? Where do you come from?" they demanded to know. "And what have you done that could have brought such evil upon us?"

Jonah looked at the sailors and sighed. There wasn't an Israelite among them. They were pagans, one and all. Pig eaters. Idol worshippers. How could they possibly understand?

"I am a Hebrew," he explained. "And I worship the Lord God, the God who made the earth and sea – and everything else that is! He is the One I am running from. He is the One who is responsible for this storm."

The sailors trembled. "What can we do, then? Tell us – how do we appease your God? How do we stop the storm?"

"There is only one way," said Jonah slowly, "You must throw me into the sea."

It didn't make any sense. The sailors should have jumped at Jonah's offer. They should have chucked him overboard and gone safely on their way. But they didn't. Instead, they took up their oars and rowed even harder for shore, hoping to outrun the storm.

"Was it possible?" Jonah wondered. "Were these pig eaters, these idol worshipers, actually trying to save him?"

Whatever the intention, their efforts proved futile. For the harder they rowed, the higher rose the sea around them. Until, at last, they were left without a choice. Either Jonah would drown, or they all would.

So they fell to their knees again – and Jonah could hardly believe this – they prayed not to their own gods, but to the Lord!

"God, God of heaven and earth!" they cried, "forgive us for what we are about to do."

Then they tossed Jonah overboard, and immediately the sea grew calm. And as the prophet sank deeper and deeper beneath the waves, they worshipped the prophet's God and offered sacrifices to his name.

It didn't make any sense. Somehow, Jonah was still alive! He could hear himself breathing. He could feel his heart beating. And the smell – phew! – he had never smelled anything so awful in his life! But when he opened his eyes, everything was dark.

He shook his head and tried to remember. He remembered the crashing waves. He remembered struggling for the surface and saving each tiny bit of breath. And then, just before he passed out… he remembered! The fish! The biggest fish he had ever seen! And it was swimming straight for him.

"Was it possible?" Jonah wondered. "It must be. It had to be! He was sitting in the belly of the fish!"

And, no, it still didn't make any sense. Jonah had disobeyed God. He knew he deserved to die. And yet, God had preserved him, sent this fish – he was sure of it! And that meant, surely it meant, that God still had work for him to do, and that he would see the light of day, again!

And so Jonah prayed a prayer. Not a prayer for help, but a prayer of thanksgiving, as if the help had already come. As if the belly of this fish were a temple, and he was seated in the midst of it – ribs standing tall like pillars, the odour of entrails rising like incense.

"I cried to God," prayed Jonah,
I cried to him and he answered me.
From the belly of hell I cried
And the Lord God heard my voice!

It was he who cast me in the sea,
Far beneath the crashing waves,
With the waters roaring round me,
And the surface like the sky.

And so I thought
that I had been banished,
Cut off from God
And his temple forever.

Down I went,
Down deeper and deeper,
Down to the feet of the mountains,
Seaweed wrapped around my head.

Down, still further down,
Down, and no escape.
And that is when you touched me
And rescued me from the watery pit.

In the nick of time,
Just when all hope had gone,
You heard my prayer, O Lord,
Far, far away, in your holy temple.

Idol worshippers don't understand.
Their petitions count for nothing.
But I will give you thanks,
Offer sacrifices in your name,
For you are my great deliver!

Three days and three nights. That's how long Jonah waited in the belly of the fish. Then it belched him up on dry land, and those words came pouring into his head again: "Go to Nineveh, the great city, and tell them that I have seen their wickedness."

It still didn't make any sense. Not to Jonah. But he wasn't about to argue this time. So he travelled east, all the way to Nineveh. And when he got there, his mission made less sense than ever!

"This city is enormous!" sighed Jonah. "It will take me days just to walk across it. How can my message possibly make any difference?"

But Jonah was determined not to end up in another fish's belly. So he started to preach.

"Forty days!" he said to anyone who would listen. "Forty days to change your ways. Or else God is going to destroy your city."

"This is useless!" Jonah sighed. "These pig eaters, these idol worshippers, are never going to change."

But day after day, he preached. And day by day, the people of Nineveh began to take notice. There were just a few, at first, but soon the whole city was on its knees – from the humblest servant to the king himself – weeping and praying and asking God's forgiveness.

"This doesn't make any sense!" Jonah grumbled.

"No sense at all!" Jonah groused.

"You had the perfect opportunity, God, to destroy your enemy, and the enemy of your people. But you let it pass, and now – look at them – pig eaters and idol worshippers, praying, confessing, repenting, and asking for forgiveness!

"Can you see, now, why I ran away? This won't last. They'll be up to their old tricks again, in no time – you'll see! And then they'll be out to destroy us all over again."

And at that moment, Jonah got an idea.

"I'll get out of the city," he said to himself, "I'll get out of the city and sit on the hillside and watch. Watch and wait for them to turn from God again. And then maybe then – God will destroy the Ninevites once and for all!"

"Jonah," God called.

"Jonah!" God beckoned, "Do you really think it's right for you to be angry with me?"

But Jonah paid God no attention. He was too busy building a little tent and stocking it with provisions, ready to watch the city's ruin.

So God got Jonah's attention another way. He made a tree grow up over Jonah's tent, to shade him in the heat of the day. And just as Jonah had started to appreciate the shade, God sent a worm in the night to kill the little tree.

"This doesn't make any sense!" Jonah moaned. "This tree was here one day, and gone the next. Now I'll have to sit and sweat. Life is so unfair!"

And that's when the voice, the unmistakable voice, the voice of God himself, came pouring, once again, into Jonah's head.

"I'll tell you what makes no sense, Jonah," the voice began. "You grieve at the death of this tree, but you have no concern, whatsoever, for the lives – the thousands of lives – who dwell in the city below.

"Yes, they are idol worshippers, so far from understanding me as a child is from knowing its right or left hand. But I love them. And I have forgiven them. And if my ways are ever going to make any sense to you, then you will have to lay aside your prejudices and learn to love them too."

The New Testament

1

Lights and Bells

Matthew 1–2; Luke 1 – 2:1–21

*Just a little Christmas poem of mine that might fit nicely into a Christmas
Eve or Christmas morning service.*

Telling tips

You might just want to read this one on your own – it's very short. Or you could
get the group to do the "Lights and bells, Bells and lights" parts with you.

Lights and bells,
Bells and lights.
Cold pale mornings,
Long dark nights.
As winter's grey
Grabs hold and bites,
Christmas comes
With sounds and sights.
Lights and bells,
Bells and lights.

Lights and bells,
Bells and lights.
Angel songs,
Stars like kites.
Good News rings out
From Heaven's heights.
And Jesus comes
With sounds and sights.
Lights and bells,
Bells and lights.

Lights and bells.
Bells and lights.
Stable rafters
And starry brights
Paint shadow crosses
On wood uprights.
The baby turns…
Turns wrongs to rights.
Lights and bells,
Bells and lights.
For you and me
Turns wrongs to rights.
Lights and bells,
Bells and lights.

2

Foxes, Fish Food, and Flying Things

Matthew 8:19–27

OK, here's the deal. This reading was written, originally, for a church I pastored in England. And, over there, there is a long-established television character called Basil Brush. He's a fox puppet and his signature phrase (don't ask me why; I don't know!) is "Boom! Boom!" So, for a British audience, a fox who goes "Boom! Boom!" works nicely with a thundery storm that does the same. If you want to do this reading, you might explain that to your crowd (hey, a little insight into British TV culture won't hurt anyone. Then again…). Or, you could just tell them to go "Boom! Boom!" at that point and hope they don't ask why!

Telling tips

Divide your crowd into four groups and teach each group a different sound: "Boom! Boom!", "Zoom! Zoom!", "No room!", and (in a grave voice) "Tomb-tomb!" Then bring each group in at the appropriate times, remembering to quieten them down to a whisper at the end.

A teacher – a teacher of the Jewish law – came up to Jesus and said, "I will follow you wherever you go."

The man sounded serious. He sounded dedicated. He sounded keen. But Jesus wanted to make sure that the man knew exactly what he was getting himself into.

So he turned to him and said, "Wherever I go? Really? Well, let me tell you then. Foxes (*Boom! Boom!*) have holes to hide in, and birds of the air (*Zoom! Zoom!*) can always return to their nests. But I have nowhere (*No room!*) to lay down my weary head."

Another man said to Jesus, "I want to follow you, too. But my dad has just died and I need to go to his funeral."

And I know this sounds harsh, but Jesus wanted the man to know just how important, how life-changing, how costly this decision was. So he turned to him and said, "Then follow me. Follow me, now. And let the dead bury the dead." (*Tomb-tomb!*)

It's not easy to follow. I think that's what Jesus was trying to say. Not a walk in the park. Not a piece of cake. Not a bowlful of cherries. Or any of the other "happily-ever-after" clichés we sometimes build in to our appeals.

And to prove his point (could it be?), he boarded a boat with his followers and sailed right into a storm.

The thunder crashed. (*Boom! Boom!*)

The waves rushed by. (*Zoom! Zoom!*)

And his followers cried, "Lord, save us! We're going to die." (*Tomb-tomb!*)

"There's no place (*No room!*) for fear, here," said Jesus. "Trust me, and you will see."

So Jesus stood up, stood up in the boat in the middle of the storm.

And he silenced the thunder. (*Whisper – Boom! Boom!*)

And he stilled the waves. (*Whisper – Zoom! Zoom!*)

And nobody died. (Whisper – Tomb-tomb.)

For there was no place (*Whisper – No Room*) for anything but wonder and awe.

3

A Table Story

Matthew 9:9–13

Sometimes it's just a word that helps you find your way into a retelling. And in this case, as you will see, it's the word "count".

Telling tips

This is definitely meant to be a solo piece. When I first did this reading, I sat behind a table on a stage and did it from there. I think it helped to give a sense of the story's setting. And because I hadn't memorized the story, it also gave me somewhere to put the text!

Matthew looked around the table and counted.
Ten guests.

Six dishes.

Five stacks of thin, flat bread.

And eight – no, nine – bottles of his best wine.

Matthew couldn't help himself. Counting was on his mind. Counting was in his blood. Counting was his business.

Counting. And tables.

Matthew had sat behind the one and done the other for as long as he could remember. Because counting was what a tax collector's job demanded.

So much for the masters back in Rome.

So much for the men who watched his back.

And so much, of course, for Matthew!

Matthew grinned as he remembered.

Count well, and you could count on a pretty good living. And if the taxpayers should complain, or the accountants in Rome grow suspicious, then you could usually fob them off with just a little more creative counting!

"A few more denarii, please!"

"Another pile of coins, sir!"

"Yes, that's right, ma'am, I need both of your chickens. It's hardly my fault that they're the last you've got."

"Not enough! Not enough! Not enough!" That was his mantra. And his bully boys were always there to back up those words with a broken arm or a twisted neck. Was it any wonder then that he was hated and despised and left to socialize with the rest of society's outcasts?

Matthew looked around the table and counted. The table was full of outcasts. But how many of his friends had imagined that they would ever be sitting here?

Not Adam, for a start, Galilee's best brothel keeper. Nor Daniel, drunk from the day he could carry a bottle. Nor Caleb the conman. Nor Benjamin the womanizer. Nor Jacob the thief.

But here they were, eating and drinking and joking around with a rabbi, of all people! A rabbi, for heaven's sake! A rabbi!

It didn't add up.

No matter which way Matthew counted.

He'd never had any time for religion.

Dos and Don'ts.

Rights and Wrongs.

Following the rules. Keeping the traditions.

It was just another kind of counting, as far as he could tell.

The scribes and the priests and the Pharisees sat behind their tables too. They called them altars, of course, but it was just the same. And they stacked up good deeds and bad deeds as if they were piles of coins.

"Too much drink."

"Too many women."

"Too much gambling."

"Too many lies."

And in the end, when the counting was done, their answer was always the same.

"Not good enough! Not good enough! Not good enough!"

So what was the point? If he couldn't be good enough for them, how could he ever be good enough for God? Surely, then, it made sense to stay away from their tables altogether.

Yet, here he was, at the table with a rabbi.

Matthew looked around the table and counted.

There was not one of his friends that anyone would even think of calling good. They were rogues, one and all. Rogues, himself included. And not even lovable rogues!

They were dishonest, perverted, selfish and mean. But this rabbi was still sitting there among them.

And that's what counted the most.

Matthew's friends had all asked him, "Why?"

"Why did you leave your job?"

"Why did you give up your fortune?"

"Why did you leave it all to follow him?"

And the answer was here – at the table.

Rabbi Jesus was a good man. Matthew had no doubt of that. But unlike so many other religious people whom Matthew had met, Jesus did not make his goodness an excuse for judgment.

He could be holy, somehow, without being holier-than-thou. He could eat with good people and bad people alike, and treat them all with respect, treat them all the same. And if that's what lay at the heart of this new kingdom that Jesus was always going on about, then Matthew wanted to be a part of it.

Because, when it came down to it, Matthew was tired of counting. Wherever he had been, whatever he had done, somebody was always counting.

Counting the taxes to see who owed the most.

Counting the profits to see who was the richest.

Counting the bad deeds to see who was the worst.

Counting the good deeds to see who was the purest.

But at this table – the table where Jesus sat – nobody was counting. And when nobody was counting, then everybody counted!

Good or bad. Rich or poor. Sinner or saint. God loved them all and welcomed them all to his table. Surely that's what Jesus was trying to say.

And as for change – changing to be more like Jesus? Yes, who wouldn't want to be like him? Love life as he did. See through the hypocrisy. Cut to the heart of things. Surely that invitation – to come and follow and be changed – was part of the equation as well.

Matthew looked around the table again. Looked at all his friends. Would they stay with Jesus? Would they follow? Would they change?

Matthew couldn't tell. But one thing he did know – there was no chance of them following Jesus without some kind of welcome in the first place.

Without his acceptance.

Without his invitation.

Without this table.

4

Peter Walks on Water

Matthew 14:22–33

I sort of stumbled across this particular storytelling technique by accident. I wanted the crowd to really enjoy the participation, but discovered that they didn't always "catch on" first time. So I thought I'd do it again. And once more for good measure! And if I was leading them in their bit three times, why not do the set-up lines in the same way? So what should really be a rather short story becomes a longer one – and the repetition and participation help the story to sink (sorry!) in.

Telling tips

Before the story begins, teach the crowd the following words and actions:
- "Boo!" (Make ghost motions and sounds.)

- "Phew!" (Wipe forehead in a relieved motion.)

- "Canoe" (Make a paddling motion.)

- "You" (Point index finger.)

- "Two" (Put up two fingers, like a peace sign, in the air.)

- "Shoe" (Point at your foot.)

- "Oh, poo!" (Say this sadly.)

- "Woo-hoo!" (Say this joyfully.)

- "It's true!" (Point finger in air.)

After I teach the actions, I sometimes ask the crowd if they can figure out the Bible story. I've had some great (but mostly wrong!) answers.

Lead them in these motions during the course of the story – and don't worry if they don't catch on first time; they're probably just watching you to see what you do. As I said above, the repetition is there for them to really enjoy their part. And when you repeat your lines at the start of each verse, make sure you say the line differently, each time, for effect or for emphasis, or to build the tension in the story.

Peter and his friends were sailing one night,
Peter and his friends were sailing one night,
Peter and his friends were sailing one night,
When they thought they spotted a ghost – Boo!
When they thought they spotted a ghost – Boo!
When they thought they spotted a ghost – Boo!

"That ghost looks like Jesus," said Peter to his friends.
"That ghost looks like Jesus," said Peter to his friends.
"That ghost looks like Jesus," said Peter to his friends.
And all of his friends were relieved – Phew!
And all of his friends were relieved – Phew!
And all of his friends were relieved – Phew!

"But if it's Jesus," said Peter, "then he's walking on the water!"
"But if it's Jesus," said Peter, "then he's walking on the water!"
"But if it's Jesus," said Peter, "then he's walking on the water!"
"Without the aid of a canoe!"
"Without the aid of a canoe!"
"Without the aid of a canoe!"

"If you're really Jesus," said Peter to the ghost-man,
"If you're really Jesus," said Peter to the ghost-man,
"If you're really Jesus," said Peter to the ghost-man,
"Then let me come walk with you."
"Then let me come walk with you."
"Then let me come walk with you."

"Step out of the boat," said Jesus to Peter.
"Step out of the boat," said Jesus to Peter.
"Step out of the boat," said Jesus to Peter.
"There's room out here for two!"
"There's room out here for two!"
"There's room out here for two!"

So Peter stepped out and walked to Jesus,
So Peter stepped out and walked to Jesus,
So Peter stepped out and walked to Jesus,
With nothing but sea under his shoe.
With nothing but sea under his shoe.
With nothing but sea under his shoe.

Then Peter got scared and stopped trusting Jesus.
Then Peter got scared and stopped trusting Jesus.
Then Peter got scared and stopped trusting Jesus.
And he started to sink – Oh, poo!
And he started to sink – Oh, poo!
And he started to sink – Oh, poo!

So Jesus helped Peter back into the boat.
So Jesus helped Peter back into the boat.
So Jesus helped Peter back into the boat.
And all of his friends cheered, "Woo-hoo!"
And all of his friends cheered, "Woo-hoo!"
And all of his friends cheered, "Woo-hoo!"

"You're somebody special!" they said to Jesus.
"You're somebody special!" they said to Jesus.
"You're somebody special!" they said to Jesus.
"The Son of God – it's true!"
"The Son of God – it's true!"
"The Son of God – it's true!"

5

Two Answers

Matthew 16:25

My tenth-grade social studies teacher was a guy named Dave Shrecengost. We called him Shrec for short, but he was no ogre. On the contrary, he was one of those teachers whom you could feel close to and yet still respect. And, better still, he was the kind of educator who understood that his job was not simply to pass on facts and figures, but to teach you how to process and think about them. He's the one who asked the question. And the fact that one of his students is still working on the answer some fifty-five years later shows just how good a teacher he was!

Telling tips

You could either do this one by yourself, or tell it with someone else – with one doing the verse and the other the text in between. You could also put the Bible verse up on a screen and have the group read it at the appropriate times. (This is better than having them do it from their Bibles, simply because they will, more likely than not, have different translations, and then it just sounds like church in the Tower of Babel! It will work, though, if everyone is reading from pew Bibles.)

Jesus said, "Whoever wants to save their life will lose it, but whoever loses their life for me will find it."

When I was at school, when I was only fifteen, one of my teachers asked the class a question: 'What do you want to do with your life?'

Jesus said, "Whoever wants to save their life will lose it, but whoever loses their life for me will find it."

The answers broke down into roughly two groups.

Half of the class simply wanted to be happy.

And the other half wanted to do something that would make the world a better place.

> Jesus said, "Whoever wants to save their life will lose it,
> but whoever loses their life for me will find it."

Thirty years have passed.
Thirty years and more.
And I've watched my classmates.
And my friends.
And my family.
And my workmates.

And I've finally figured it out.
Only just figured it out.
Those weren't two answers.
Not two answers at all.
No, those answers were one and the same!

> Jesus said, "Whoever wants to save their life will lose it,
> but whoever loses their life for me will find it."

6

One Out of a Hundred

Matthew 18:12–14

This is a really short reading, but it's the brevity, I think, that makes it powerful. It's one of those readings that can be dropped into a service, like a little surprise, to make a really big point.

Telling tips

One to do on your own, or you could have another reader do the Scripture verse.

One out of a hundred.
A penny on the ground.
You'd hardly bother if you dropped it,
Or bend down to pick it up.

But God would.

One out of a hundred.
Statistically insignificant.
Well within the margin of error.
Hardly worth counting.

But God would.

One out of a hundred.
A face in a crowd.
A voice in a chorus.
You'd hardly notice if they were missing.

But God would.

What do you think? If a man owns a hundred sheep, and one of them wanders away, will he not leave the ninety-nine on the hills and go to look for the one that wandered off? And if he finds it, truly I tell you, he is happier about that one sheep than about the ninety-nine that did not wander off. In the same way your Father in heaven is not willing that any of these little ones should perish. [NIV]

Not even one.
One out of a hundred.

The Apostle Paul and Sir Isaac Newton

Matthew 28; Luke 24; John 20; 1 Corinthians 15

The idea for this very short reading came from a song by Julie Miller called "The Speed of Light", on her Broken Things *album. I just love the way she links together the spiritual and the physical, the emotional and the scientific, and thought that a similar approach might work in this situation too.*

Telling tips

It's short, really short – and that's its strength. So do it on your own. Play with the repetition. And then slow down and take your time over the end. I think this works very well either to start an Easter service or to finish it.

The tomb was sealed.
But the tomb couldn't hold him.

The guards were armed.
But the guards couldn't hold him.

Three days had passed.
But time couldn't hold him.

The man was dead.
But death couldn't hold him.

Mary Magdalene tried.
But she couldn't hold him.

The door was shut.
But the room couldn't hold him.

And when he walked to the top of the hill
And bid his friends goodbye, gravity,
Even gravity could not hold him.

So how come we can hold him
Closer than a brother?
How come we can hold him
Where two or three are gathered?

Death has been swallowed up in victory.
That's how.
And even gravity is no match for love.

8

So Sow!

Mark 4:1–20

I wrote this originally for an event that celebrated the work of Sunday school teachers and children's leaders. The parable of the sower set the theme for the day and I wanted to do a retelling that reflected both the realism and the hope of that story.

So Go!
So Sow!
And Know
The seeds you throw
Are seeds not sown in vain.

Yeah, some of them will fall along the path
Miss the soil altogether

And have no chance to hear
As Satan's sneaky sparrows steal them all away.
But others will land on the good earth
And seeds will sprout and buds will blossom
And fruit will weigh down branches
Thirty and sixty and a hundred times more!

So Go!
So Sow!
And Know
The seeds you throw
Are seeds not sown in vain.

And, yeah, some will fall on the rocky ground
Sink down and take root right away.
Till trouble comes like a scorching sun
And the soil is not deep enough
To save them from the withering day.
But others will land on the good earth
And vines will grow and wine will flow
And grapes will weigh down branches
Thirty and sixty and a hundred times more.

So Go!

So Sow!
And Know
The seeds you throw
Are seeds not sown in vain.

And, yeah, some will fall on the thorny ground
And the weeds of worry
And the weeds of wealth
Will strangle and shut out the light.
But others will land on the good earth
And rising right up to an elephant's eye
(or so the song says anyway)
The corn will reach to the sky
Thirty and sixty and a hundred times high.

So Go!
So Sow!
And Know
The seeds you throw
Are seeds not sown in vain.

9

A Little Shining, A Little Sowing

Mark 4:21–32

Just a little reading, this one – tying together three of Jesus' sayings about the kingdom. Probably more of an all-age service piece.

Telling tips

Teach everyone the chorus first – you might want to put it up on a screen so they will remember. You might also want to teach them a few actions to go along with the words.

- "A little shining" – hands open beside face in a glowing motion.

- "A little sowing" – pretend to toss seeds in a sowing motion. (It wouldn't hurt to explain this. You can't take it for granted that everyone will know what "sowing" is, and because knowing that is pretty much essential to understanding the reading – and what Jesus has to say – it's important that the whole group is clued in to this from the start.)

- "The kingdom of God keeps growing and growing" – reach out arms, wider and wider, or reach above head, taller and taller.

- A little shining, a little sowing,
  the kingdom of God keeps growing and growing.

"If you have a lamp," said Jesus, "you've got to let it glow. Under a bowl. Under the bed. It's no use there at all! But put it on a lampstand – for everyone to see – and all that once was hidden is revealed!

"If you have a lamp," said Jesus, "you've got to let it glow."

A little shining, a little sowing,
the kingdom of God keeps growing and growing.

"If you have a seed," said Jesus, "you've got to let it go. Drop it into the ground. That's your part, and God will do the rest. Seed to stem. Stem to stalk. Stalk to bushy head. You couldn't make it happen if you tried.

"If you have a seed," said Jesus, "you've got to let it go."

A little shining, a little sowing,
the kingdom of God keeps growing and growing.

"So plant your seed," said Jesus, "then stand back and watch it grow! A mustard seed is small. The smallest seed of all. But it grows into a great big bushy... bush! With great big bushy branches for birds to roost and rest. So plant your seed," said Jesus, "then stand back and watch it grow!"

A little shining, a little sowing,
the kingdom of God keeps growing and growing.

10

Angel Surprise

Luke 1:26–38

This story was originally in my book Angels, Angels All Around. *That book
is out of print now, so I wanted to make sure that my favourite stories in
that collection continued to be available (not just on eBay!). This one might
actually be my absolute favourite of that bunch. I know a lot of people like the
Easter Angel story, but the thing I like about this one is the angel Gabriel.
I realize that there is no way of knowing how an angel thinks or what an
angel feels. Entering into that experience imaginatively was what lay at
the heart of that book in the first place. But I found the idea that an angel
might get tired of the shocked and petrified reaction to his sudden appearance
really compelling. And also the idea that an angel might be capable of being
shocked, in his own right.*

It's a great piece for an early Advent service. Enjoy!

Telling tips

This is definitely one to tell or read on your own. It could be read with actors
miming the parts, but it would have to be done very sensitively.

The angel Gabriel sat in the corner and watched.

The girl was only thirteen. Fourteen at most. Barely a woman, by the shape
of her. With long, dark hair and bright olive skin. Not beautiful, but far from plain.
Pretty.

Gabriel hugged his knees and scrunched himself back into the corner. The last
thing he wanted to do was scare her, but that's what always seemed to happen
when angels appeared. And maybe that's why Gabriel hated these surprise visits.

The girl was whistling now. Doing her ordinary, everyday tasks – as if this was
some ordinary afternoon, and not the most extraordinary day of her life.

The angel rested his chin on his knees. Think, Gabriel, think. She's young.

She's innocent. She's fragile. So how do you do it? How do you tell her that God is about to change her whole life, without scaring her to death?

Mary swept as she whistled. And as the dust motes danced in front of her broom, catching the sun and changing shape, Gabriel had an idea. What about a vision, he wondered. The dust rises and takes on the form of a man. "Mary," the dust-cloud-man says, "you are going to be the mother of the Son of God!"

Gabriel shook his head, then buried it in his arms. No, no, no, he decided. Still too scary. And besides, all it takes is a strong breeze, and the poor girl has to sweep her floors all over again!

It was too late now, anyway. Mary had put her broom away and was across the room, preparing dinner. Gabriel climbed up out of the corner and stretched. Then he followed her to the table.

Bread. She was making bread. And as Mary mixed the ingredients, another idea started to knead itself together and rise in Gabriel's head.

He could write the message in the flour on the table. Of course! A hand from heaven, like the one that scratched those letters on the wall in Babylon. But it would have to be brief, because there wasn't much time. Mary's parents were gone, and there was no telling when they'd come back through the door. He wouldn't want to be surprised in the middle of his message. Gabriel hated surprises!

But wait, thought Gabriel. Maybe he could be the one at the door. An unexpected visitor with an important message. But what if she got scared and slammed the door in his face? Or what if some passer-by saw them? (She'd have enough explaining to do when the baby arrived. She wouldn't want to have to make excuses for some mysterious stranger.)

Gabriel had run out of ideas. He was running out of time. So he sighed. A long, frustrated angel sigh.

Perhaps it was that sigh. Maybe it was something else that Mary heard. For whatever reason, she spun around and seemed to hang suspended in the air for a second, her hair flung out behind her, her feet barely touching the floor. And her eyes, her eyes looked right into Gabriel's.

They should have looked right through him, but they didn't. Somehow she could see him. Somehow she knew he was there.

"Hello, Mary," he said finally, because there was nothing else to say. "God is with you, and wants to do something very special for you."

Mary didn't say anything. But she didn't faint, either. And that was a great relief to the angel. She just stood there, shaking ever so slightly, and stared at her guest.

"There's no need to be afraid," Gabriel assured her, although it was hard to know exactly what she was feeling. Was she trembling with fear? Or was it more like excitement? Gabriel couldn't tell. And he didn't like that one bit. This girl was nothing like what he had expected. This girl was a bit of a surprise.

"Look," he continued, "God is very pleased with you. So pleased, in fact, that he wants you to be the mother of a very special child – Jesus, the Messiah, the deliverer whom your people have been waiting for all these years."

Surely this would shock her, Gabriel thought. And he was ready to catch her if she should fall. But all she did was sit herself down to think. She played with the hem of her dress, folding and unfolding it. She twisted her hair.

Say something, thought Gabriel. Say anything!

And finally she did.

"I don't understand. How can this happen? How can I become someone's mother when I'm not yet someone's wife?"

This was the last question the angel expected. This girl wasn't hysterical. She wasn't even alarmed. Her question was plain, straightforward, and practical.

So Gabriel answered her the best he could. "The Holy Spirit will visit you. You will be wrapped in the power of the Almighty. And you will give birth to the Son of God."

Mary had never heard of such a thing. And it showed. In her bright brown eyes it showed.

"God can do anything," said Gabriel. "Think about your cousin Elizabeth. Well past child-bearing age. Barren, by all accounts. And yet, she's expecting a son!"

Mary looked up at the angel and shook her head. She was still trying to take it in. But she wasn't afraid, he could tell that much. She was strong, this girl. A doer. A coper. A fighter. And when she finally weighed it all up, Gabriel knew what her answer would be even before she gave it. Those eyes of hers were shining, fierce, and bold.

"I'll do it," she said. "I'll do it. I'll be whatever God wants me to be."

Gabriel nodded. Then he turned to leave. He reached out to open the curtain – the curtain between heaven and earth – and saw that his hand was trembling.

He turned back to look at Mary one last time. And in the mirror of her eyes, Gabriel saw one shocked angel face.

Mary smiled at him. He smiled back. Perhaps surprises aren't so bad after all, he thought.

Then Gabriel pulled the curtain behind him and said goodbye to the girl.

The girl who had surprised an angel.

And who would one day surprise the world.

11

"Magnificent" – Mary's Song

Luke 1:46–55

I have tried to be faithful to the spirit and the sense of what we have come to call "The Magnificat". That's one of the reasons the song/poem is in the third person (it works addressed to God, as well, and I have put that version at the end), 'cause that's how Mary phrases it.

I don't see any problem with just reading it as a version of the passage, but feel free to add a tune, if you like!

Telling tips

Nothing much, really. You might want to have your group read the chorus as one while you do the verses.

Mighty One, Holy One, merciful forever.
Age to age, each generation spent.
Faithful One, Patient One, whose love cannot be severed.
There's no other word for him: Magnificent.

My soul cries out, my spirit sings
In praise of God, my Saviour,
Who looks at me and sees me as I am,
Then lifts me up on angel wings,
Hands that never waver,
And makes me part of his eternal plan.

Mighty One, Holy One, merciful forever.
Age to age, each generation spent.
Faithful One, Patient One, whose love cannot be severed.
There's no other word for him: Magnificent.

He shakes the proud and breaks the crown
And makes the strong man stumble.
He sets the rich man begging in the street,
Then reaches down and from the ground
Lifts up the poor and humble
And welcomes them to his forever feast.

Mighty One, Holy One, merciful forever.
Age to age, each generation spent.
Faithful One, Patient One, whose love cannot be severed.
There's no other word for him: Magnificent.

Second person version

Mighty One, Holy One, merciful forever.
Age to age, each generation spent.
Faithful One, Patient One, whose love cannot be severed.
There's no other word for you: Magnificent.

My soul cries out, my spirit sings
In praise of God, my Saviour.
You look at me and see me as I am
Then lift me up on angel wings,
Hands that never waver,
And make me part of your eternal plan.

Mighty One, Holy One, merciful forever.
Age to age, each generation spent.
Faithful One, Patient One, whose love cannot be severed.
There's no other word for you: Magnificent.

You shake the proud and break the crown
And make the strong man stumble.
You set the rich man begging in the street
Then reach right down and from the ground
Lift up the poor and humble
And welcome them to your forever feast.

Mighty One, Holy One, merciful forever.
Age to age, each generation spent.
Faithful One, Patient One, whose love cannot be severed.
There's no other word for you: Magnificent

12

A Christmas Eve Service for Those Who Don't Feel Like Celebrating

Luke 2:8–18

My dad died in the autumn of 2002, following a long and painful illness, and by the time that Christmas rolled around, I really didn't feel like celebrating very much. Maybe it was selfish, but I wrote this piece for our annual Christmas Eve service that year and, from the response I got, even people who did feel like celebrating found it helpful.

Telling tips

The individual sections are best read by you, or a variety of readers, taking the sections in turn. During the gaps in the text, I inserted carols and prayers that reflected the themes in the section I had just read. I think we lit candles, as well, as the reading suggests.

Every now and then, I read a familiar passage from the Bible, and something strikes me for the very first time. A line I've never really heard before – or never really thought about. There's a line like that at the end of the passage that we're going to focus on now. I'd like you to listen for it as I read Luke 2:8–18. (*Read Luke 2:8–18.*)

The shepherds spread the word. They went and told people what they had seen and heard. Friends. Relations. Citizens of Bethlehem. And when those people heard the story, they were amazed. Well, who wouldn't be?

But were they moved? Convinced? Or changed? That's a different thing altogether, isn't it? And it's true for us as well.

Because sometimes, even though it's Christmas – maybe even the first Christmas – we're just not in a Christmas-y mood. We just don't feel like celebrating.

The shepherds' first port of call is the local pub. "Bethlehem's Best" – that's the brew they serve. And while the punters sit and sip, the shepherds tell their story.

There's a lot of ooh-ing and aah-ing and "Never!" But when the shepherds repeat the angels' message – "Good news of great joy!" – a man in the corner grunts and gulps down what's left of his pint. He's a merchant, travelling up and down the land of Palestine and beyond. And he knows, because he's seen it, that good news is in very short supply.

Famine to the east. Rebellion to the west. Higher taxes and even higher crime. Hospital queues. Inadequate transport. Falling pensions. Failing schools.

And, just like us, he wonders: How do you do it? How do you celebrate good news – how do you even believe in the possibility – when all the news you hear is bad?

So let's light a candle. And let's pray. For everyone who wonders with him. For everyone this Christmas who struggles to believe that the news – any news – can be good.

"Good news of great joy!" the shepherds repeat. And they're standing on the tables now and flapping pretend wings!

Some punters laugh. Some punters cheer. But the barmaid turns round and wipes her eyes with a dirty towel. Her husband is out of work. One of her children is seriously ill. And just last week, her grandmother died. Everything seems to be falling apart. Everywhere she looks is dark. She wants to share the shepherds' excitement – or at least she feels she should. But she can't. Not now. Because everything is still too painful, too close, too hopeless, too sad.

And just like us – because we've been there, or one day will be – just like us she wonders: How do you sing "Joy to the World" when all you feel is sadness?

So let's light a candle. And let's pray a prayer. For everyone who wonders with her. For everyone this Christmas who's sad.

The shepherds are in full swing now. And even though they can't begin to sound like angels, the message is the same. "Glory to God in the highest. And peace to people on earth."

One punter has had enough. It's not just their singing he can't stand. Nor the disruption of a quiet night's drink. It's that line that galls.

"Peace on earth," he mutters. And he slams the door on his way out. "Peace on earth? While the Romans rule over us? While they crush us and control us and lay claim to God's own land? Peace on earth? Impossible!"

How can we possibly sing about peace on earth, when there's always some place somewhere in that world that seems to be on the brink of war?

So let's light a candle. And let's pray a prayer. In the hope that, one Christmas, the angels' song might come true.

The shepherds' tale is almost done. But the punters are losing interest. Angels are one thing – strange, exotic, amazing! But a baby? Everyone's seen a baby. And so the end of the story is a bit of a dud.

But it's also the beginning of an answer. The answer to all we have felt and worried over and wondered about. You see, Christmas promises are one thing. Sometimes, by God's grace, they come true. And sometimes, foiled by man's stubbornness and sin, they fall short. Their complete fulfilment lies ahead – in the kingdom to come.

Christmas promises are one thing. But a Christmas present is something else. For God's gift to us is God himself. God in a very specific way:

God in a manger.
God in a stable.
God vulnerable and fragile and small.
God like us, in fact.
God with us in the bad news.
God with us in the sadness.
God with us when we cry for peace.
God with us when the promises come true.
And God with us when they don't.
God in a cradle. And God on a cross.
God puts himself in our hands. To suckle and to nurture. To receive or to reject.
God's gift is God himself.

So let's light a candle. And let's pray a prayer for everyone who wants God's gift this Christmas. For everyone who longs for God himself.

13

Midnight – A Meditation for Christmas or Good Friday

Luke 2:1–20; John 3:1–21; Luke 22

This is one of the oldest readings in the book. I wrote it for a Christmas Eve service twenty years ago or so, but, as the title suggests, I think it would also work nicely on Good Friday. It needs that lights-down, candles-burning, crowd-huddled-in-the-dark atmosphere to really work.

Telling tips

You could have a different reader for each of the three sections, if you didn't want to read it all yourself. And it works really well to insert songs and prayers and Scripture readings between the sections – perhaps even introducing each section with the Bible passage to which it refers. In that case, you probably will want someone else to read the Scripture, just for a bit of variety.

Midnight One

It's midnight, and the stillness is ripped by the first wailing breath of a newborn baby. A traveller, asleep in the inn, stirs and turns over and pulls his blanket up around his shoulders. A dog sits up and barks. A child, sickly and half-awake, calls for a drink of water.

It's midnight, and on a hillside outside the town only the sheepdogs have heard the cry. Their masters are stretched out around the campfire, talking and laughing and sharing a drink – keeping the night at bay, along with the wolves and bears. But they're tired and so, gradually, their talk winds down to a murmur. The hillside is still now. Still, like the town. It's midnight. And things happen at midnight.

As if to echo the baby's cry, or maybe even to answer it, the silence is torn again – but, this time, by a very different kind of voice.

"Don't be afraid," the voice says. And if the shepherds weren't so terrified, they might just burst out laughing. Don't be afraid? Don't be ridiculous! The blanket of night has been yanked off their backs and replaced by a vision of heaven-only-knows-what! And it tells them not to be afraid.

"Listen," the voice goes on. "I have good news for you, and for everyone else, as well. Today is the Messiah's birthday. And Bethlehem is his birthplace!"

What can the shepherds say? What can they do? They know how to deal with thieves and bears, but night visitors like this are well beyond their expertise.

"Here is how you will know what I say is true," the angel continues. "Look for a cowshed. Look for a manger. And that's where you'll find the baby!"

And the shepherds are even more confused – for it's not the place that any of them would have thought of finding a baby, much less a Messiah. But then, there's not much time to think, because the next few moments are like a multiplication table of the first – more angels, more light, more sound, and a song this world won't hear the likes of again until eternity.

When it's all over, the shepherds hurry off, flock and all, as fast as feet and hooves will carry them. Innkeepers are awakened and late-night revellers stopped until the shepherds finally find directions to the stable they've been looking for.

The angel was right, of course – right down to the swaddling cloth! And there he is – the baby, the sign, the Messiah!

What follows is a lot of handshaking and backslapping, and baa-ing and barking to boot. And then, not waiting around for the wise men (as some tableaux suggest!), the shepherds rush off to share their good news with the rest of the town.

They didn't understand fully what they had just experienced. And they wouldn't for another thirty years or so. But they were sure of one thing. It was midnight. And at midnight, things happen. God breaks the back of night and calls forth a brand new day.

Midnight Two

It's midnight, and there's a baby crying again. Two men, deep in thought and discussion, lift their heads and listen. One of them thinks, "Why doesn't somebody shut that kid up?" The other one just smiles. It's midnight. And he knows – at midnight, things happen.

"Nicodemus," he says, "If you're ever going to see the kingdom of God, you're going to have to be born all over again. Like a newborn baby, you're going to have to start fresh – seeing God and this world and yourself in a completely new and different way."

Nicodemus can't quite get his head round that. The baby's still crying – there's a light on now – and what began as a secret midnight rendezvous between a radical rabbi and a highly respected member of the religious establishment is in danger of being seriously compromised. Born again? Born again? What do nappies and baby wipes have to do with God?

Jesus tries again.

"The world is in darkness," he says. "Dark as midnight. People go their own way and do their own thing without regard for the needs of others or the will of God."

Nicodemus has read the papers. He watched *Newsnight* before he came out. The darkness he understands.

"Thirty years ago, Nicodemus, God sent a light into this dark world, a light to chase away the darkness and lead us to a brand new day. I am that light, Nicodemus, but I've got to tell you that we have all developed such good night vision that some of us are still going to prefer the darkness. That's why I say that you must be born again. Because anything short of a brand new start – any compromise with the darkness – is a return to midnight."

Scurrying home, darting from pillar to pillar, Nicodemus still doesn't quite understand what he has just heard. But he's sure of one thing. It's midnight. And at midnight things happen. God is up to something here. And he wants to be part of it – to leave the darkness behind and find that brand new day.

Midnight Three

'Tis midnight, and on Olive's brow,
The star is dimmed that lately shown:
'Tis midnight in the garden now,
The suff'ring Saviour prays alone.
"Tis Midnight, and on Olive's Brow",
Lyrics by William Bingham Tappan (1794–1849);
music by William Batchelder Bradbury (1816–68)

It's midnight, and at midnight things happen. Thirty-three years on, and the baby whose first breath disturbed Bethlehem's sleep is less than twenty-four hours from his last. One of his closest friends has betrayed him. There is a crowd coming to arrest him. And the followers who have sworn to defend him are asleep. There are no shepherds on the way, no guiding star above. For all practical purposes, he is alone.

What the angels sang about so joyfully all those years ago must now come to pass. He must be the Messiah, redeemer, and saviour, but in a way that not even the angels could have imagined. He smiles at the irony of it. To be the Prince of Peace has little to do with living a peaceful life. There has been plenty of bother and misunderstanding and controversy – and now, finally, this.

There is a part of him that wants to run off – off into the darkness. But he is confident, because he has prayed, that nothing but his death will bring that darkness to an end.

He can see torches now, slicing through the night in his direction. He is a torch, as well, about to be consumed for his father's sake, and for the sake of the world.

As the arresting soldiers obey their orders, they have no idea what they are doing – and understand even less what God is doing. For it's midnight, and he is up to something again. He sent the baby to Bethlehem, the rabbi to the religious leader, and now he sends his own Son to a cross, that those soldiers and a world just like them might have their darkness turned to light.

Because it's midnight. And at midnight, things happen.

One day ends. And a brand new day is born.

14

Old Shepherd

Luke 2:8–20

There are a lot of potential "what ifs" in the Bible, and this is one of them. It's unlikely, obviously, that something like this actually happened, but it does give the opportunity to let one familiar Bible story inform another and help us, perhaps, to better understand them both.

Telling tips

Definitely one to do on your own. I dropped this into the end of a Christmas Candlelight service originally, and it was really effective.

The old shepherd climbed the hill just as he'd climbed up hills a hundred times before. And as he climbed he looked, this way and that, for his one lost little lamb.

At the top of the hill he stopped to catch his breath. And that's when he saw the woman.

"I know you," he said, struggling for breath, and surprised that the words had even come out. But he was so shocked to see her that he could not help himself.

"It has been many years," he went on. "But you are the woman, I'm sure of it. The woman the angel led us to. The woman in the stable."

The woman wiped the tears from her eyes and nodded. But she did not look at the old shepherd, not even for a second. For her gaze was fixed on her own little lamb. Fixed on him as he hung there in the air.

"And your baby?" the shepherd continued, following her gaze. "Is that your baby there?"

Again the woman nodded. Yes.

"The angel seemed so certain," mused the old man after a while. "The Saviour. Christ. The Lord. That's what he told us. And that is why my companions and

I ran with such haste to see you – with my own little boy leading the way. But, surely, the angel…"

"The angel was not wrong," the woman interrupted. "God was at work then, all those years ago. And God is at work now. I believe it. I must."

"But how?" whispered the shepherd. "How, in the face of this?"

"Hush," said the woman. "He's trying to speak."

"Today," said the man in the air. "Today," he said to the man hanging next to him. "Today, you will be with me in Paradise."

And as he watched, and as he listened, the old man's eyes filled with tears, as well.

"Do you see?" said the woman. "Even now. Even here. The angel's words ring true. Who else could make such a promise to a dying man? Who else would even care?"

"I must go," said the shepherd. "I have found what I was looking for."

"But you haven't told me," said the woman. "Whatever happened to your son? The little boy with the lamb?"

"Yes, well…" the old man faltered. "I suppose you could say that he fell in with the wrong crowd and wandered away."

"I see," said the woman. "I'm sorry. Do you know where he is now?"

"Now?" answered the shepherd, looking one last time into the sky. "Now he is on his way to Paradise. I guess our angel was right, after all."

And with that he turned and climbed back down the hill, just as he'd climbed down hills a hundred times before.

15

A Night the Stars Danced for Joy

Luke 2:8–20

Here's a story from Angels, Angels All Around *that I wanted to keep... well... around.*

Telling Tip

One to do on your own.

The shepherd, the shepherd's wife, and the shepherd boy lay on their backs on top of the hill. Their hands were folded behind their heads, and their feet stretched out in three directions like points on a compass. Their day's work was done. Their sheep had dropped off to sleep. And they had run out of things to say.

So they just lay there on top of that hill and stared lazily into the night sky. It was a clear night. There were no clouds for shy stars to hide behind. And the bolder stars? For some reason, they seemed to be shining more proudly than any of the shepherds could remember. Suddenly, what must have been the boldest star of all came rushing across the sky, dancing from one horizon to the other and showing off its sparkling serpent's tail. "Shooting star," said the boy dreamily. "Make a wish." The shepherd and his wife said nothing. They were too old for games and too tired tonight, even to say so.

But they were not too old for wishing.

The shepherd fixed his eyes on a cluster of stars that looked like a great bear. And he thought about the cluster of scars on his leg – jagged reminders of a battle he'd fought with a real bear long ago. A battle to save his sheep.

There were other scars, too, mapped out like a hundred roads across his back. Souvenirs of his battles with that Great Bear, Rome. The land of Israel belonged to his people, not to the Roman invaders. So why should he bow politely to their soldiers and surrender his sheep for their banquets? Greedy tyrants. Uniformed thieves. That's what they were.

And even their claw-sharp whips would not change his mind.

And so the shepherd made a silent wish. He wished for someone to save him. From violence. From greed. From bears.

The shepherd's wife had her eyes shut. This was the hardest time of the day for her. The time when there was nothing to do but try to fall asleep.

The time when the wind carried voices back to her. Her voice and her mother's. Angry, bitter voices. Voices hurling words that hurt. Words she wished she'd never spoken. Words she couldn't take back now, because her mother was dead, and there was no chance to say she was sorry. And so the shepherd's wife made a silent wish, too. She wished for peace, for an end to those bitter voices on the wind.

The shepherd boy grew tired of waiting.

"All right," he said finally. "I'll make a wish, then. I wish, I wish, I wish something interesting would happen for a change. Something exciting. I'm tired of just sitting on this hill night after night. I want something to laugh about. To sing and dance about."

The shepherd turned to look at his wife.

The shepherd's wife opened her eyes and shook her head.

But before either of them could say anything, something happened.

Something that suggested the shepherd boy just might get his wish.

Like tiny white buds blossoming into gold flowers, the stars began to swell and spread, until their edges bled together and the sky was filled with a glowing blanket of light. And then that blanket of light began to shrink and gather itself into a brilliant, blinding ball that hung above them.

The shepherds dared not move. All they could do was stare into that light. They watched it slowly change again. Shining rays stretched into arms. Legs kicked out like white beams. And a glowing face blinked bright and burning. The light sprouted wings. It took the shape of an angel. And it spoke.

"Don't be afraid," the angel said, "but sing and dance for joy! I have good news for you. Today, in Bethlehem, your Saviour was born – the special one whom God promised to send you. Here's the proof: if you go to Bethlehem, you will find the baby wrapped in cloths and lying in a feed trough."

The shepherds were still too shocked to speak. But that didn't keep them from thinking.

"Don't be afraid?" thought the shepherd. "He's got to be joking."

"A baby in a feed trough?" thought the shepherd's wife. "Why, even our boy got better treatment than that."

"Sing and dance for joy?" thought the shepherd boy. "Now that's more like it!"

And as if in answer to the boy's thought, the angel threw his arms and legs wide, like the first step in some heavenly jig. But instead, he flung himself – could it be? – into a thousand different pieces of light, pieces that scattered themselves across the dark blue of the night and landed where the stars had been. Pieces that turned into angels themselves, singing a song that the shepherds had never heard before, to a tune that had been humming in their heads forever.

"Glory to God in the highest!" the angels sang. "And peace on earth to all."

Some plucked at lyres. Some blew trumpets. Some beat drums. Some banged cymbals. There were dancers, as well – spinning and whirling, larking and leaping across the face of the midnight moon.

Finally, when the music could get no louder, when the singers could sing no stronger, when the dancers could leap no higher, when the shepherd's mouths and eyes could open no further, everything came to a stop.

As quickly as the angels had come, they were gone. The sky was silent and filled once more with twinkling stars. The shepherds lay there for a moment, blinking and rubbing their eyes.

At last the shepherd struggled to his feet. "Well," he said, "looks like we'd better find this baby."

The shepherd's wife pulled herself up, shook the grass off her robe and ran her fingers absently through her hair.

And the shepherd boy leaped eagerly to his feet and shouted, "Hooray!"

When they got to Bethlehem, things were just as the angel had said. A husband and a young mother. And a baby in a feed trough. A family much like the shepherd's, in fact. Was it possible, the shepherd wondered, for one so small, so poor, so ordinary, to be the Saviour? The Promised One? Then the shepherd told the young mother about the angels. And that's when he knew. It was the look in her eyes. The look that said, "How wonderful!" but also, "I'm not surprised." There was something special going on here. The mother knew it. And now the shepherd and his family knew it, too.

"Well," said the boy as they made their way back to the hill, "my wish came true. Too bad you didn't make a wish."

The shepherd said nothing. But he ran one finger gently along his scars. Was he imagining things, or were they smaller now?

The shepherd's wife said nothing. She was listening. There were no bitter voices on the wind now. There were songs – heaven songs – and the cry of a newborn child.

"Glory to God in the highest!" she shouted suddenly.

"And peace to everyone on earth!" the shepherd shouted back.

Then the shepherd boy shouted too – "Hooray!" – and danced like an angel for joy.

16

Mary Went Looking for Jesus

Luke 2:41–50; John 19:25

Sometimes writers get a "gift" – and this piece is one of them. I was at an Eastertime conference a few years ago, and the Scripture for one of the evenings was the passage from Luke 2 about the young Jesus in the temple. I was talking with some of the leaders in the afternoon, and they asked me if I had a reading that would fit. I didn't, but said I'd be happy to put something together. So I went back to my room and prayed, and the Luke 2 story and the Passion story just sort of came together. As I said, a gift.

Telling tips

This is definitely one to do on your own. You need to read the Bible passage at the start really well, and "sell" the idea that the Luke 2 story is what you're doing. I always pick up the pace and the sense of desperation as Mary looks for Jesus, and then slow it right down with "And finally she found him. But it wasn't like that other time", because you need to give your group the time to make the transition to the other story with you. You also need to make sure you leave time for some reflection or response at the end. I've found that it just needs working through – some quiet time or a quiet song works best.

Every year his parents went to Jerusalem for the Feast of the Passover. When Jesus was twelve years old, they went up to the Feast, according to the custom. After the Feast was over, while his parents were returning home, the boy Jesus stayed behind in Jerusalem, but they were unaware of it. Thinking he was in their company, they travelled on for a day. Then they began looking for him among their relatives and friends. When they did not find him, they went back to Jerusalem to look for him.

Mary went looking for Jesus. Her heart was pounding, her hands sweating. She hadn't seen him for days.

Mary went looking for Jesus. "Have you seen my son?" she asked. "Have you seen my son? My boy?"

Mary went looking for Jesus. The hot wind biting her face, chasing the tears from the corners of her eyes.

Mary went looking for Jesus. Up and down, and in and out, the crowded streets of Jerusalem.

Mary went looking for Jesus. And suddenly she remembered. The same search. The same crowded streets. But, oh, so long ago.

Mary went looking for Jesus. And finally she found him. But it wasn't like that other time. Not at all.

Then, she had looked down at his twelve-year-old face. Now, she was forced to look up.

Then, the temple teachers had praised him, amazed! Now, they shouted and swore.

Then, his face was adolescent fresh. Now, it was covered in blood.

Mary went looking for Jesus. "Why are you looking for me?" he'd asked. And he'd fixed her with a look both innocent and wise. A look that said: "I'm sorry you're worried. I know what I'm doing. Everything will be all right.

'Didn't you know that I'd be here in my Father's house, doing my Father's will?'

Mary went looking for Jesus. He was looking at her now as well. And it was the same look. The very same look. The bright boy. The dying man. "I'm sorry you're worried. I know what I'm doing. Everything will be all right."

They say you never stop being your mother's son.

Or your father's either, I guess.

Mary went looking for Jesus. And she found him in a temple. And she found him on a cross. Where she always knew he'd be – doing his Father's will.

17

Hometown Boy

Luke 4:14–30

Having preached in my hometown church, I think I have some sympathy both for what Jesus had to deal with and also for the woman in this story. (The other voice is most definitely a woman – older – a widow, sitting in the back of the room where she can't quite see or hear.) The desire is to wish the best for the hometown boy, to say you knew-him-when if he's doing well. And all that comes up in this piece. I read somewhere that there were probably no more than 100–120 people living in Nazareth at that time, so it wasn't just some people who knew the hometown boy, it was probably everybody. That makes this whole event even more extraordinary, and the woman's reaction even more amusing!

Telling tips

You'll need one person to read the Bible passage in a straightforward way, and another person to play the part of the woman who is whispering (loudly) to the woman sitting next to her.

Jesus returned to Galilee in the power of the Spirit, and news about him spread through the whole countryside. He taught in their synagogues and everyone praised him.

He went to Nazareth, where he had been brought up, and on the sabbath day he went into the synagogue, as was his custom. And he stood up to read.

"Ooh, look! Isn't that Jesus – Joseph and Mary's son?"

The scroll of the prophet Isaiah was handed to him.

"He looks good, doesn't he? I like what he's done with his hair!"

Unrolling it, he found the place and began to read.

"He played with my boys, you know – Abraham, Samuel, and little Judas."

"The Spirit of the Lord is on me…"

"Always creeping up and tripping him, he was. Sneaky little beggar, my Judas."

"Because he has anointed me to preach good news to the poor..."

"We had him for dinner on more than one occasion."

"He has sent me to proclaim freedom for the prisoners..."

"Absolutely adored my baked beans. But they didn't agree with him, poor boy."

"And recovery of sight for the blind..."

"'You can make those noises in a carpenter's shop,' I'd say, 'but not in this house!'"

"To release the oppressed..."

"Has a clear speaking voice, doesn't he?"

"To proclaim the year of the Lord's favour."

"You don't have to strain to hear – not like some I could mention."

Then he rolled up the scroll, gave it back to the attendant and sat down.

"And look at that body language. Poised. Confident. He'll go far."

The eyes of everyone in the synagogue were fastened on him.

"I bet his mother's pleased."

And he began by saying, "Today this scripture is fulfilled in your hearing."

"That was nice, wasn't it? A lovely sentiment."

All spoke well of him and were amazed at the gracious words that came from his lips.

"So well spoken. Such gracious words. Is he wearing a little gloss on his lips?"

"But isn't this Joseph's son?" they asked.

"Actually, I've heard rumours about that. But I'll say no more."

Jesus said to them, "Surely you will quote this proverb to me: 'Physician, heal yourself!'"

"This is so nice, isn't it?"

"'Do here in your hometown what we have heard that you did in Capernaum.'"

"Hometown boy, reading and preaching. Brings a tear to the eye, doesn't it?"

"I tell you the truth," he continued, "no prophet is accepted in his hometown."

"Somebody you know. Somebody you can trust. Somebody who won't rock the boat."

"I assure you, there were many widows in Israel in Elijah's time, when the sky was shut for three and a half years and there was a severe famine throughout the land. Yet Elijah was not sent to any of them, but to a gentile widow in Zarephath in the region of Sidon."

"Gentle Jesus, meek and mild. We used to call him that, you know. He was lovely!"

"And there were many in Israel with leprosy in the time of Elisha the prophet, yet not one of them was cleansed – only Naaman the Syrian – the gentile."

"No trouble. No trouble at all."

All the people in the synagogue were furious when they heard this.

"It's getting a little noisy in here. Are we finished already?"

They got up…

"Where's everyone going? His mother's planned a little reception, of course!"

… drove him out of the town and took him to the brow of the hill on which the town was built in order to throw him down the cliff.

"To the cliffside, you say? Is that where we're going? For a little picnic, I imagine."

But he walked right through the crowd and went on his way.

"I don't know about you, but I think it's lovely to see a hometown boy do well!"

18

Poor, Hungry, Sad, and Unpopular

Luke 6:20–26

It was the "Whoah/Woe" thing that started this one off. And the "Bless" just followed along. And because this version of the Beatitudes is less familiar than the one from Matthew, it was easier to "play" with.

Telling tips

After the "Blessed" lines, look at the person next to you, and say "Bless!" (Maybe even put your arm around their shoulder!)

After the "Woe" lines, pull on imaginary reins, like you are slowing down a horse, and say "Whoah!" Explain that putting a stop to the kind of life that has no need for God is at the heart of both "Woe" and "Whoah!"

Are you poor? Then you are blessed, (*Bless!*)
For God will give you his kingdom.

Are you hungry? Then you are blessed, (*Bless!*)
For God will fill you up.

Are you weeping? Then you are blessed, (*Bless!*)
For God will bring a smile to your face.

Are you hated, excluded, rejected, persecuted? Then you are blessed, (*Bless!*)
Because that's how God's messengers are always treated. And they get God's reward!

Or are you wealthy? Then woe, (*Whoah!*)
You have all the comfort you're going to get.

Are you full? Then woe, (*Whoah!*)
For you will feel the pangs of hunger.

Are you laughing? Then woe, (*Whoah!*)
Tears will flow from your eyes.

Are you popular? Then woe, (*Whoah!*)
So were the false prophets, who had no word from God.

So God wants us poor, hungry, sad, and unpopular (a bit like high school!)?
Looks like it. Because then, and only then, do we reach out in need for him.

19

Having His Way

Luke 7:1–10; Matthew 8:5–13

Sometimes it's a phrase that jumps out of a reading, that sums the whole thing up for you. That's where this one started – with the centurion's authority and his recognition of a similar quality in Jesus.

Telling tips

Probably one to do on your own. Make sure you emphasize the first line in each section.

He was accustomed to having his way.

There were a hundred soldiers under his command, each one obliged to do whatever he wanted.

And as for the civilian population, there wasn't one of them who even dared to look him in the eye.

Fear? Hatred? It didn't matter – or so his fellow officers had often said. The point was to keep the peace. And if the odd busted head or broken arm or well-timed execution was the means it took to do that, so be it.

He was accustomed to having his way.

But in his experience, the stick was, on the whole, less effective than the carrot in that regard. And so, unlike some of his comrades, he took a more irenic approach to controlling the population of Palestine.

Yes, there were marches. Yes, there was a regular and visible military presence. But there were conversations, as well – particularly with the religious leaders. And the occasional contribution to some local cause.

Respect. That's what he was looking for. That's what he hoped he had achieved.

He was accustomed to having his way.

And then, one day, one of his servant boys fell ill. Deathly ill. And there was nothing he could do. No way to have his way. Not this time.

Somehow, word reached the synagogue. And the local religious officials paved the way for him to meet an itinerant teacher called Jesus.

The name was not strange to him. Protocol required keeping tabs on such men. They had a way of gathering crowds, then followers, then the kind of passionate momentum that had sometimes led to violence.

This man had the reputation for working miracles. And since a miracle was precisely what the centurion required, meeting the man seemed the thing to do.

He was accustomed to having his way.

That's the first thing the centurion thought when he saw Jesus.

The teacher did not look down. Not like the others. He looked the centurion in the eye, like they were equals. Maybe even like he was in charge.

On another occasion, the centurion thought, he might have taken this as a warning sign. But not now. Not when he needed what this man's reputation suggested he could provide.

And so it was the centurion who lowered his eyes.

"My servant is ill," he explained. "Paralysed and in great pain. I understand that you have the power to heal him."

"I do," said Jesus. "And I will."

There was no doubt in the centurion's mind. The man said it. He would do it.

He was accustomed to having his way.

It wasn't a religious thing. It was more a matter of recognition. One man of power acknowledging the same trait in another.

And so, before Jesus could even take a step, the centurion held out his hand and said, "There's no need for you to come to the house. We are both men of authority. We know how this works. I tell my soldiers what to do, and they do it. The same is true of you. So say the word, and my servant will be healed."

And now it was the teacher's turn to be impressed.

"Did you hear that?" said Jesus to the crowd. "This man doesn't even share our faith, but there is not one of you who trusts me like he does. One day, I tell you, people just like him, from all over this world of ours, will come and feast with our forefathers in the kingdom of heaven!"

The centurion noted that the crowd did not seem to be particularly impressed by this. But their murmuring did not, for a moment, dampen the teacher's enthusiasm.

"Go," he said. "Your servant is already well."

The centurion had no doubt that he would find his servant healed. As for the teacher's confidence that people like him would find themselves in the company of his God, one day, the centurion was less sure.

But who knew?

The man was, after all, accustomed to having his way.

20

Sowers and Soil and Seeds

Luke 8:1–14

This one pretty much speaks for itself. It's a relatively straightforward retelling of Jesus' parable. It works really well in an all-age service.

Telling tips

I have included the tips in the text, so they are easier to follow. Divide your group into four sections – that's probably the best way to do this. Then introduce the actions and practise them with each section before you start the story. Remember, the more fun you have with each action as you demonstrate it, the more likely it is that they will join in and enjoy it, too.

Jesus walked out of the house. He went to the lake – the lake of Galilee. But he didn't go to swim or to catch himself some fish. He went there to teach.

And when he sat down – 'cause that's what teachers did in those days – when he sat down, a huge crowd gathered round. So huge that they couldn't possibly see him, much less hear him.

So he borrowed a boat and pushed off a little way from shore. And when the people could see and when the people could hear, he told them a story, a particular kind of story we call a parable, a story with a special, hidden meaning.

"A farmer went out to sow some seed – tossing it here and there on the ground. Some of the seed fell on the hard, foot-worn path. And as soon as it did, the greedy birds swooped down and ate it up" *(gobble, gobble, gobble – hee-hee-hee – mmm).*

"Some of the seed fell on rocks, where the soil was very shallow. The plants sprang up quickly" *(leap up to standing position – Ta-da! – or Hooray!).* "But because the soil was shallow, their roots did not sink deep. And when the sun came up, it scorched them, and they withered and died" *("I'm melting! I'm melting" – à la Wizard of Oz – "Nooo!!" Drop into seat).*

"Other seeds fell among the thorns" *(Uh-oh!)* "which grew up and choked the plants" *(put hands round own throat – GAAAH!).*

"But some of the seed fell on good soil. And that produced a crop. A hundred, sixty, thirty times what was sown" *(cheer, "Fruit, fruit, that's what we're for. Thirty, sixty, a hundred times more! Goooo fruit!").*

Jesus' disciples, his students, his apprentices, came to him and asked: "Why do you tell the people parables? Why not spell it out?"

"It gives them something to think about, to pray about, to puzzle over," said Jesus, "and if they have the ears to hear what God is saying, they'll get it. So here's what the parable means."

"The seed is the message of God's kingdom – all that I have come to teach you. When someone hears about it and does not understand it, he is like the seed on the path. The devil comes, like a greedy bird, and snatches it away" *(bird actions).*

"The one who received the seed on the rocky place hears the message of the kingdom and accepts it with joy" *(stand up – Ta-da!).* "But because he has no root, when trouble comes, he quickly withers away" *(wither motion).*

"The next one accepts the message, too. And it sinks in and he grows. But then worry – worry about having too much stuff, worry about having too little, worry like a patch of thorns" *(Uh-oh!)* "comes along to choke him."

"And the last one is like the seed sown on good ground. He hears the message of the kingdom. He understands it. And his life is good and fruitful as a result" *(cheer, etc.).*

21

Glow, Moses, Glow!

Luke 9:28–36

First of all, apologies to Graham Kendrick. He's a nice guy with a good sense of humour, so I'm hoping he will understand that when I was asked to write a song about the Transfiguration, there was really no other choice. "Shine, Jesus, Shine!" That's what it's all about. So "Shine, Jesus, Shine!" had to be at the heart of it. Yes, I nicked the odd lyric just for familiarity's sake. And, yes, seeing as Elijah is knocking about in the story, I had to nick the odd line from Robin Mark as well (again, apologies). But people really like this song. It's loads of fun. So enjoy!

Telling tips

Sing it to the tune of "Shine, Jesus, Shine". Simple as that. And even though it's a parody, you mustn't forget to mark it down on your music licence sheet. Graham deserves something for all this abuse, after all!

Jesus said to Peter, "Let's go up the mountain."
Took so many steps that he could hardly count 'em.
James and John came along for the journey.
Suddenly Jesus started to transform, he
Shone like the sun, shone like the sun.

Shine, Jesus, shine,
Fill this land with the Father's glory
Glow, Moses, Glow,
Look! He's stood there, as well!
These are the days, are the days,
Hey look, there's the prophet Elijah!
He's shining, too
And we're all feeling swell!

Peter said to Jesus, "Why not build three tents near?
One for you and these other two gents here?
Then God came down in a big shiny cloud.
"This is my Son," he said. "He's made me proud.
Listen to him (I want you to) Listen to him!"

Chorus

When the cloud had lifted Jesus stood there alone.
They went back down the mountain, Peter walked on his own.
"Oh dear," he thought, "I've gone and put my foot in it."
But then he reconsidered. "Hey, wait just a minute!
I know what Jesus means. I said it back in Matthew chapter 16!"

Chorus

22

Foxes, Funerals, and Furrows

Luke 9:57–62

A little reading, this one, but I think it sums up nicely the intent of these three sayings.

Telling tips

One to do on your own.

"Foxes have holes," said Jesus. "Birds have nests. But I have nowhere to lay my head. No furniture, no flat, no financial security. Know that first, if you would follow me."

"Funerals are for dead men," said Jesus. "Even a funeral as important as your father's. But the Kingdom of God is more important still. Put that first, if you would follow me."

"Furrows in a field need to be straight and true," said Jesus. "And facing forward is the only way to plough them. You'll never do it looking back. The future comes first, if you would follow me."

Foxes, Funerals, and Furrows.

Come and follow me.

23

Not a Story about Loving

Luke 10:25–37

I love it when I find something in a really familiar story that I never noticed before. That's what occasioned this retelling of the story of the Good Samaritan. I hope at least some of you will be surprised as well!

A man asks Jesus a question.
    "How do I inherit eternal life?"
So Jesus gives him an answer.
"Love God with all you've got. And love your neighbour as yourself."
This sounds hard, and a bit extreme. Like a room without walls. A country without boundaries. "Surely there are limits," thinks the man.
So he asks a follow-up question.
"Who, exactly, is my neighbour?"
And Jesus tells him a story.
But it's not a story about loving.
It's not about loving, at all.

A man walks down a dangerous road. From Jerusalem to Jericho. And he has a nasty surprise.
He is set upon by thieves. Robbed and left for dead. Hopeless.
It's not a story about loving.
It's not about loving, at all.

So two men come along, a priest and a Levite. It's starting to sound like a joke. But they don't walk into a bar. And the wounded man is definitely not laughing.

And instead of helping him, they pass by, presumably because they are both temple officials and they don't want to make themselves unclean. And touching blood (of which there is plenty) or touching a dead body (of which there is quite possibly one – they don't get close enough to check!) would do just that. And so, in order to keep one of God's laws, they violate another. And they leave the man alone.

This is, of course, one of the official explanations for their behaviour. The only problem I have with it is that they are walking away from Jerusalem, which means they have already done their jobs, which means that helping the man wouldn't have kept them from performing their temple functions, which means they could have touched him, which means, at the end of the day, that maybe, just maybe, they didn't actually give a monkey's!

So it's still not a story about loving.

It's not about loving, at all.

And then another man comes by. A Samaritan man. A man whom the wounded man would quite likely have considered a heretic and a half-breed, well outside of God's love and grace. In fact, it's quite possible that the wounded man was on that road in the first place because it was the best road for avoiding the territory of the Samaritan man. Ironic, yeah?

But the Samaritan man helps the wounded man. He dresses his wounds, and bundles him onto his beast, and takes him to the nearest emergency room, and pays for both his treatment and the rehab that follows.

And it's still not a story about loving.

It's not about loving, at all.

Because if it were about loving, then surely the roles would have been reversed. The Samaritan would have been the wounded man. And the man on the donkey would have been – I don't know – the man who asked the question. The man who wanted to know how far love should go.

But Jesus knew his heart. And he knows ours too. He knew that if the Samaritan had been the victim, and the other man the helper, then his message might still have been missed.

Help a hated enemy? Stoop to give aid to a foe? It looks like love, sure. But it might just be condescension or pity – another way of looking down on someone, even as you're reaching down to pull them up.

But when you are the one who is in trouble, who is left for dead, who is left without hope unless someone helps, then "loving your neighbour" is all that matters. Or rather, receiving love from him. And that's the point of the story. And it's genius.

Because it's not a story about loving, at all.

It's a story about being loved.

24

Buzz-y

Luke 10:38–42

This is a quick reading – and all the more appropriate for it! It would make a lovely introduction to a sermon about Mary and Martha, and works really well right across the age range.

Telling tips

Teach the chorus to your crowd, first of all, and make sure they can do it quickly (and that you repeat it each time). Do it ever more quickly as the reading progresses, to give a sense of Martha's increasing busyness and frustration. And then slow it right down when Jesus speaks. Let them join you on the first two lines of the last chorus (which you can do a little more slowly), and then cut them off and do the last two lines yourself.

Busy, busy, busy,
Busy as a bee.
Martha was so busy,
She could hardly even breathe!
(x2)

Wash the dishes, cook the meals,
Put the kettle on.
Clean the windows, sweep the floor,
Work is never done!

Busy, busy, busy,
Busy as a bee.
Martha was so busy,
She could hardly even breathe!
(x2)

Jesus came to visit once,
She put on such a spread!
Home-made bread and fancy cakes
And pickled chicken heads.

Busy, busy, busy,
Busy as a bee.
Martha was so busy,
She could hardly even breathe!
(x2)

"I do all the work," she moaned,
"It all comes down to me!
While sister Mary chats with Jesus
Idle and carefree."

Busy, busy, busy,
Busy as a bee.
Martha was so busy,
She could hardly even breathe!
(x2)

"Slow down, Martha," Jesus smiled.
"Take it easy, please.
Hospitality is good,
But you still need time to breathe.
Time to think and time to pray,
Time to spend with me.
So join your sister Mary,
And then we'll sort out tea."

Busy, busy, busy,
Busy as a bee.
So Martha sat and listened
And at last found time to breathe.

25

Thinkin' 'bout Ravens

Luke 12:22–34

I got into this little "thinkin' 'bout" groove, and the following three readings were the result.

Think about ravens for a minute.
Oversized crows. Edgar Alan Poe. Got it?
Now answer me this:
Have you ever seen a raven ploughing a field?
Thought not.
Or driving a combine harvester?
Nope.
Forking hay into a barn? Filling a silo?
Not even "nevermore". Just plain "never".
Yet God feeds them all they need.

Now think about lilies.
Tall white Easter lilies. Stripy orange tiger lilies. Pad-perching water lilies. Got it?
Now answer me this:
Have you ever seen a lily looking for work?
Thought not.
Or doing that Rapunzel thing with a spinning-wheel?

Nope.
Or picking through a rack full of clothing?
And, speaking of fashion, lilies last just about as long as the latest style.
Yet God makes them beautiful.

So don't worry. God will do the same for you.
And now I know what you're thinking. I don't even have to ask.
That's crazy. That's barmy. That's nuts!

And so I'll ask again.
Think about ravens.
Think about lilies.
Are they crazy?
Nope (unless you want to count pecking out the innards of roadkill).
They do what God made them to do and let him take care of the rest.
And that's all he asks of us.

To do what he made us for.
Love him.
Love one another.
Look for his kingdom.
And leave him to take care of the rest.

Consider the ravens.
Consider the lilies.

26

Thinkin' 'bout Mustard

Luke 13:18–21

This one's a little longer – a bit of a sermon, really ('cause that's how it started). It gets there in the end, though – and there's plenty of food for thought. Well, plenty of mustard and bread, anyway.

Telling tips

Don't forget to do the 1 Corinthians reading near the end. It won't make much sense otherwise.

Think about mustard for a minute.
That's right. Mustard.

English. French. The bright yellow hot-doggy stuff. Whatever.

Jesus said that the kingdom of God is like a mustard seed. Maybe the smallest seed of all. But a seed that grows into an enormous tree, where birds build their homes in the branches.

So you need to know something about mustard.

And you need to know something about bread. Well, yeasty bread – no pittas permitted.

So think about bread.

White. Wheat. Whatever. Roll-shaped. Baguette-ish. Loaf-like.

It's yeast that makes it rise. Leaven is what Jesus called it. And he said that the kingdom of God is like leaven. And when just a little of it gets mixed into the dough, it makes enough to feed a crowd.

So you need to know something about bread.

And finally, I suppose, you need to know something about the kingdom of God. Now I could go on and on. Plenty of theologians have. But this is supposed to be a reading, not a lecture, so let's borrow Jesus' definition. You can find it in the prayer he taught us.

"Thy kingdom come"? It's when God's will is done – on earth as it is in heaven.

So, given a little space – a mustard-seed-sized door, a leaven's worth – surrendering to the will of God can result in some very big changes – to you and me, to our communities, to our churches, to the world.

And there you have it. Except of course, you don't. Because that surrender thing doesn't come easy. Not to any of us.

And what is more, mustard seeds don't grow into trees. Not big ones with bird-burdened branches. No, mustard seeds grow into shrubs. And not very pretty shrubs, as it happens. Quite weedy shrubs, in fact, that people used to yank out of their gardens.

So what's up? Did Jesus get it wrong? Does divine knowledge not extend to horticulture?

I can't answer that one. But I can say that there is just the chance that Jesus had a different tree in mind, altogether.

You see, there's this vision in the book of Daniel. One of King Nebuchadnezzar's vision. And the vision – are you still with me? – is of a tree! A great big tree. A great big tree with birds in its branches. A-ha!

And what does Daniel say that the great big tree stands for? A great big kingdom!

So maybe what Jesus is really saying to his listeners is this: the tiny little mustard seed, which you think is just a weed, will grow into the biggest kingdom you ever heard of!

And then, to add insult to injury, he brings up yeast. Yeah, yeast. I've got no problem with yeast. You've got no problem. But to his listeners, yeast was the thing that made bread bad. Because all sacred bread was yeast-less. Un-leavened. Pure.

So maybe what Jesus is really saying is this: God's kingdom is like yeast – the thing you think is impure will be the thing that works its way into the dough and feeds a multitude.

Weeds and seeds and impure stuff – that's what's at the heart of God's kingdom. That's what makes the difference. That's what leads to the surrender. That's what makes the kingdom come.

And how is that? I think Paul had it all figured out. *(Read 1 Corinthians 1:20–25.)*

> The Mustard seed. The weed.
> The leaven – no taste of heaven.
> The cross. The loss. The curse.
> From such the kingdom comes.
>
> You just need to know something about mustard.
> And you need to know something about bread.

27

Thinkin' 'bout Foxes and Chickens

Luke 13:31–35

One more to think about. It's an interesting contrast, don't you think?

Think about foxes for a minute.
That's right. Foxes.
Sly as a fox.
Crazy like a fox.
Cute little heartbreaker. Sweet little lovemaker.
Foxy Lady.
Sleek. Sexy. Self-sufficient.
Foxes.

Think about foxes. Now think again.
'Cause Jesus called King Herod a fox.
And, by implication, all those religious leaders in Israel's sad and long history who relied on their instinct and their cunning and their wiles to save their nation. And who put the prophets to death for simply suggesting that trusting God and doing his will and turning back to him might be a more effective course.

So the prophets died. And, ironically, the leaders did too. For sleek and sexy and self-sufficient so often leads to slavery.

Now think about chickens.

That's right. Chickens.

"Don't be a chicken!" your friends jeer, when you're the only one who hasn't jumped off the diving-board.

"Don't be a chicken!" your dad chides, when your knuckles are white on the side of the slide.

Nobody wants to be a chicken.

Cowardly.

Cringing.

Kentucky-fried.

Think about chickens. Now think again.

'Cause that's what Jesus hoped and prayed those prophet-killing foxes might become. Chickens. Chicks. Running towards him like he was their mother hen. Wings outstretched. To protect. To comfort. To save.

So we can be foxes. Sleek and self-sufficient. Making our own way. Cleverly paving a path to destruction.

Or we can be chickens. Running to him. Running his way. Safe under his arms. Outstretched.

Don't be a chicken?
Don't be an idiot.
Don't be a fox.

28

A Lost Sheep

Luke 15:1–7

I love the three "lost" stories, and the way they build.
One out of a hundred. One out of ten. One out of two. Or maybe two
out of two. And God's grace there throughout. To rescue. To return. To save.
Given the fact that they work together, I thought it would be fair to tell them
in the same way. The Rhyming Way!

Telling tips

See "Peter Walks on Water" (New Testament, chapter 4) for suggestions on
how to tell this kind of story.

There once was a shepherd who had a hundred sheep.
There once was a shepherd who had a hundred sheep.
There once was a shepherd who had a hundred sheep.
They skipped and they frolicked and they leaped.
(Leap – even if just little!)
They skipped and they frolicked and they leaped.
They skipped and they frolicked and they leaped.

But one of the sheep was more curious than the rest
But one of the sheep was more curious than the rest
But one of the sheep was more curious than the rest
And away from the others he creeped.
(Make a little creeping-away motion with hands.)
And away from the others he creeped.
And away from the others he creeped.

"Someone's missing," said the shepherd, when he counted up that night.
"Someone's missing," said the shepherd, when he counted up that night.
"Someone's missing," said the shepherd, when he counted up that night.

"Until I find him, I shall not go to sleep!"
(Head on hands, sleeping motion.)
"Until I find him, I shall not go to sleep!"
"Until I find him, I shall not go to sleep!"

So the shepherd left the ninety-nine and set off in the dark,
So the shepherd left the ninety-nine and set off in the dark,
So the shepherd left the ninety-nine and set off in the dark,
And behind every boulder he peeped.
(Peeping motion – hands above eyes.)
And behind every boulder he peeped.
And behind every boulder he peeped.

And finally he found him – that lost and lonely sheep,
And finally he found him – that lost and lonely sheep,
And finally he found him – that lost and lonely sheep,
Trapped in thorns, where the path was rough and steep.
(Pretend you're on the edge of a precipice, looking down, and frightened – say "steep" with a little shriek.)
Trapped in thorns, where the path was rough and steep.
Trapped in thorns, where the path was rough and steep.

So the shepherd freed the sheep and set him on his shoulders.
So the shepherd freed the sheep and set him on his shoulders.
So the shepherd freed the sheep and set him on his shoulders.
"Man," he thought. "I sure could use a Jeep!"
(Pretend you are turning steering wheel.)
"Man," he thought. "I sure could use a Jeep!"
"Man," he thought. "I sure could use a Jeep!"

So the shepherd took the sheep and put him with the others
So the shepherd took the sheep and put him with the others
So the shepherd took the sheep and put him with the others
In a white-and-woolly, happy-hundred heap.
(Make shape of heap with hands.)
In a white-and-woolly, happy-hundred heap.
In a white-and-woolly, happy-hundred heap.

Then the shepherd threw a party for his neighbours and his friends.
Then the shepherd threw a party for his neighbours and his friends.
Then the shepherd threw a party for his neighbours and his friends.
They skipped and they frolicked and they leaped.
(Repeat first motion.)
They skipped and they frolicked and they leaped.
They skipped and they frolicked and they leaped.

29

A Maths Problem

Luke 15:1–2; 8–10

There's an awful lot of arithmetic in the Bible. Two by two. Seventy times seven. Ninety-nine sheep out of a hundred. In fact, one of these days I'm going to write a whole book of Bible maths stories, so that kids can learn about Deuteronomy and long division all in one go! In the meantime, here's a story in which the numbers really matter.

Telling tips

Before the story begins, teach your group the little counting rhythm. Let them use their fingers if they have to – it's more fun, anyway! Then bring them in at the appropriate times.

Jesus was talking with the tax collectors and their friends. But the Pharisees and their friends (who always seemed to be eavesdropping) were listening as well.

"Look at that!" they muttered. "He says he's a religious man, but he spends all his time with sinners!"

So Jesus turned to the Pharisees and said, "I've got a maths problem for you. Add, subtract, multiply, divide. Use your fingers, use your toes if you like. Here's the problem: 'What number makes an angel smile?'"

The Pharisees groaned. They hated maths – and those word problems in particular. So while they were undoing their sandals, Jesus told them a story.

Once there was a woman who had ten coins. And each coin was worth a day's wage. One afternoon, she went to count her coins. And suddenly, she had a maths problem too!

One, two, three.
Four, five, six.
Seven, eight, nine, and ten.

That's how many there were supposed to be. But somehow, someone had done some subtracting. And now there were only nine!

Desperate for a solution, the woman tackled the problem at once. She lit a lamp. She swept the floor. She lost track of how much time it took. Inch by inch. Metre by metre. Cubit by cubit. The woman looked carefully into every crack and crevice. And finally, she found it!

Her deficit diminished. Her budget balanced. The woman counted her coins again.

> One, two, three.
> Four, five, six.
> Seven, eight, nine, and TEN!

And then she smiled. For that one last coin had made all the difference.

What number makes an angel smile? The answer is the same.

One.

Just one.

Each one.

Every one.

One missing soul swept out of the darkness and into the light. One lost sinner found. Do the maths. Add, subtract, multiply, divide. Use your fingers, use your toes if you like. You'll see that it all adds up.

30

Just Waiting

Luke 15:11–32

Working on similar tellings of this and the previous two "Lost" stories got me thinking about their similarities and their differences. And also prompted the question that drives this piece.

Telling tips

One to tell on your own.

Did you ever wonder why he didn't go?

Why he just stood there, waiting?

The shepherd went. He left the ninety-nine behind and went out in the country, went out all alone. He went, and he searched, until he found his lost sheep.

So why not the father? Why didn't he go? Why did he just stand there, waiting?

The woman went. Her coin was lost, so she lit a lamp, and grabbed a broom and went and swept and searched until she found her lost coin.

So why not the father? Why didn't he go? Why did he just stand there, waiting?

I think it's because there is a difference – a difference between a lost sheep and a lost coin and a lost son.

The sheep is unlikely to come home on its own. With some varieties of pigeon, and the odd Disney dog and cat, you have a chance. But a sheep? A sheep is not hard-wired to return to the pen. A sheep is more likely to get stuck, or slaughtered, or slip off a mountainside.

So you have to go out and find him.

Same with a coin. It's a rare bit of currency that leaps out of that crack in the floor, shouting, "I'm here! Look! Pick me up, please!"

Doesn't happen. Not in my experience. And, for the record, it's true of car keys, as well. You have to go out and find them.

But sons? Sons make choices. They decide to go away. And unless they decide to come back, there's not much point following them to that far country and dragging them home.

I think the father knew that. He knew that until his son was ready to make that choice – until he was fully and finally fed up with the path he had chosen – there was no point in trying to force him onto another path.

Mind you, I'm sure he wanted to. I bet it took every bit of energy just to stand there, every ounce of strength to wait, particularly on those days when his mind was occupied with the inevitable "what ifs?"

What if he's hurt?

What if he's in jail?

What if I had done something differently?

What if there is something I can do, today, now, to save him?

The "what ifs" and "the waiting" were just holding him there, in some kind of terrible tension, like an enormous rubber band, stretched near to breaking.

And maybe that is why, when his son finally appeared on the horizon, the father literally took off in his direction, robes flying, arms outstretched, the words hurtling out of his mouth: "You're back! You're alive! Welcome home!"

Because now there was something he could do.

Something more than waiting.

31

There Was an Old Woman Who Pestered a Judge

Luke 18:1–8

I really got a kick out of writing (and performing) this one. The story of the Persistent Woman and the Unjust Judge is one of those more puzzling narratives and one, therefore, that doesn't seem to get addressed that often. I simply wanted to get across the idea of persistence – the never-ending nagging that Jesus suggests she used to get the judge to vindicate her. And that's when the song popped into my head – "There Was An Old Woman Who Swallowed a Fly…"

I cheated a bit, I must admit. "Pudge" is a little forced. It's short for "pudginess", of course – and I suspect she lost it due to her incessant activity and worrying (a point I made when I reached that verse and needed a breath).

Feel free to comment along the way – it just gets more and more ridiculous, and that's all part of the fun.

Telling tips

Sing to the tune of "There Was an Old Woman Who Swallowed a Fly". You can put the words on a screen, but I found that folks gave up after a while and I was on my own anyway. It does need a lot of practice to work well – and at speed.

There was an old woman who pestered a judge
To keep from her record a character smudge,
But he wouldn't budge.

There was an old woman who niggled and nudged.
I don't know why she niggled and nudged.
She niggled and nudged to pester a judge
To keep from her record a character smudge,
But he wouldn't budge.

There was an old woman who tramped and trudged.
I don't know why she tramped and trudged.
She tramped and trudged to niggle and nudge.
She niggled and nudged to pester a judge
To keep from her record a character smudge,
But he wouldn't budge.

There was an old woman who slipped on the sludge.
I don't know why she slipped on the sludge.
She slipped on the sludge as she tramped and trudged.
She tramped and trudged to niggle and nudge.
She niggled and nudged to pester a judge
To keep from her record a character smudge,
But he wouldn't budge.

There was an old woman whose life was a drudge.
I don't know why her life was a drudge.
Her life was a drudge 'cause she slipped on the sludge.
She slipped on the sludge as she tramped and trudged.
She tramped and trudged to niggle and nudge.
She niggled and nudged to pester a judge
To keep from her record a character smudge,
But he wouldn't budge.

There was an old woman who harboured a grudge.
I don't know why she harboured a grudge.
She harboured a grudge 'cause her life was a drudge.
Her life was a drudge 'cause she slipped on the sludge.
She slipped on the sludge as she tramped and trudged.
She tramped and trudged to niggle and nudge.
She niggled and nudged to pester a judge
To keep from her record a character smudge,
But he wouldn't budge.

There was an old woman who lost all her pudge.
I don't know why she lost all her pudge.
She lost all her pudge 'cause she harboured a grudge.
She harboured a grudge 'cause her life was a drudge.
Her life was a drudge 'cause she slipped on the sludge.

She slipped on the sludge as she tramped and trudged.
She tramped and trudged to niggle and nudge.
She niggled and nudged to pester a judge
To keep from her record a character smudge,
But he wouldn't budge.

There was an old woman who swallowed some fudge.
I don't know why she swallowed that fudge.
She swallowed the fudge 'cause she lost all her pudge.
She lost all her pudge 'cause she harboured a grudge.
She harboured a grudge 'cause her life was a drudge.
Her life was a drudge 'cause she slipped on the sludge.
She slipped on the sludge as she tramped and trudged.
She tramped and trudged to niggle and nudge.
She niggled and nudged to pester a judge
To keep from her record a character smudge,
But he wouldn't budge.

"I'm tired of this song, now," complained the judge,
"And tired of that woman (what's her name?), Miss Margery Mudge."
She swallowed the fudge 'cause she lost all her pudge.
She lost all her pudge 'cause she harboured a grudge.
She harboured a grudge 'cause her life was a drudge.
Her life was a drudge 'cause she slipped on the sludge.
She slipped on the sludge as she tramped and trudged.
She tramped and trudged to niggle and nudge.
She niggled and nudged to pester a judge
To keep from her record a character smudge.
"So at last I'll budge!"

32
Kids, Camels, and the Kingdom of God

Luke 18:15–30

Here are two stories from Luke 18 that are linked together by the disciples' very different response to the people who came to see Jesus. The alternative ending makes the reading a bit more specific, and may not work in every situation, but I have included it in case it works for you.

Telling tips

There are two motions at the heart of this reading – "welcoming" (arms open wide, ready to receive) and "pushing away" (hands out in front, pushing). Teach these to your group and then lead them in doing the motions at the appropriate points in the text.

When the women came to Jesus with their children, the disciples pushed them away. But Jesus opened wide his arms and said, "Don't keep the kids away from me. The kingdom of heaven belongs to them. They're little and powerless, dependent and small. And you need to be like them to find your way in!"

But when the ruler came to Jesus, with his goodness and his goods, the disciples welcomed him with open arms. "If this man can't be saved," they said, "then who can?"

Jesus welcomed the man as well. But this is what he said: "The only goodness there is, is God's. And as for your goods – give them to the poor!"

So the man walked sadly away.

Jesus was sad as well. So he turned to his friends and said, "The rich own many things. But not the kingdom of God. It does not belong to them. They are big and powerful, strong and independent. And, like a camel shoved through the eye of a needle, they find it hard to let go of enough hump and hoof to squeeze in!

God's values are different from ours. That's all Jesus was trying to say. He welcomes those we push away. And those we welcome, he welcomes too. (They just can't push their way in!)

It sounds difficult. It sounds complicated. But it's simple really.

It's all about kids and camels and the kingdom of God.

(Alternative ending – pick up after "… hump and hoof to squeeze in!")

So when the rich man came to our church, we welcomed him with open arms. We gave him a cup of coffee and a comfy seat in a state-of-the-art sanctuary.

And when the children came, we welcomed them as well. We let them stay in the sanctuary (for the first thirty minutes). Then we sent them to the corner of the fellowship hall (which, admittedly, could use a coat of paint), with Mrs Robertson, who has served the Sunday school faithfully for ages (on a fifty-pound-per-year budget).

And that's when Jesus came to our church too. "This is not hard," he said. "I'll go through it slowly if you like, because so much depends on you getting this." And he told us again about kids and camels and the kingdom of God.

33

He Was a Rich Man

Luke 18:18–25; 19:1–10

Sometimes it helps to look at two stories together. It gives you a better idea of what each of them is about.

A & B: He was a rich man.
A & B: He was looking for Jesus.
A: So he walked up to Jesus, one day.
B: So he crept out of his house, one day.
A: And he asked Jesus a question.
B: And he climbed up a tree.

A & B: He was a rich man.
A & B: He was looking for Jesus.
A: Everyone respected him.
B: Everyone despised him.
A: Because he was so good at being good.
B: Because he was so good at being bad – a tax collector, a traitor, and a cheat.

A & B: He was a rich man.
A & B: He was looking for Jesus.
A: "What must I do, Jesus," he asked, "to inherit eternal life?"
B: "What should I do?" he wondered. "If the crowd spots me here, I could lose my life."
A: "You know the law," Jesus answered. "No adultery. No murder. No stealing. No lying. Honour your dad and your mum."
B: "I need somewhere to eat," Jesus announced. "Where shall I go for my tea?"

A & B: He was a rich man.

A & B: He was looking for Jesus.

A: "I have done all those things since I was a boy," the rich man said.

B: "There's no reason he'd want to come to my house," the rich man sighed.

A: "Then there's just one thing you lack," said Jesus, looking him in the eye. "Sell all you have and give it to the poor. Then come and follow me."

B: "Come down!" said Jesus, looking up through the leaves. "I'm staying at your house today."

A & B: He was a rich man.

A & B: He was looking for Jesus.

A: And the rich man looked down at the ground.

B: And the rich man climbed down from the tree.

A: And the rich man was very sad.

B: And the rich man was very glad.

A: And the rich man declined the offer.

B: And the rich man came up with an offer – half his possessions to the poor, and four times back what he had stolen.

A: And Jesus said, "How hard it is for the rich to enter the kingdom. It's easier for a camel to go through the eye of a needle than for a rich man to enter the kingdom of God."

B: And Jesus said, "Today salvation has come to this house, because this man too is a son of Abraham. For the Son of Man came to seek and to save what was lost."

A & B: He was a rich man.

A & B: He was looking for Jesus.

34

The Anatomy of Faith

Luke 18:35–43

This is just a quick and punchy way of telling the story of the blind beggar Jesus healed. And because it's so physical, it helps us to understand both the man's infirmity and his strengths. And maybe to see him as a whole person – and not just a blind beggar.

Telling tips

You might just want to point to your ears, mouth, head, and heart as you work your way through the reading. And then do it again, at the end, finishing off with your eyes.

He couldn't see. But there was nothing wrong with his ears.
"Who's there?" asked the blind beggar. "What's going on? There's a crowd on its way, isn't there?"
"Jesus is coming," said a beggar nearby. "The crowd's with him."

He couldn't see. But there was nothing wrong with his mouth.
"Jesus!" he shouted. "Jesus, son of David, have mercy on me!"
And when there was no answer, he shouted even louder. "Jesus!"
"Quiet!" said the people in the crowd. "Stop your shouting, beggar!"

He couldn't see. But there was nothing wrong with his head.
He knew all about squeaky wheels. And grease.
So he shouted louder still, "Jesus, son of David, have mercy on me!"
So Jesus stopped.
"What would you like me to do for you?" he asked.

He couldn't see. But there was nothing wrong with his heart.
    "I don't want to be a blind beggar," he said. "I want to see."
    And Jesus said, "So be it then. Your faith has made you whole."

And now there was nothing wrong.
    Not with his ears.
    Not with his mouth.
    Not with his head.
    Not with his heart.
    And not with his eyes either.
    Not any more!

35

The Ballad of a Little Man

Luke 19:1–10

Apparently, in Middle Eastern societies, one is honoured not so much by being invited to the home of someone important as by having that someone accept an invitation to your house. This retelling of the story of Zacchaeus is built upon that premise, with the "great and the good" of Jericho lined up to invite Jesus into their homes. I think it makes his decision to eat his supper with the diminutive tax collector even more outrageous and even more profound.

Telling tips

I generally just read this on my own. But you might want to get some helpers to play Abraham and Nathanael, and even someone small for Zacchaeus. They could just mime their parts (it will take a bit of practice). And as for the sycamore tree, well, you could always use a chair or a pew or a very tall deacon! Just check your insurance cover first!

Abraham was the town butcher.
He stood tall. He was honest and kind.
He sold chicken and cow.
The folks loved it – and how!
(And he never touched fried bacon rind!)

But Zacchaeus was a wee little man,
And a wee little man was he.
He was hated and feared.
No one wanted him near.
He was Jericho's taxman, you see!

Nathanael was the town baker.
A big man, with five strapping sons.
All Jericho slobbered
And globbered and drooled
At the smell of his freshly baked buns.

But Zacchaeus was a wee little man,
And a wee little man was he.
For a few pennies more
He'd cheat you for sure
He'd do anything to increase his fee.

Now the word went around
Old Jericho Town
That Jesus was coming for tea.
'Twas an honour, a treat
For this teacher to eat
At one's house – so they lined up to see.

"Come eat with me!"
Tall Abraham said.
"We'll have drumsticks and lamb chops and beef!"
But Jesus just smiled
And passed on through the crowd,
Leaving Abraham stricken with grief.

"To my house he'll come,"
Nathanael explained
To those standing 'round, with a boast.
But when he was asked
Jesus wandered right past.
Nate's mood turned as black as burned toast.

Many others came next.
I suppose that you've guessed –
Jesus said "no" to each of them too.
In fact, he said "nay"
To all good folk that day,
And shaded his eyes for a view.

Zacchaeus, meanwhile,
With a chimpanzee's style,
Had climbed up a sycamore tree.
He was just curious
But the crowd might get furious
If they saw him. So he hid there safely!

Jesus looked down,
Quite close to the ground,
And failed there to find his prey.
A rustle. A cry.
So Jesus looked high.
The branches were starting to sway.

"So that's where you're hiding,
You wee little man.
I'm hungry, and that's why I say:
Put your feet on the ground.
ZACCHAEUS, COME DOWN!
I'm eating at your house today."

Zacchaeus was shocked.
And you could have knocked
The crowd over with a feather. And so,
Honoured and humbled,
He climbed down then stumbled
Homeward, with Jesus in tow.

The crowd muttered and moaned.
"A sinner!" they groaned.
"A scoundrel, a swindler, a swine!
It's a scandal, a curse.
It couldn't be worse!
Jesus sharing his bread and his wine."

They talked all through tea.
What they said, no one knows.
No keyhole to hear or peep through.
But when they came out,
Jesus said, with a shout,
"Zacchaeus has now changed his view!"

"He's different, he's sorry.
He's forgiven. He's saved.
He's brand-spanking, fresh-smelling new.
He's still rather small.
But his heart's ten feet tall.
And now he will prove it to you."

"To those that I've cheated,"
Said Zac with a smile,
"I'll pay back times two – no, times four!

And I've emptied my coffers.
I've got some great offers
For anyone out there who's poor."

The people applauded.
They couldn't believe it.
"He's gentle and kind as a dove!"
Jesus said, with a grin.
"See, there's no one whose sin
Takes them out of the reach of my love."

36

Three

Luke 22:54–62

I keep having to remind myself how young these guys were. OK, nineteen or twenty in the first century was probably "older" than it is today, but still, Peter's youth and relative inexperience make this story a lot more understandable. Excusable? That's what Peter had to wrestle with. And I think I know what his answer would be.

Telling tips

One to do on your own.

One.
One man.
One courtyard.
One newly kindled fire.
One servant girl.
"You look like one of his lot," she says.
And Peter – Peter doesn't hesitate for even one minute.
"I don't know him," he says at once.

Two.
Too long waiting.
Too exposed.
Yet too tired and worried and confused to walk away.
And so, a second voice: "I saw you, too. You were with him."
And a second denial in reply: "You're mistaken, man, it wasn't me."

Three
Three parts to Palestine. And three distinct accents.
"You're a Galilean," says a third man. "Just like Jesus. I can hear it in your voice."
And three thoughts fight for control in Peter's head.
Run. Admit it. Or…
The third choice. "I don't know what you're talking about."

And then, one, the rooster crows.
And, two, Jesus turns and looks at him.
And, three, Peter leaves the courtyard.
And there's no counting the tears that fall from his face.

37

Travail

Luke 23:26–49

This is another one of those readings that juxtapose two familiar stories in the hope of making better sense of each of them.

1: It was a long journey.
2: It was a hard journey.

1: Step by agonizing step.
2: Desperate for a rest.

1: There were stops, sure.
2: But not for long.

1: They just kept going.
2: On and on.

1: Until they arrived.
2: At last!

1: The place was crowded. No room.
2: And then, there it was, the spot.

1: So she lay herself down.
2: And so did he.

1 & 2: And, oh, the agony!
1: The pain came sharp and fast.
2: One, two, three bursts – in quick succession.

1: And then, that dropping feeling.
2: The sudden jolt of it.

1: The surprise.
2: The shock.

1: More waiting followed.
2: Hour after hour.

1: And more pain.
2: So much to bear.

1: And then, when it seemed like it would never be over,
2: Never ever end,

1 & 2: It happened.
1: And the angels burst forth.
2: And the angels held back.

1 & 2: As he opened his mouth and cried,
2: "Father, into your hands I commit my spirit."

1: And his eyes opened.
2: And his eyes shut.

1: And it began.
2: And it was done.

1 & 2: And his mother bowed her head and wept.

38

Women!

Luke 24:1–12

It's the little phrases, that usually just slide by in the text, the ones that get you thinking when you finally take the time to consider just what they mean – it's one of those phrases that kicked off this reading.

Telling tips

Do it on your own – with feeling. Or you might like to make it a radio play kind of thing – to bring out the different characters.

"What do you mean, you don't believe us?" sobbed Mary Magdalene. "We were there!"

"You're upset," said John. "Look at you. It's been a very difficult few days. No one could blame you for getting a little… hysterical."

"We're not hysterical!" shrieked Joanna.

"We can see that," said James, winking at the others.

Joanna lowered her register, more than a few notches, and then, slowly and deliberately, she said, "We are not hysterical because of what we saw. We are hysterical because you won't believe us!"

"We don't believe you," said Peter, even more slowly, "because dead people don't come back from the grave."

"Lazarus did!" countered the other Mary. "And that boy from Nain. And Jairus's daughter!"

"Because Jesus was there to bring them back from the dead," replied Peter, more slowly still, like he was talking to an imbecile.

"That's right," added Andrew, desperate to help. "Jesus brought them back from the dead when he was alive. So now that he's dead, he can't bring anybody back to life, particularly himself, because he's dead. And not alive… to… to… bring himself back… to life… from… the dead. I think."

"You don't have to spell it out for us," sighed Mary Magdalene. "We're not stupid. But we saw what we saw. Why don't you just believe us?"

"It was dark when you arrived, wasn't it?" asked Peter.

And the women nodded.

"And you were upset. So surely there was a part of you that *wanted* to see him alive again."

"And that's why you imagined it," Nathanael concluded. "Nothing wrong with that."

"Imagined an open tomb?" asked Joanna incredulously.

"And a blinding light? And angels?" said Mary Magdalene.

"And what about the rest?" added the other Mary. "What they said – all those things about Jesus being delivered into the hands of sinful men and being crucified and returning on the third day. It sounds like a lot of what Jesus himself said!"

"Jesus said a lot of... symbolic... things," countered Peter. "And the fact that you remembered one or two of them still doesn't prove that he's alive."

"We saw it! Every one of us!" cried Mary Magdalene. "What other proof do you need? Why won't you just believe us?"

Peter sighed. "All right, then. How about this. How about I go to the tomb and have a little look round?"

"I don't know," said John. "There are soldiers everywhere out there. I don't think it's safe."

"Oh, terrific – but it was all right for us to go?" said Joanna, in a huff.

"Well, you're just, you know – women," said Andrew, trying hard again. "It's different with us men. The soldiers wouldn't be looking... for..." And then he looked around. The women's arms were crossed in front of them. The men were looking at the ceiling. Someone was whistling. "And... and... maybe this isn't the time," he finished.

"I'm going," said Peter. "If the soldiers get me..."

"No, no... they won't," added the other Mary. "There was an earthquake as well – I remember it now – it knocked them out."

"Very convenient," Peter sighed. "It gets better with every telling. So as I said, I'm off. Pray I get back in one piece."

So Peter left. And Peter went to the tomb. And what he found were strips of linen, lying on their own. So he went away, wondering. But sometime later that day, says Luke, Jesus appeared to him, alive!

What did Jesus say? We don't know. But there's a part of me that would like to believe that the first thing he did was to put his hand on his friend's shoulder, lean over, and whisper in his ear: "The women, Peter. Why didn't you just believe them?"

39

Angel of Death and Life

Luke 24:1–12

Some stories are gifts. There is nothing. You have hardly thought about what you want to write. And then, out of the blue, an idea comes. That's how it was with this story. So all I have ever been able to do is to be grateful for it.

Telling tips

For years, when my brother and I told it, he would play one angel and I would play the other. So if you can find someone to tell this with you, it could work really well. Otherwise, one to tell on your own.

The angel sat in the dark and waited.

This was the most unusual assignment he had ever received. Up till now, his missions had always been straightforward – keeping children from falling into wells, helping lost travellers find their way. Typical guardian angel kind of stuff.

But this job was different, very different. A quick beam of light to mark the location, and a strange set of orders that simply said he should wait for his partner to arrive. Partner? He'd never had a partner before. He was big and strong and could do most things on his own. So he couldn't help wondering what this was all about.

And then the angel saw something.

The sun reached one long finger over the horizon and, sure enough, there was someone coming towards him, wading slowly through the darkness as if it were a thick, black sea. Could this be his partner? If so, it was the most unusual angel he had ever seen.

No song. No shimmer. No shine. There was hardly a hint of heaven about him. Instead, he was thin and tired – a small grey mouse of an angel. Barely an angel at all, it seemed.

The first angel raised his hand in greeting. "Hello," he said. "My name is Candriel. Who are you?"

The second angel sat down beside his partner, but it was a minute or two before he spoke. And when he did, it was a mouse's whisper that matched his looks.

"My name is Destroyer," he said solemnly. "I am the Angel of Death."

An early morning breeze blew past the angels, but it was not the breeze that made Candriel shiver. He'd heard of this angel. Everyone had. How he'd killed Egyptian firstborns and set God's people free. How he'd slain, single-handedly, 185,000 Assyrian soldiers in one night. But to look at him now, sitting there all small and grey and quiet, it hardly seemed possible.

Could this really be the Angel of Death? Candriel wondered. And what kind of mission was this going to be?

"I suppose you have the orders?" said Candriel uncertainly.

The Angel of Death nodded a laid a bony hand on one of his pockets. "I do," he sighed. "But I was told not to open them until he saw women coming up the hill. It's got something to do with a secret surprise."

A partner. A signal. A surprise. This job gets stranger and stranger, thought Candriel. But all he dared say was, "What do you suppose the orders are?"

The Angel of Death shook his head. "Oh, that's not hard to guess. All you have to do is look around."

The sun's bright scalp edged over the horizon, and Candriel looked. They were in the middle of a graveyard.

"Death again," Destroyer sighed. "Seems like death is always part of the job for me. So I guess it makes sense that I should play some part in his death, too. The saddest death of all."

Candriel looked again. The sun was a little higher now, and he could see it all clearly. The garden graveyard. The sleeping soldiers. The city of Jerusalem off in the distance. The huge stone that sealed the tomb beneath them.

"So you've guessed who's in the tomb we're sitting on," said Destroyer.

"Jesus," whispered Candriel. "It's Jesus, isn't it? It's God's son."

A soldier grunted in his sleep. A bird whistled in the distance. And the Angel of Death just nodded.

"I saw it happen, you know," said Candriel after a while. "I saw him die on the cross. Our whole battalion was ready to burst through the sky, beat the stuffing out of those soldiers, and save him. Uproot that cross, tear it right out of the ground – that's what I would have done. But they wouldn't let us do anything. They said the signal had to come from Him. And the signal never came."

Destroyer turned a grey face to his partner. "I didn't watch," he said softly. "I couldn't. I've seen too much death already. I'm sure He had a reason. He must have. But that didn't make it any easier. Didn't ease the terrible hurt."

"No," agreed Candriel. "He suffered a lot. You could see that. They did some awful things to him."

"That's not what I mean," said Destroyer. "I mean the other kind of hurt that comes with death. Saying goodbye to your friends, to the ones you love. They say that even his mother was there."

Candriel said nothing. He looked puzzled.

"You're a guardian angel, aren't you?" asked Destroyer. "Big and strong – the rescuing type."

"Right," said Candriel. "And I'm good at what I do."

"I'm sure you are," said the Angel of Death. "And I'm also sure you feel a lot of joy and gratitude from the people you rescue."

"Oh, yes!" Candriel smiled.

"Well, it's different when you're the Angel of Death. Take the Assyrian army, for example. They had the city of Jerusalem surrounded. They were going to slaughter most of God's people and make slaves of the rest. It was my job to stop them."

"That must have been difficult," Candriel interrupted, "To kill many of them. I mean, with you being so small."

The Angel of Death looked up at his partner and slowly shook his head. "No," he sighed. "Doing the job was the easy part. A quick breath in the face. That's all it took. Then their eyes glazed over and their hearts grew still.

"The hard part was the thoughts – those thousands and thousands of sad goodbye thoughts:

"My wife... I'll never see you again."

"I'm sorry, Mother. I promised you I would come back."

"Grow up well, my son... I will miss you."

"Missing. Death is all about missing. That's what I remember most about that night. And that's what I think must have been so hard for Jesus and his friends."

Candriel looked at his partner. And what he saw was sadness. Sadness like some great thick shell that seemed to crush and shrink Destroyer.

"I just wish," the Angel of Death concluded, "I just wish that once I could have a mission where I remembered not sadness and loss, but the kind of joy and gratitude that you have felt so often."

Candriel didn't know what to say. But he was a guardian angel, after all. So at least he knew what to do. He opened up one shining silver wing, and reaching through the sadness, he wrapped it around the Angel of Death.

They sat there together in the sadness and the new day's light. And then Candriel spotted the women.

"That's the signal," he said. "It's time to read the orders."

The Angel of Death reached into his pocket and handed the scroll to his partner. "You read it," he said.

Candriel took the scroll and started to unroll it. "It's probably very simple," he said. "The women are coming. They're friends of Jesus. We're probably supposed to protect them from these soldiers. It's going to be all right. You'll see."

And then he read the scroll out loud.

"'Candriel,'" the orders said. "'Guardian Angel kind and strong: you wanted so badly to free my Son from his cross. But that was not within your power. What is now within your power is to roll away the stone. Open his tomb and show the world that the one who died on the cross is now alive – free from death for ever! As for you, Destroyer, faithful servant, Angel of Death: someone needs to tell these women that the one they miss is alive. Who better to share this joyful news than the one who understands their sadness and loss?'"

It took hardly a second. Candriel dropped the orders, leaped off the tomb, and rolled away the stone.

Destroyer was right behind, climbing down after him into the grave. It was empty.

It was empty!

And that's when Candriel saw his partner change.

The soldiers said it was an earthquake. They said they saw a flash of lightning. But Candriel knew different.

The sound that cracked the morning stillness was a sad whisper exploding into a shout of joy. And the light that stunned the soldiers was a grim, grey shadow bursting bright to white.

"He is not here. He is risen! He is alive!" Destroyer shouted to the women.

And the Angel of Death became, forevermore, the Angel of Life.

40

The Tree of Life or The Tale of Three More Trees

Genesis 3; Matthew 27:11–66

Just a bit of speculation here. If the Tree of Life stood in the heart of Eden, then perhaps it also stands at the heart of our return. I think I wrote this about the same time as I was writing Angels, Angels All Around.

Telling tips

This is very much one for you to tell on your own. It would be fitting at Easter, but I think you could probably use it at any time. It's a more dramatic reading than many of the others in this collection, so it needs practising and careful pacing.

And the angel who guarded the gates of Eden took one last look at Adam. He burned those features for ever in his mind – sad eyes, sorry brow, the face of loneliness and rejection – then raised his fiery sword into the sky. And there he remained, blocking the entrance to the Garden and the path to the Tree of Life.

Age after age, he stood at his post, the beauty of the Garden all about him. He knew its smell and its taste and its sounds, but he had no time to enjoy it. For all he could do was watch, in case the face of Adam should return.

And perhaps that is why, one day, the impossible finally happened.

It wasn't a sound that caught his attention. It was more like a feeling. A sense, deep inside the angel, that something was wrong. And that is why he lowered his sword, turned and ran through the Garden. And that is how he discovered that the Tree of Life was gone!

Only a ragged hole remained, as if the tree had been torn out by its roots. The angel drove his sword into the ground, its flaming orange dimmed to a flickering blue. Then he knelt beside it and buried his face in his hands.

What was he going to do? Guarding the tree had been his responsibility. But somehow he had failed. And there was only one course of action he could take: he must find the Tree of Life and watch over it once again.

So like Adam before him, he walked sadly out of the Garden of Eden. But he did not wander over the unploughed wilderness of the world. No, he opened his wings and flung himself through the fabric of time and space – in search of the Tree of Life.

There was a smell to Paradise – a purity, a freshness – that he was certain he could recognize. And so he sniffed his way through aeons and epochs until, finally, he picked up the scent. Then he raised his sword and sliced his way into one particular time and place.

The air was cold, the clouds icy with the promise of winter. Below the clouds there were hills, mile after mile of them, portioned off by rivers and valleys. And trees? There were more trees than the angel had ever seen. But they were stripped bare of leaves. All but one, that is, whose pointed branches burned bright from the window of a single house. That was the one he headed for, until his senses picked up something else – chimney smoke and the sound of human voices.

"Adam!" the angel cursed, as he flew, invisible, into the house and hovered next to a small plastic replica of himself.

Adams were everywhere below, their hands full of bright and shiny things. The angel looked long and hard, but he could find no one who resembled the sad Adam he had chased from the Garden.

Instead, these Adams were laughing – big ones and little ones, brown ones and pale ones – all together. Then finally, they settled themselves on the furniture and on the floor, and one of the Adams spoke.

"Let us give thanks to God!" he said. "For the gift of his Son, for the gifts we hold in our hands, and for the gifts we are to each other."

That is when a voice whispered to the angel from among the bright branches. "I am not the tree you seek," it said. "I am the Tree of Laughter. Where sadness turns to joy, where tears give way to smiles, where all that oppresses or frightens is conquered by hope and peace, that is where you will find me. But you must look elsewhere if you would find the Tree of Life."

And so the angel left the Tree of Laughter, and the merrymakers gathered in its shade, and burst the curtain of time once more – in search of the Tree of Life.

It was not long before he caught the scent again. So he pulled out his sword and slashed a path into another place.

The sun was red against the horizon – red as the angel's sword – and it burned the land brown and bare. Except for one tree, that is, whose leaves hung cool and green over the banks of a sleepy river.

There were noises beneath this tree as well. Strange, muffled sounds – human sounds that made the angel cautious.

"Adam!" he whispered, and invisible once more, he hovered closer to have a look.

They were Adams, certainly – a male and a female, skin black as the river's edge. And they were holding one another and caressing one another and pressing their lips together. And then they just sat there and stared at each other and said nothing for hours and hours. Nothing at all.

"I am not the tree you seek," the branches quivered at last. "I am the Tree of Love. Watch and you will see."

And in a moment, the sun rose and fell, thousands upon thousands of times! The two Adams became four, then ten, then a hundred. Their hair bleached white, their bodies bent and stooped, and they held children and grandchildren and great-grandchildren in their ever-more-feeble arms. But they never grew tired of staring into each other's eyes and saying nothing for hours. Nothing at all.

"Where there is tenderness," the tree continued. "Where there is commitment and kindness and passion, that is where you will find me. But you must look elsewhere if you would find the Tree of Life."

And so the angel resumed his search, determined that he would not be foiled again. This time, however, the scent was nowhere to be found. He had almost given up hope, in fact, when he smelled it – the faintest odour of Paradise. Sceptical, he stopped and sniffed, and the longer he waited, the stronger the scent became. The Tree of Life was near. He was sure of it. So he drew his sword and ripped, one more time, through the fabric of heaven and earth.

And immediately, he was sorry that he had.

The sky shuddered dark around him. Thunder clapped. A fierce wind blew. And below all was lifeless and grey. Surely he had made another mistake.

But the scent was stronger than ever. So he plunged, invisible, toward the earth. And all at once, he knew. He was in the right place after all. For there, on a hill, stood Adam!

Sad eyes. Sorry brow. The face of loneliness and rejection. He would recognize those features anywhere!

"Adam!" he bellowed. "Adam!" he cursed. "What have you done with the Tree of Life?"

But Adam would not answer. His head lolled heavily to one side. His lips were blistered and bruised.

"He cannot hear you," whispered a voice. "He hears no one. He is dead."

"Dead?" the angel wondered. "Adam? Dead?"

"Not Adam," the voice replied. "But Adam's son. And the Son of God as well. Sent by the Maker himself to undo Adam's damage and repair the path to Paradise."

"And who... who are you?" the angel asked. But there was no need to wait for an answer. All he had to do was look – beyond the face, beyond the hands, beyond the outstretched arms of the man before him. And, sure enough, there was wood.

Wood cut and shaped. Wood hammered and pierced. Wood stripped bare of all beauty and blossom and life.

"No!" the angel cried, falling to his knees. "This is not possible. Who could have done this to you?"

"The Maker of all things," the voice said softly. "It was he who plucked me from the Garden. He who brought me here. He who planted me in this place. For where evil is overwhelmed by goodness, where failure is comforted by grace, where sins are forgiven and debts are repaid and darkness is blinded by light, that is where you will find me. For I am what the Maker always intended me to be. I am the Tree of Life."

"And what about me?" the angel pleaded. "What am I to do now? What am I to be?"

"What the Maker made you for," answered the fading voice.

And so the angel climbed slowly to his feet and, with his sword raised like lightning to the sky, stood guard on the hill of death and watched over the Tree of Life.

41

Three Men and a Fig Tree

John 1:43–51

*Sometimes it's the characters who help you find your way into a retelling.
Sometimes it's the setting. In this case, it was both! The differences between
the characters of Jesus, Nathanael, and Philip are the key to understanding
this passage. But the fig tree is pretty important, too! So I thought I'd wrap
them up together in a kind of chorus to make that clear. This piece was
originally written for a family service at the church across the street, so it
works well across a wide age range.*

Telling tips

Divide your crowd into four groups: one for Jesus, one for Nathanael, one for
Philip, and one for the fig tree! Teach them the following actions before the
story begins:

- Jesus – arms wide open, in a welcoming gesture.

- Nathanael – arms crossed in a defensive posture, suspicious look on
  his face.

- Philip – waving, as if to say "Come with me."

- Fig tree – arms as branches – either waving or fixed in a "branchy",
  contorted manner.

Then, as you read the story, have each group do its motion in turn, during
the "Jesus, Nathanael, Philip, and the fig tree" chorus lines.

The other option, which is more chaotic (but also more fun!), is to teach
everyone every motion and then point to a group when you say each name
in the "chorus", but do it randomly – so they never know what's coming! The
only downside is that this might distract their attention from the rest of the

reading. Probably not a good thing if you want them to actually remember the story! A milder version of this is to teach each group the fig tree motion, only, and move that around, from group to group, during the 'chorus'.

Jesus said to Philip, "Follow me!"
Jesus, Nathanael, Philip, and the fig tree.
So Philip found his friend, sitting under a tree.

"We've found him, Nathanael! The one we've been waiting for!"
Jesus, Nathanael, Philip, and the fig tree.
"The Messiah, promised by Moses and the prophets!"

"His name is Jesus – Jesus of Nazareth."
Jesus, Nathanael, Philip, and the fig tree.
Nathanael scoffed. He was a bit of a snob.

"Nothing good has ever come from Nazareth!"
Jesus, Nathanael, Philip, and the fig tree.
"You'll see!" said Philip. "Just come and see!"

So they left the fig tree and went to find Jesus.
Jesus, Nathanael, Philip, and the fig tree.
And when Jesus saw them coming, he opened his arms.

"Nathanael!" he said. "Nathanael, I know you!"
Jesus, Nathanael, Philip, and the fig tree.
"You speak your mind. You mean what you say."

"And when you see the truth, you want to embrace it."
Jesus, Nathanael, Philip, and the fig tree.
"A true Israelite – with nothing false about you."

Nathanael was puzzled. "But how do you know me?"
Jesus, Nathanael, Philip, and the fig tree.
"We've never met. Not that I can recall."

"I saw you," said Jesus. "Underneath the fig tree."
Jesus, Nathanael, Philip, and the fig tree.
"I saw you while Philip was on his way."

Nathanael was amazed – amazed and astounded.
Jesus, Nathanael, Philip, and the fig tree.
"Then you must be the Messiah – the Son of God!"

"Surprised?" said Jesus. "We've only just started."
Jesus, Nathanael, Philip, and the fig tree.
"You'll see angels in heaven by the time we're done."

So Nathanael followed Jesus, just like Philip.
Jesus, Nathanael, Philip, and the fig tree.
And off they went. What adventures they had!
Jesus, Nathanael, Philip, and the fig tree.

42

The Wedding at Cana

John 2:1–11

There are any number of stories I could have chosen to demonstrate the importance of a teller and his crowd "working together" to create the story. In fact, any story that involves participation would do. But this particular form of repetitive story is absolutely dependent upon the audience taking part. It's built for that.

Telling tips

Each section is a bit like a verse (only this isn't poetry) made of two repeated sentences. The first three lines in each "verse" are yours to say. I always try to say the line a little differently each time, to keep it interesting and also to milk the line of all its meaning.

The second three lines are for your group. They also have an action to perform (described in parenthesis at the end of the "verse"). Lead your group in that action each of the three times they say that second line. I find that the repetition gives the crowd the chance to "catch up" if they haven't got it the first time. You will need to start the story by teaching all the actions. It's fun, and it also piques their curiosity – what will this story be about?

Jesus and his mum went to a wedding in Cana;
Jesus and his mum went to a wedding in Cana;
Jesus and his mum went to a wedding in Cana;
The bride and the groom looked just divine.
The bride and the groom looked just divine.
The bride and the groom looked just divine.
(Action – fingers like halo above head)

But halfway through the party, everything went wrong.
But halfway through the party, everything went wrong.
But halfway through the party, everything went wrong.
"Jesus," said his mum. "There's no more wine!"
"Jesus," said his mum. "There's no more wine!"
"Jesus," said his mum. "There's no more wine!"
(Action – pretend to hold wine glass)

"What am I supposed to do, Mum?' said Jesus with a sigh.
"What am I supposed to do, Mum?' said Jesus with a sigh.
"What am I supposed to do, Mum?' said Jesus with a sigh.
"You want a miracle, I know, but it's not yet time."
"You want a miracle, I know, but it's not yet time."
"You want a miracle, I know, but it's not yet time."
(Action – point to wrist, to watch, or to a clock in the room)

But Mary was persistent and she told some passing servants,
But Mary was persistent and she told some passing servants,
But Mary was persistent and she told some passing servants,
"I want to you obey this son of mine."
"I want to you obey this son of mine."
"I want to you obey this son of mine."
(Action – point to self)

"Do you see those six stone jars?" said Jesus to the men.
"Do you see those six stone jars?" said Jesus to the men.
"Do you see those six stone jars?" said Jesus to the men.
"Fill them with water to the top-most line."
"Fill them with water to the top-most line."
"Fill them with water to the top-most line."
(Action – draw pretend horizontal line in air)

So they filled them to the brim, thirty gallons each.
So they filled them to the brim, thirty gallons each.
So they filled them to the brim, thirty gallons each.
In one accord with Jesus' Grand Design.
In one accord with Jesus' Grand Design.
In one accord with Jesus' Grand Design.
(Action – pretend to look at blueprint – or reference TV show)

"Now draw some out," said Jesus, "and give it to your master."
"Now draw some out," said Jesus, "and give it to your master."
"Now draw some out," said Jesus, "and give it to your master."
"I think you'll be surprised by what he finds."
"I think you'll be surprised by what he finds."
"I think you'll be surprised by what he finds."
(Action – hand over eyes, looking for something)

So they drew a little out and gave it to their master,
So they drew a little out and gave it to their master,
So they drew a little out and gave it to their master,
And a shiver ran right up and down his spine.
And a shiver ran right up and down his spine.
And a shiver ran right up and down his spine.
(Action – draw spine-like line, or just shiver)

"This isn't water!" he exclaimed. "Nor any cheap old plonk."
"This isn't water!" he exclaimed. "Nor any cheap old plonk."
"This isn't water!" he exclaimed. "Nor any cheap old plonk."
"It's the finest Chardonnay. This stuff's sublime!"
"It's the finest Chardonnay. This stuff's sublime!"
"It's the finest Chardonnay. This stuff's sublime!"
(Action – make that fingers from mouth movement)

"Others serve their best wine first," he whispered to the groom.
"Others serve their best wine first," he whispered to the groom.
"Others serve their best wine first," he whispered to the groom.
"But you saved the best for last – you're so refined."
"But you saved the best for last – you're so refined."
"But you saved the best for last – you're so refined."
(Action – pretend to straighten pretend moustache – or twist curly bit at the end – nose in air, of course)

So Jesus did a miracle, the first in a long line –
So Jesus did a miracle, the first in a long line –
So Jesus did a miracle, the first in a long line –
A sign to show he really was divine.
A sign to show he really was divine.
A sign to show he really was divine.
(Action – repeat divine/halo action from first verse)

43

I Am the Bread

John 6:1–15, 25–29; Luke 24:13–35

This reading would make a nice introduction to any of the stories it references, or perhaps even an effective Communion meditation.

Telling tips

Not much for the crowd to do here. Maybe you could have them "mumble and grumble" and "groan and moan" at the appropriate places! Otherwise, it might be best just to read it on your own.

Verse 1

There was no bread on the mountain.
On the mountain there was no bread.
Only groaning bellies,
And grumbling tummies,
And one little lad who was willing
To share his McDonald's "Filet o' Fish Happy Meal".

So Jesus took the bread rolls.
And Jesus took the fish.

"Here is the bread!" he said.
He said, "Here is the bread."
And he spoke a prayer and broke it.
And every belly was full.

Verse 2

There was no bread at the seaside.
At the seaside there was no bread.
Only moaning crowds,
And mumbling Pharisees,
Who wanted to see
An all-singing, all-dancing miracle show.

"Our fathers ate bread in the desert!" they cried.
"What kind of sign will shine from you?"

So Jesus looked at the crowd.
Then Jesus shook the crowd.

"I am the bread!" he said.
He said, "I am the bread.
And if you swallow me and follow me,
Then you will live for ever!"

Verse 3

There was no bread on the road to Emmaus.
On the road, there was no bread.
Just a long sad walk
And a stranger who talked
As if he knew nothing of the death of their friend.

So when Cleopas and his friend
Arrived at last at their home
They urged the stranger to stop and have some tea.

The stranger broke the bread
And he spoke a prayer, as well.

"Thanks for the bread," the stranger said.
The stranger said, "Thanks for the bread."
Their eyes were opened.
They knew who he was!
And like a ghost or a phantom
Or an English summer sun,
He disappeared at once from their sight.

Verse 4

So here we are – traipsing up life's mountain.
Here we are – simply sailing life's sea.
Here we are – in the middle of life's journey,
A long, long way from home.

Walking and talking,
Groaning and moaning,
Grumbling and mumbling,
And fumbling together for... what?

A bit of sunshine?
A McDonald's "Happy Meal"?
An all-singing, all-dancing miracle show?
Or a life that's worth living,
Maybe worth living for ever?

"I am the bread," says Jesus.
He says, "I am the bread.
Walk with me. Talk with me.
Swallow Me. Follow me.
Come and taste and live."

44

I Am the Good Shepherd – Three Sheep Stories

John 10:1–21

This is one of my favourites! Like the previous reading, it is built around Jesus' "I Am" sayings in the Gospel of John. You can either do the reading as a whole to introduce a sermon, or weave it into the sermon, commenting on the passage after each section. It could also be the framework for a whole service, with songs and prayers and brief comments between each section.

Telling tips

This one is both simple and fun! You say the "And (all of) the people" line first – "And all of the people said, 'Baaa!'" Say it with as much enthusiasm as you can. And the crowd just repeat "Baaa" after you, in the same way you did it! Practise one of the lines with them, before you start the story – just so it's clear where they come in. But don't give the rest of the lines away. It will spoil the surprise!

The sheep thief

"I've got something to say about sheep," said Jesus.
  And all of the people said, "*Baaa!*"

"Let's start with the sheep thief," said Jesus. "That rotten, no-good rustler"
  And all of the people said, "*Boo!*"

"How does the sheep thief get into the pen?" asked Jesus. "Not through the gate, that's for sure. He creeps over the wall, in the dead of night, when nobody else is looking."

And all of the people said, "*Sneaky!*"

"And what is he there for?" asked Jesus. "I'll tell you – he's up to no good. He has knives and shears and lashings of mint sauce. He comes to steal and to kill and to destroy."

And all of the people said, "*Nasty!*"

"But the shepherd," said Jesus, "the shepherd is different!"

And all of the people said, "*How?*"

"He comes through the gate," said Jesus. "The right way. The proper way. The honest way. And he comes not to kill, but to lead the sheep to pastures green and gently flowing waters."

And all of the people said, "*Nice!*"

"I am the Gate of the sheep pen," said Jesus.

And all of the people said, "*Huh?*"

"I am the Gate!" said Jesus. "I'll protect you from anything and anyone that sneaks in to steal your joy. And if you go through me, you'll find life and find it to the full."

The stranger

"Now let's talk about strangers," said Jesus.

And the people said, "You should never talk to strangers!"

"Exactly!" said Jesus. "And every sheep knows that. If a stranger calls, the sheep will not follow, because they do not recognize his voice."

And the people said, "*That's smart!*"

"But the shepherd," said Jesus, "the shepherd is different."

And all of the people said, "*How?*"

"The sheep recognize his voice," said Jesus. "And they follow him wherever he goes. And he knows them, too. Knows each of them by name!"

And the people said, "*That's lovely!*"

"I am the Good Shepherd," said Jesus. "And I know my sheep, too. There are some of you here, and others I have yet to meet. And I know you all by name."

The hired hand

"And finally," said Jesus, "let's talk about the hired hand."

And all of the people said, "*Show me the money!*"

"That's it!" said Jesus. "The hired hand is in it only for what he can get. It's not the sheep that are important to him – it's the pay cheque and what he can buy with it."

And the people said, "*Bling-bling.*"

"So when the wolf comes," said Jesus, "what does he do? He runs away, to save his own skin."

And the people said, "It's more than his job's worth!"

"But the shepherd," said Jesus, "the shepherd is different."

And all of the people said, "*How?*"

"The sheep belong to the shepherd," said Jesus. "Each and every one of them is special to him. So when the wolf comes, he faces it and fights it off. He risks life and limb. And if he has to, he lays down his life for his sheep."

And all of the people said, "*Wow!*"

"I am the Good Shepherd," said Jesus. "And I lay down my life for you."

45

His Towel

John 13:1–17

My friend Mark was being ordained into the ministry and asked me to kick off the service with a reading of some kind. This is for him.

The Lord said, "Go and preach the word."
I asked him, "Tell me how."
He reached into his toolbox
And handed me a Trowel.

"It's Living Stones you're working with.
A Living Message, too.
Be careful not to chip and gouge
When you cement the two."

The Lord said, "Go and preach the word."
I asked him, "Tell me how."
He reached into his toolbox
And handed me a Trowel.

The Lord said, "Go and preach the word."
I asked him, 'Tell me how.'
He spoke to Rachel Riley
And she handed me a Vowel.

"'I'"s the one that you'll prefer.
'I' want. 'I' know. 'I' say.
But 'U' will make a better choice.
'U' reign. 'U' have your way."

The Lord said, "Go and preach the word."
I asked him, "Tell me how."
He spoke to Rachel Riley
And she handed me a Vowel.

The Lord said, "Go and preach the word."
I asked him, "Tell me how."
He placed a basin at my feet.
And reached for an old Towel.

"I'll wash you, make you clean and new,
I'll serve you best I can.
And then you do the same
For those I place into your hand."

The Lord said, "Go and preach the word."
I asked him, "Tell me how."
He washed me, made me clean and new,
Then handed me his Towel.

46

I Am the Vine:
A Communion Meditation

John 15:1–17

One more "I Am"! And, as the title suggests, this one makes a very nice Communion meditation.

"I am the vine," said Jesus to his friends.
He said, "I am the vine.
And my Father? My Father tends the vineyard.
He strims and trims,
He grooms and prunes,
And shapes each grape-bearing branch."

"I am the vine," said Jesus to his friends.
He said, "I am the vine.
And you? You are the branches.
Let me flow in you.
Let me grow in you.
And we will make grapes together."

"Here is the wine," said Jesus to his friends.
He said, "Here is the wine.
It pours out just like blood.
Drink of me – when you come together.

Think of me – and never forget
That love gives up its life for a friend."

"I am the vine," said Jesus.
"Here is the wine," said Jesus.
"I live my life,
I give my life
For you."

47

Jesus Looks Down

John 19:1–37

A year ago, I was asked to do a retelling of the crucifixion story with a very large group of children and adults. It needed to have a lot of participation and yet communicate the solemnity and sense of that event. There's always the risk, with participation in a serious story, of something unexpected happening, or of giggles at just the wrong time. So I chose four really simple actions and hoped they would keep us all active and together and bring us into the heart of the story. I think it worked.

Telling tips

You will need to ask your group to stand and drape their arms over the shoulders of the people standing next to them. You need to stretch your arms out too – as if you were Jesus on the cross. Or, if you think that's too difficult for your crowd, simply have them stand with their arms to their side. Then simply ask them to look "up" and "down" and "right" and "left" with you, when you do. When you reach that point in the text, ask them to close their eyes with you as well.

JESUS LOOKS DOWN (*Look down.*)
There are people down there who want him dead.

The Roman soldiers who nailed his hands and his feet to this wooden cross, and are gambling for what little he has left in this world.

And the religious leaders too – laughing their heads off and making fun of him.

"You thought you were somebody special."

"You thought you knew better than us."

"Well, just look at you now."

JESUS LOOKS RIGHT (*Look right.*)
There's a thief hanging on the cross next to him. And his words are filled with hate as well.

"You saved other people – the blind, the sick, the lame. So why can't you save yourself – and me with you?"

JESUS LOOKS LEFT (*Look left.*)
There's another thief hanging there. But his words are very different.

"Leave him alone!" croaks the second thief to the first. "We're here because we deserve it. But this man has done nothing wrong."

And then he looks Jesus in the eye. "Take me with you, please – to a better place when I die."

And Jesus looks back. And nods. And says, "Today you will be with me in Paradise."

AND THEN JESUS LOOKS DOWN AGAIN (*Look down.*)
His mum is standing there.

His mum – who talked to an angel
and had a baby in a stable
and watched that baby grow into a man
and turn water into wine
and talk to thousands at a time
and now stands there watching him die.

There are tears in her eyes. And so Jesus calls to his friend.

"John," he says. And it hurts so much to talk. "Take care of my mum for me, please. Just as if she was your mum too."

AND FINALLY JESUS LOOKS UP (*Look up.*)
The sky is dark. The rain is falling. It's as if there are tears in his Father's eyes too.

"I've done what you asked me," he says to God. "I've told them about you. I've showed them how to live. And now, with my death, I'm taking away all the bad things anyone will ever do. It's finished. It's over. It's done."

AND THEN JESUS CLOSES HIS EYES (*Close your eyes.*)
And, for you and for me, he dies.

48

Make the Wind Blow

Acts 2:1–41

I don't often do requests, but when a friend asked me if I had a reading for Pentecost that might work in an all-age service, and I didn't – I figured it was time to put something together. I've used it loads of times, ever since. And it always goes down well. So thanks, Tony!

Telling tips

You need to teach the chorus before you begin. I have included the actions in the text. At the end, I always repeat the chorus at least twice. Or even three times. And then slow it down for emphasis on the final "Take the words from your lips and put them on our lips and speak them out to the whole of the world." I think it just helps to make Pentecost really personal.

Jesus' friends were watching and praying.
Praying for the present that he had promised.
Praying together in the city of Jerusalem.
Praying on the Feast of Pentecost.

Jesus' friends were watching and praying
When all of a sudden, their prayers were answered.
They heard the roar of a rushing wind.
And tongues of fire licked their heads.

Make the wind blow. (Wave hands like the wind.)
Make the fire glow. (Make shape with hands like fire.)
Take the words from your lips (Pretend to touch God's lips.)
And put them on our lips (Touch own lips.)
And speak them out to the whole of the world. (Make shape of world.)

Jesus' friends were watching and praying
When the Holy Spirit came upon them
Filled them, thrilled them, and spilled right out of them
With words they did not know.

"What's going on?" asked the people of Jerusalem.
"What can this possibly mean?
These are plain Galileans, ordinary folk,
Speaking words they could never have learned."

Make the wind blow.
Make the fire glow.
Take the words from your lips
And put them on our lips
And speak them out to the whole of the world.

"We come from the north, the south, and the east.
We come from all over the world!
Yet we all understand the things that they say
As they tell out the wonders of God."

But some of the crowd were not so impressed.
Some even said they were drunk!
And that's when Peter, Jesus' friend,
Stood up and put them right.

Make the wind blow.
Make the fire glow.
Take the words from your lips
And put them on our lips
And speak them out to the whole of the world.

"Filled with wine?" he said. "Not likely!
But we're filled with something else!
Filled with God's own Holy Spirit –
The power the prophets promised."

"And how did this happen?" asked Peter.
"I'll tell you plain and true.
This is the gift of Jesus, the Messiah,
Whom you killed just six weeks ago!"

Make the wind blow.
Make the fire glow.
Take the words from your lips
And put them on our lips
And speak them out to the whole of the world.

The people were sorry, sad, and ashamed.
And they cried, "What can we do?"
"Repent and be baptized," said Peter plainly.
"And this gift will come to you!"

So the people repented, the people were baptized.
Three thousand people – or so!
And the word spread from there to the rest of Judea
And on to the rest of the world!

Make the wind blow.
Make the fire glow.
Take the words from your lips
And put them on our lips
And speak them out to the whole of the world.

49

A Joke at Midnight

Acts 12:6–17

Here's another example from Angels, Angels All Around. *When I tell this one, I make a big deal of the character voices – particularly the "pretend" old man. Ooh – and I've got a great song parody which you can have for free and that works a treat with this story. It's called "Help me, Rhoda" and is set to the tune of the Beach Boys' song, "Help Me, Rhonda".*

Telling tips

There aren't really any actions for this story, and it's one you can tell on your own.

Peter was asleep. His head thrown back, his mouth wide open. Singing a roaring, snoring song.

Peter was asleep, but he wasn't home in bed.

Peter was in prison. Peter the fisherman, the follower, and friend of Jesus. There was a guard on his right and a guard on his left. And his arms were chained to the wall.

Peter was dreaming. He dreamed about King Herod who had shut him up in prison for talking about Jesus. King Herod, who was going to have him killed in the morning.

He dreamed about his friends, who were praying for him at that very moment, praying that he would be set free.

And then he dreamed another dream – a most unusual dream. Peter dreamed he saw a beam of light shoot into his cell, straight down from the ceiling to the floor. And an angel slid down that beam, like a boy shimmying down a tree. The angel was small and slim, no bigger than a boy. And he wore a wide mischievous grin – as if he was about to play some kind of enormous joke on someone.

Peter wanted to watch, but as so often happens in dreams, he fell back to sleep again. The next thing he knew, someone was thumping him on the side.

Those guards, he thought peevishly. Couldn't they let him have one last night's rest? He turned his head to the left and opened his eyes. The guard was asleep. He turned his head to the right. That guard was asleep too. Puzzled, he looked straight ahead. And there, not a hand's breadth from his face, was that mischievous grin he'd seen in his dream.

Was Peter dreaming, now? He couldn't tell.

The angel wrapped his small hands around two of Peter's fat fisherman's fingers and jumped back, pulling Peter to his feet. Then the angel skipped away a few steps and motioned for Peter to shake his hands.

This has got to be a dream, thought Peter. But he shook his hands, like the angel showed him. And his chains fell off!

Quick as a child, the angel leaped to catch them before they rattled to the floor. Then he gently set them down, grinning and giggling all the while.

Peter grinned too. What a dream this is! he thought.

Suddenly, from out of nowhere, Peter's clothes came flying across the cell and hit him smack in the face.

"Put them on," a small voice giggled.

Peter put them on. And just as he'd finished, his sandals dropped lightly – one, two – in front of his feet.

"These, too," the voice giggled again. "It's time to go."

Peter looked at the angel. He looked at the sleeping guards. He looked at the empty chains. A wonderful dream, indeed! he thought.

The angel slipped through the bars of the cell door and motioned for Peter to follow. Peter tried to slip through, but his full fisherman's figure got in the way.

Chuckling, the angel reached up and snapped out two of the metal bars.

Peter sucked in his belly and tried again. Finally, with a shove and a grunt, he burst through.

He started down the hall and then remembered with a shock that two guards were always stationed outside his cell. Peter stopped and turned around slowly. He wondered for a moment if this dream would turn into a nightmare.

The guards were still there all right. Standing to attention. But their eyes stared blindly ahead. And in their hands, where their spears should have been, the angel was placing the iron bars he had snapped from the cell door.

The angel stood between them, his arms crossed and his head tossed back, laughing a laugh that Peter might have called "naughty", had he not known it came from heaven.

"An amazing dream!" said Peter.

The angel slipped past him and headed down a long hall towards the prison gates, waving for Peter to follow. Together they crept, the tiny bright angel, toes barely touching the floor, and his dark-cloaked shadow, lumbering behind on flat fisherman's feet.

As they approached the first gate, the angel whispered into Peter's ear, "Do you like to play make-believe?"

Make-believe? When Peter was a small boy – smaller even than this angel – he used to pretend that he was with his father out on the sea. He'd drag a piece of old net across the beach and haul in catches of flat stone fish.

"Sure," Peter whispered. He liked to play make-believe.

"Good," said the angel. "You can pretend to be Amos, the old man who cleans out the cells. It should get us past the next guards."

"But I don't look anything like him," Peter protested. "And I don't sound anything like him. What will I do if they ask me a question?"

"Just stoop over," ordered the little angel, "and put your hand on your back, as if it's sore. Now walk very slowly, as if you're afraid of falling down."

The angel pulled Peter's cloak over his head, making a hood to hide his face. "That's good. That's very good," he sniggered. "And don't worry about how you'll sound. Leave the talking to me."

Peter stooped and shuffled his way to the first gate.

But when he saw the guards, he wondered if it wasn't time to pinch himself and wake up from this dream.

Too late! A voice was already echoing out from somewhere inside his cloak. "Evening boys," it quivered. "Another late night and – oh! – my back is killing me."

" 'Old Amos,' my wife says, 'you're too old to be scrubbing out those cells. Think of your rheumatism. Think of your legs. Think of the diseases you could pick up in that place!'"

" 'Ah, but old Agatha,' I says back, 'the king needs me. The prisoners need me. Those guards – those brave young boys – they need me. And they're always so kind to me,' I says, 'very kind, indeed.'"

One of the guards swung open the gate, and the other chuckled and reached into his belt. "Here you go, old man," he said. And he tossed Peter a small coin.

Peter started to reach out and catch it, but the angel quietly slapped his hand and whispered, "No, let it drop. Now stoop to pick it up, but watch out for the guard's…"

BOOT! The guard's foot found Peter's behind and sent him sprawling.

The angel made small clucking noises inside Peter's cloak. "Tsk! Tsk! You boys will have your fun."

Peter climbed slowly and shakily to his feet. Then, chased by the guards' laughter, he skittered down the hall like an old spider.

"Never mind them," grinned the angel. "We'll have the last laugh."

By the time they reached the main gate, the one that led out of the prison and into the city, Peter was really enjoying his dream. The gate was massive, so there was no need for any guards. Who could possibly break out of it? And who would want to break in?

Peter looked down at the angel and smiled. "Now what?" he said. "Let me guess. You just wave your hand and the gates swing open, right?"

The angel smiled back. "You're catching on." And with a giggle, he waved his hand. The gate swung open.

Together they walked through dark, deserted streets towards the house where Peter's friends were praying.

And they filled those silent streets with laughter.

They sniggered as they imagined how those guards would feel when they woke up.

They cheered when they thought about the reaction of Peter's worried friends.

And they snorted and guffawed as they pictured the look on Herod's face when he heard the news.

"This has been great fun," said the angel as they reached the house of Peter's friends. "But now it's time for me to go."

"And time for me to wake up, I suppose," Peter sighed.

"No," the angel giggled as a beam of light shot down from the stars. "That's the best joke of all. You've been awake the whole time!" And with a snap of his fingers, he slid up the beam and out of sight.

Peter stood there for a moment staring up into the sky. A cool breeze ruffled his hair and sent a shiver down his spine. He looked around. The street was empty.

Then he reached out and touched the solid stone wall of his friends' house. He rapped his knuckles against their hard wooden door. And he listened to the astonished voice of the young girl who answered it.

"It's Peter!" she gasped. "It's Peter! He's free!" And she ran inside to tell the others, leaving Peter standing outside.

So it was true. And not a dream at all. The guards. The broken bars. The angel.

Peter shook his head. He had escaped. He could hardly believe it. What a night! What a rescue! What a joke!

Then a smile found its way onto his fisherman's face. And he stepped inside to share the joke with his friends.

50

A Visit to Lystra

Acts 14:8–18

The nice thing about this reading, from a storyteller's point of view, is that it requires you to remember only twelve lines! The repetition and the actions fill up the bulk of the time and make the piece work.

Telling tips

This is one of those stories where you explain the story before you actually tell it! Say that it's about Paul and Barnabas and their first visit to Lystra. They see a lame man, and at that point we all grab our legs and say, "OW!" The lame man is healed, so we all throw our arms wide and say 'WOW!' The people in the town think Paul and Barnabas are gods, so we all act like ancient Greek gods, throw thunderbolts and shout, "KAPOW!" The people bring them offerings, so we hold our fingers against our temples like horns and everyone will pretend to be a COW. Paul and Barnabas are horrified by this behaviour. They are not gods, they explain. We join them by stamping our feet and demanding that the people take the gifts away right NOW! And then, as Paul and Barnabas seize the opportunity to talk about their faith, we will join them as they point their audience to the True God, unto whom they should BOW. The repetition in each verse is there both to build some tension (as you say it a bit louder each time) and to give the crowd the chance to really get into the participation.

Paul and Barnabas were preaching in Lystra.
Paul and Barnabas were preaching in Lystra.
Paul and Barnabas were preaching in Lystra.
When they spotted a lame man. (OW!)
When they spotted a lame man. (OW!)
When they spotted a lame man. (OW!)

"You can be healed!" said Paul to the lame man.
"You can be healed!" said Paul to the lame man.
"You can be healed!" said Paul to the lame man.
And the man jumped up and walked. (WOW!)
And the man jumped up and walked. (WOW!)
And the man jumped up and walked. (WOW!)

"These men must be gods!" cried the people of Lystra.
"These men must be gods!" cried the people of Lystra.
"These men must be gods!" cried the people of Lystra.
Gods like Hermes and Zeus. (KAPOW!)
Gods like Hermes and Zeus. (KAPOW!)
Gods like Hermes and Zeus. (KAPOW!)

So they brought them gifts and sacrifices.
So they brought them gifts and sacrifices.
So they brought them gifts and sacrifices.
Fancy wreaths and a COW.
Fancy wreaths and a COW.
Fancy wreaths and a COW.

"We are not gods!" cried Paul and Barnabas.
"We are not gods!" cried Paul and Barnabas.
"We are not gods!" cried Paul and Barnabas.
Take these away right NOW!
Take these away right NOW!
Take these away right NOW!

"We worship the God who made heaven and earth."
"We worship the God who made heaven and earth."
"We worship the God who made heaven and earth."
"Unto him you should BOW."
"Unto him you should BOW."
"Unto him you should BOW."

OW, WOW, KAPOW, COW,
NOW unto him you should BOW.

51

The Angel in the Storm

Acts 27

One last story from Angels, Angels All Around.

Telling tips
And, much like the other stories from that collection, one to tell on your own.

They stood on the deck together: the merchant, the captain, the soldier and the prisoner.

"I'm for going on," the merchant argued. "It's the only way to save the ship. If another storm brews up, this little port we're in won't begin to protect us."

"Aye," agreed the captain. "Winter's coming, and the stormy season with it. There are safer ports on the other side of the island."

"Just so long as we get there," the soldier added impatiently. "We should have been to Rome by now."

"Well, if you ask me," said the prisoner staring out at the dark skies, "if we set off in this weather, we're going to lose this ship – and most of us as well. We're safe here. I say we should just stay put." Then he turned and hobbled away.

The other three watched him go, watched his skinny legs and hunched back and unruly hair disappear into the fog.

"Who does he think he is?" snapped the merchant. "This is my ship, and I say where she goes."

"Bandy-legged landlubber!" the captain huffed. "What does he know about the sea?"

"His name is Paul," the soldier said. "I'm taking to Rome to stand trial before Caesar. Seems he's caused trouble in Jerusalem teaching about some new god called Jesus."

"Well," The merchant muttered, "he'll need all the help his new god can give him if he doesn't keep his nose out of other people's business. Captain, let's shove off."

And so the boat left the port and headed out to sea.

A week later, they were on deck again. But no one was standing this time.

They held onto the ropes. They held onto the rails. They held onto anything sturdy enough to keep them from being blown into the water.

"A Northeaster!" shouted the captain. "The fiercest storm there is. But in all my seafaring days, I've never seen one so fierce as this."

"We've done all we can," moaned the merchant. "But the storm is still driving us. We're miles off course, heading straight for the deadly swamps along Africa's shore. There's no hope for us."

"No hope?" asked the soldier.

"Oh, I wouldn't say that," answered the prisoner. In many ways he looked just like the other three. His clothes were drenched, his hair lay slick against his head. And he, too, was bent double by the fierce winds and rain. But where the other three wore worried frowns, he sported a broad smile.

"Everything is going to be fine," shouted Paul against the storm. "I've just seen an angel. Over there. On the other side of the ship. His eyes were lightning. His voice thunder. His hair wild like the waves.

"'Paul,' he told me, 'don't be afraid. You will be safe – you and everyone else on board. You're meant to appear before Caesar, and so you will. You have God's word on it.'

"So, you see," Paul smiled, "all we need to do is stay on the ship and trust God. He will take care of the rest." Then Paul staggered away.

"He's been out to see too long," muttered the merchant.

"Barnacles for brains," the captain sputtered, "that's what he's got. Everybody saved? It'll take the luck of Neptune to see even ten of us safely on shore."

"I don't know," mused the solder. "He was the one who told us not to leave in the first place."

Seven more days passed. Driven by the wind, the ship drifted blind through a moonless night. There were sailors on deck, scurrying about in the dark like rats.

"There's land ahead, captain," the first sailor squeaked. "We've checked and the water's getting shallow."

"But there's sure to be rocks ahead too," squeaked another. "We wouldn't be able to steer past them. The wind's too fierce. The waves too high. We'll wreck for sure."

"Gather round, lads," the captain called. "I have a plan."

Several moments later, the sailors scurried to the side of the ship and started to load the lifeboat.

"Quiet now, lads," the captain whispered. "We don't want to wake anyone.

Before long, we'll have this little boat through the rocks and be safe on shore."

And they might have done just that... if someone hadn't been watching them. He might have been out for a bit of fresh air. Maybe he couldn't sleep. Or perhaps he hoped to meet another angel.

In any case, Paul saw them loading the boat and ran to tell the soldier. "You've got to stop them," he warned. "In order for the angel's promise to come true, we must all stay on the ship."

The soldier looked hard at Paul, then he called his men. Together they raced to the deck.

"Hold it right there," he called to the sailors. "Where do you think you're going?"

"Ah, well..." mumbled the captain. "We were just off to drop an anchor from the front of the ship. Keep her from drifting, you know. Right, lads?"

The sailors squeaked. Their heads bobbed up and down.

The solder pointed at Paul. "This man tells me you were about to abandon the ship."

"What? Him?" the captain grunted. "The man who sees angels? He's crazy as a loon."

The soldier glanced into the lifeboat and spotted the ship's remaining food and water. He lifted the bundle out.

"Perhaps he is crazy as a loon," said the soldier, swinging his sword through one of the ropes from which the lifeboat hung. "Perhaps he's not," he continued, cutting through another. "What I do know is that all of us are riding out this storm together." And he cut through the last rope.

Together the men watched the empty lifeboat bounce and bob away until it was swallowed by the dark sea. After that, no one could go back to sleep.

"Listen," Paul announced to them all. "I saw an angel. With a face like the moon. Hands big as clams. White gull wings. He promised we would all come safely to land. The shore is near, so we need to build up our strength. Now is the time to dig into our remaining supplies, to eat and get ready for landing."

The merchant looked at the soldier. "He's a strange one, all right. He's got some nerve."

The soldier looked at the merchant. "Yes, he has. But he hasn't steered us wrong so far."

The captain did not dare to say a thing.

"All right," called the merchant. "Eat whatever you want. Then throw what's left overboard and get some sleep."

So Paul gave thanks to God, and together they ate.

Next morning they all stood on the deck. But the deck was falling apart. The ship had struck a sandbar.

"We've run aground!" called the captain.

"We'll have to swim for it!" cried the merchant.

The soldier called for his men. "Gather the prisoners," he ordered. "We need to swim ashore."

"But sir," asked one of his men, "what if they escape?"

"Yes," said another. "The punishment is death for the soldier who lets a prisoner escape. Unless, of course, the prisoner dies."

"That's right," agreed a third. "If they die, they can't escape. Why don't we just kill the prisoners right now?"

The soldier looked at the prisoners. They were a raggle-taggle bunch. Except for the strange one – the man who's seen an angel.

Gull wings. Lightning eyes. Hair like the waves.

Had Paul really seen such a messenger from heaven, the soldier wondered. Well, his words had come true, hadn't they? He'd been right about the storm, about the sailors – about most everything, really.

"No," the soldier ordered. "We've come this far together. We'll finish the journey together, too. Ready? One. Two. Three. JUMP!"

They stood on the beach together. Every single one of them. All present and accounted for.

"Well, we made it," sighed the merchant. "I just wish I could say the same for my ship."

"We're alive!" shouted the captain as he kissed the ground. "Who could have guessed it? Who could have guessed it?"

A green wave curled up against the shore. A gull cried overhead. And in the distance, lightning flashed.

The soldier watched the wave and the gull and the lightning. Then he looked across the beach to where Paul was praying.

"The prisoner could have," he said softly, "that's who. The strange one. The man who saw the angel."

52

Clouds and Crowds and Witnesses

Hebrews 11, 12

I know that, strictly speaking, the idea of the 'cloud of witnesses' in Hebrews is not that they should be watching us, but that we should be looking to them as our examples of faith and sacrifice and steadfastness. Having said that, I think that, by pushing the Chariots of Fire racing imagery, this reading does what the author of Hebrews intends. It uses the lives of the 'saints' who have gone before us as an encouragement for us to 'stay the course' as well.

Telling tips

The cheering is obviously the key participation device here. I usually just bring the crowd in with a cheer after each time I say 'They're cheering (BIG CHEER!). Can you hear them?' It's as simple as that, though it might help to warm them up with a few practice cheers ahead of time – and to tell them that the cheers need to get a little bit bigger each time. When you get to the part where Jesus throws his arms open in the shape of a cross, do that, just as if you're crossing the finishing line! And, yes, if you want to get someone to play the theme from *Chariots of Fire* in the background, it probably won't be all that cheesy – and just might work!

They're cheering. Can you hear them?
Like a cloud, they surround us.
The ones who've run the race before.

Abel and Enoch,
Noah and Abraham,
Isaac and Jacob and Joseph and Moses.

Look at them training.
Take note of their technique.
They'll teach us how to run the race.

They're cheering. Can you hear them?
Like a cloud, they surround us.
The ones who've run the race before.

Rahab and Gideon,
Barak and Samson,
Jephthah and David and Samuel and the prophets

Throw off everything that holds you back.
Like Noah threw off his doubt,
Like Abraham threw off his homeland,
Like Enoch threw off the weight of the world and went to walk with God.

Throw off whatever is wrong as well – whatever tempts and tangles and trips
you up.
Like Rahab threw off her idols,
Like Jacob threw off his deceit,
Like Moses threw off the pleasures of sin and chose the plight of his people.

Then run with perseverance. Run the whole course and never give up.
Like Joseph waiting for his dreams to come true,
Like Samuel's search for a king,
Like Gideon watching his army weaken to the point he could claim God's
victory.

They're cheering. Can you hear them?
Like a cloud, they surround us.
The ones who've run the race before.

And out in front, out in front of us all
Is the one on whom we fix our eyes.
He's setting the pace. He's leading the race.
The author and perfecter of our faith.

He hurdles the shame,
He fights through the pain.
It looks as if the race will be lost.
But in spite of his foes
He endures, wins, then throws
His arms wide in the shape of a cross.

So let's run the race.
Run and not grow weary.
Run for the prize that's set before us.

And when we get run down,
Let's look and let's listen.
For we don't run this race alone.

They're cheering. Can you hear them?
Like a cloud, they surround us.
The ones who've run the race before.

53

A Choosy People

1 Peter 2:9–10

I have pastored three churches over the past twenty-five years – one in the States and two in the UK. And during that time I have heard an amazing variety of reasons why the Lord calls Christians to move from one church to another! And no, before you think it, I'm not a complete loser! Yes, sometimes the Lord had his reasons for calling people away from the churches I pastored, and sometimes (just to keep things even, I guess) he had his reasons for calling them to the churches I pastored, as well. As you have probably guessed by now, I have strong suspicions about whether the Lord was actually involved in this process at all. And that is partly where this reading comes from. "Chosen" or "Choosy"? – that's the question. And I'm not sure the contemporary church has benefited much from choosing one answer over the other.

Telling tips

This is a reading for two to do. Have one person read the scripture passages (keep this quite serious) and the other the lines in between. You might want to change names and references to suit your own situation.

> *But you are a chosen people, a royal priesthood, a holy nation,*
> *God's special possession, that you may declare the praises of him*
> *who called you out of darkness into his wonderful light.*

When we first moved to town, we had a pretty clear idea of the kind of church we were looking for.

The worship had to be right, for a start.

> *But you are a chosen people, a royal priesthood, a holy nation,*
> *God's special possession.*

Post-Kendrick. Pre-Redman. A touch of Taizé. That's what we had in mind. And we thought we'd found it. But when the organist at the first church we joined played the chorus of 'Shine, Jesus, Shine' while the offering was being collected, we knew there and then that the Lord was telling us to leave.

> *That you may declare the praises of him who called you out of*
> *darkness into his wonderful light.*

The next church was better. Yes, they seemed to love God and love one another. But they weren't really in touch with the Spirit. They weren't 'moving on'. If you know what I mean.

> *But you are a holy nation, a royal priesthood.*

So we tried a church on the other side of town. Sadly, the pastor was entirely too legalistic. He wouldn't let women pray!

> *A holy nation, God's special possession.*

While the vicar at the next place was entirely too loose. He wanted women priests!

> *That you may declare the praises of him…*

So God called us on. What could we do?

> *Who called you out of darkness into his wonderful light.*

But everywhere we went it was the same story.

> *But you are a chosen people.*

The paintwork was too bright.

A royal priesthood.

The drums were too loud.

A holy nation.

The incense made me sneeze.

God's special possession.

The woman sitting next to me had a funny nose.

That you may declare the praises of him who called you out of darkness into his wonderful light.

I think the church is like a supermarket! If you don't like the quality of the produce at Tesco, you can always pop down to Sainsbury's. Or ASDA. Or even the corner shop. Choice – that's the important thing. Keeping the customer satisfied. And I'm sure that's true of church as well.

But you are a chosen people.

Let's Hear it for the Church!

I have to confess – sometimes I get a little tired of the self-flagellating routine that the church regularly puts itself through. A couple of years ago there were several high-profile books about how awful the authors' church experience was and how the church really needed to get its act together if it was going to be an adequate representative of Jesus in the modern world. I have two responses to that. The first is, "When did the church ever really have its act together – in the modern world or any other?" Not among Jesus' disciples, as far as I can tell. And not among most of the churches referred to in the New Testament, either! Oh, there are a few brief shining moments mentioned here and there. And I'll bet you could pick a few of those out from your experience of the church, as well. But the rest of the time, the church was, and continues to be, more a "work in progress" than a "masterpiece". And that brings me to my second response. I'm not at all sure that Jesus ever intended it to be any more than that. I'm not saying that Christians ought to be satisfied with hypocrisy and scandal and manipulation and apathy (see, there I go, too!), but that we ought, at the very least, to get a little less satisfaction from beating ourselves up!

I heard a sermon once where the speaker observed that in some Christian traditions the congregation believed that it hadn't been adequately preached to until it could feel the bruises of its own imperfection. But what does that say about grace? If I can't even talk about our church experience without pointing the finger of blame at the elder who shunned me, or the group leader who oppressed me, or the minister who disagreed with me, or the Sunday school teacher who passed heresy on to me, then how am I ever going to live in grace with the rest of the world? The church isn't perfect. It's never going to be, not this side of heaven. That's why it's the place for grace. Because we need it there, sometimes more than anywhere. And when we find it, well… that's what this reading is about.

Let's hear it for the Church!

OK, so it's had some negative press recently.

But where did we get the idea that it would be perfect?

Not from the Bible – that's for sure!

The church in Corinth was dirty with division and immorality.

But Paul thanked God for it.

And I want to thank God for my church, too – the church I grew up in.

For Kathy Miller and the indescribably delicious cookies she baked for every wedding and funeral and bridal shower these last thirty years.

For my dear departed and ever-so-slightly-insane grandmother, who taught the Junior Boys' Class like she was directing a B-grade horror film.

"That's right; it was the firstborn who died in the final Egyptian plague. And which of you boys are the firstborn in your families?"

And for the whole lot of them, who held us and cried with us when my dad passed away a few years ago.

There are more that I could name – and plenty that you could name, too – who were there just when you needed them.

So let's hear it – let's hear it for the Church!

And let's hear it for the Bride!

OK, so she gets shot down sometimes.

Like Uma Thurman before she slipped into that bright yellow jumpsuit.

But where did we get the idea that following Jesus would make us popular?

Not from Jesus – that's for sure!

"If they persecuted me," he said, "can you expect anything better?"

No, he dresses us up and prepares us and makes us beautiful – not for the world – but for his eyes only. And that's a different kind of beauty.

It's the beauty of a church in pain – arrested and beaten and imprisoned – in China and Africa and across the Middle East.

It's the beauty of a church with principles – that knows right from wrong and will not bend with the changing winds of social and political convention.

And it's the beauty of the person sitting next to you, as well. Who hangs in there, believing and praying and trying to do what's best when much of the rest of the population laughs and makes fun and scratches its head and simply doesn't "get it".
So let's hear it – let's hear it for the Bride!

And let's hear it for the Body!
OK, so it's a little out of shape.
Like the 'before' pictures in the latest diet-fad ad.
But where did we get the idea that it would be "pumped"?
Not from Paul, that's for sure.
Most of the churches he wrote to were "97-pound weaklings".
But that's the point. It's only by God's grace and God's power that we become what we never could have been on our own.
And the horror is not that we mess up sometimes. That's to be expected. That's what grace is for.
No, the miracle is that we sometimes get it right!
And the poor get fed.
And kids find a place where they are accepted.
And the sick get healed.
And marriages get saved.
And the grieving are comforted.
And folk just like you and me find God.
People often say to me – and I know what they mean – "I love Jesus, but I just can't stand the church."
And what I want to say, and what I ought to say, and what I'm saying right now is this:
"How? How can you say you love Jesus and not love his Body?"

So let's hear it for the Body!
All fingers and thumbs sometimes, but the Body of Christ nonetheless.
And let's hear it for the Bride!
Beautiful and broken and unbowed.
And let's hear it
Let's hear it
Let's hear it for the Church!